continued

"This story is deep with details not only of Muhammad's life journey, but with historic information about the culture of the times in Arabia. . . . Filled with rich color of the locations, culture, and people; it is a book plentiful with tales of Muhammad's life that follow logically from orphan to religious leader, but more than that, it enriches us with the details of a time and place in history."

—*New York Journal of Books*

"Hazleton sets her keen eye and her sculpted prose on one of the most fascinating and misunderstood figures in history. What she uncovers is a complex yet utterly relatable man whose personal trials and triumphs changed the course of history. This is a wonderful book."

—Reza Aslan, author of
Zealot: The Life and Times of Jesus of Nazareth

"Winning . . . A level-headed, elegant look at the life of the prophet amid the making of a legend."   —*Kirkus Reviews*

"Vivid and engaging . . . Fluid and captivating . . . invaluable for those seeking a greater understanding of Islam's message and its messenger."   —*Publishers Weekly*

"Profoundly moving."

—Imam Feisal Abdul Rauf, The Cordoba Initiative

"Hazleton has done the seemingly impossible: rendered into human proportions a man who is more often the subject of pious veneration or political vitriol. This is the most readable, engaging study of Muhammad I have ever come across."

—G. Willow Wilson, author of *Alif the Unseen* and
The Butterfly Mosque

"*The First Muslim* tells the mostly unknown story of the prophet Muhammad in a masterful, accessible, and engaging way. Hazleton's empathetic touch softens her rigorous scholarship and research as she crucially demystifies both the man himself and the birth of Islam. An absolute delight (and indispensable) for believers and nonbelievers alike."

—Hooman Majd, author of
The Ayatollah Begs to Differ and *The Ayatollahs' Democracy*

"[A] humane, audacious biography . . . An elegant narrative crafted for open-minded readers. . . . a vivid canvas of Arabian life in the early seventh century."

—*Haaretz*

"A genuine attempt to try to understand the human experience Muhammad went through . . . Hazleton queries and questions in a way that will resonate with a nonacademic audience trying to come to grips with the fastest growing religion on the planet. It is a welcome antidote to the barrage of hatred and distortion to which Islam has been subjected since the early Bush years . . . [An] opportunity for balance to be restored and for those of us who don't subscribe to the extremes to regain the middle ground."

—*Guernica*

"Hazleton . . . is in the revelation business: She's out to consider Muhammad as a mortal human, a man who lived and died and was vulnerable. . . . A world-class history teacher who contextualizes the realities of [his] far-off times . . . [She] can effortlessly distill years of research into a few conversational sentences."

—*The Stranger*

"A strikingly nuanced portrait of how Muhammad the man—fallible and complex—became Muhammad the prophet. . . . With the insight of a psychologist and the details of a historian, Hazleton portrays a Muhammad both divinely inspired and deeply human."

—*Spirituality & Health*

The

FIRST MUSLIM

The Story of Muhammad

LESLEY HAZLETON

RIVERHEAD BOOKS
New York

RIVERHEAD BOOKS
Published by the Penguin Group
Penguin Group (USA) LLC
375 Hudson Street, New York, New York 10014, USA

USA • Canada • UK • Ireland • Australia • New Zealand • India • South Africa • China

penguin.com

A Penguin Random House Company

The Library of Congress has catalogued the Riverhead hardcover edition as follows:

Hazleton, Lesley, date.
The first Muslim : the story of Muhammad / Lesley Hazleton.
p.   cm.
ISBN 978-1-59448-728-6
1. Muhammad, Prophet, d. 632—Biography.   I. Title.
BP75.H39   2013   2012038501
297.6'3—dc23
[B]

First Riverhead hardcover edition: January 2013
First Riverhead trade paperback edition: February 2014
Riverhead trade paperback ISBN: 978-1-59463-230-3

PRINTED IN THE UNITED STATES OF AMERICA

Cover design by Alex Merto
Book design by Amanda Dewey
Map by Jeffrey L. Ward

For Layla and Ian

Muhammad, say, "I am the first Muslim."

—QURAN

The inner meaning of history . . . involves speculation and
an attempt to get to the truth, subtle explanation of the causes
and origins of existing things, and deep knowledge of the how
and why of events.

—IBN-KHALDUN

I do not accept the claim of saintliness . . . I am prone to as
many weaknesses as you are. But I have seen the world. I have
lived in the world with my eyes open.

—MAHATMA GANDHI

Contents

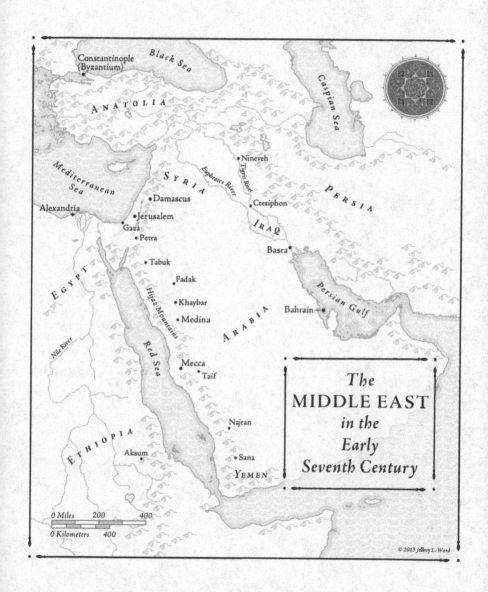

The
MIDDLE EAST
in the
Early
Seventh Century

0 Miles   200   400
0 Kilometers   400

© 2013 Jeffrey L. Ward

Part One

ORPHAN

One

I f he weren't standing lonely vigil on the mountain, you might say that there was no sign of anything unusual about him. The earliest sources describe him with infuriating vagueness for those of us who need images. "He was neither tall nor short," they say. "Neither dark nor fair." "Neither thin nor stout." But here and there, specific details slip through, and when they do, they are surprising. Surely a man spending night after night in solitary meditation would be a gaunt, ascetic figure, yet far from being pale and wan, he had round, rosy cheeks and a ruddy complexion. He was stockily built, almost barrel-chested, which may partly account for his distinctive gait, always "leaning forward slightly as though he were hurrying toward something." And he must have had a stiff neck, because people would remember that when he turned to look at you, he turned his whole body instead of just his head. The only sense in which he was conventionally handsome was his profile: the swooping hawk nose long considered a sign of nobility in the Middle East.

On the surface, you might conclude that he was an average Meccan. At forty years old, the son of a man he had never seen, he had made a far better life for himself than had ever seemed possible. The child born an outsider within his own society had finally won acceptance, and carved out a good life despite the odds against him. He was comfortably off, a happily married business agent with the respect of his peers. If he was not one of the movers and shakers of his prosperous city, that was precisely why people trusted him to represent their interests. They saw him as a man with no axe of his own to grind, a man who would consider an offer or a dispute on its merits and decide accordingly. He had found a secure niche in the world, and had earned every right, in middle age, to sit back and enjoy his rise to respectability. So what was he doing alone up here on one of the mountains that ringed the sleeping city below? Why would a happily married man isolate himself this way, standing in meditation through the night?

There was a hint, perhaps, in his clothing. By now he could certainly have afforded the elaborate embroidered silks of the wealthy, but his clothing was low-key. His sandals were worn, the leather thongs sun-bleached paler than his skin. His homespun robe would be almost threadbare if it hadn't been so carefully patched, and it was hardly enough to shield him against the nighttime cold of the high desert. Yet something about the way he stood on the mountainside made the cold irrelevant. Tilted slightly forward as though leaning into the wind, his stance seemed that of someone who existed at an angle to the earth.

Certainly a man could see the world in a different way up here. He could find peace in the silence, with just the soughing of the wind over the rock for company, far from the feuds and gossip of the city with its arguments over money and power. Here, a man was merely a speck in the mountain landscape, his mind free to think and reflect, and then finally to stop thinking, stop reflecting, and submit itself to the vastness.

Look closer and you might detect the shadow of loneliness in the corners of his eyes, something lingering there of the outsider he had once been, as though he were haunted by the awareness that at any moment everything he'd worked so long and hard for could be taken away. You might see a hint of that same mix of vulnerability and resoluteness in his mouth, the full lips slightly parted as he whispered into the darkness. And then perhaps you'd ask why contentment was not enough. Did the fact that it had been so hard-earned make him unable to accept it as a given, never to be secure in his right to it? But then what would? What was he searching for? Was it a certain peace within himself, perhaps? Or was it something more—a glimpse, maybe just an intimation, of something larger?

One thing is certain: by Muhammad's own account, he was completely unprepared for the enormity of what he would experience on this particular night in the year 610.

A human encounters the divine: to the rationalist, a matter not of fact but of wishful fiction. So if Muhammad had behaved the way one might expect after his first encounter on Mount Hira, it would only make sense to call the story just that: a fable concocted by piety and belief. But he did not.

He did not come floating off the mountain as though walking on air. He did not run down shouting "Hallelujah" and "Bless the Lord." He did not radiate light and joy. There were no choirs of angels, no music of the heavens. No elation, no ecstasy, no golden aura surrounding him. No sense of his absolute, foreordained, unquestionable role as the messenger of God. Not even the whole of the Quran fully revealed, but only a few brief verses. In short, Muhammad did none of the things that might seem essential to the legend of a man who had just done the impossible and crossed the border between this world and another—none of the things that might make it easy to cry foul, to denigrate the whole story as an invention, a cover for something as mundane as delusion or personal ambition.

On the contrary: he was convinced that what he had encountered could not be real. At best it must be a hallucination: a trick of the eye or the ear, or his own mind working against him. At worst, possession, and he had been seized by an evil *jinn*, a spirit out to deceive him, even to crush the life out of him. In fact he was so sure that he could only be *majnun*, literally possessed by a *jinn*, that when he found himself still alive, his first instinct had been to finish the job himself, to leap off the highest cliff and escape the terror of what he had experienced by putting an end to all experience.

So the man who fled down Mount Hira trembled not with joy but with a stark, primordial fear. He was overwhelmed not with conviction, but by doubt. He was sure of only one thing: whatever this was, it was not meant to happen to him. Not to a middle-aged man who had hoped perhaps at most for a simple moment of grace instead of this vast blinding weight of revelation. If he no longer feared for his life, he certainly feared for his sanity, painfully aware that too many nights in solitary meditation might have driven him over the edge.

Whatever happened up there on Mount Hira, the sheer humanness of Muhammad's reaction may be the strongest argument for its historical reality. Whether you think the words he heard came from inside himself or from outside, it is clear that Muhammad experienced them, and with a force that would shatter his sense of himself and his world. Terrgor was the sole sane response. Terror and denial. And if this reaction strikes us now as unexpected, even shockingly so, that is only a reflection of how badly we have been misled by the stereotyped image of ecstatic mystical bliss.

Lay aside such preconceived notions for a moment, and you might see that Muhammad's terror speaks of real experience. It sounds fallibly human—too human for some, like conservative Muslim theologians who argue that the account of his trying to kill himself should not even be mentioned despite the fact that it's in the earliest Islamic biographies. They insist that he never doubted for a single moment, let alone despaired. Demanding perfection, they cannot tolerate human imperfection.

Perhaps this is why it can be so hard to see who Muhammad really was. The purity of perfection denies the complexity of a lived life. For Muslims worldwide, Muhammad is the ideal man, *the* prophet, the messenger of God, and though he is told again and again in the Quran to say "I am just one of you"—just a man—reverence and love cannot resist the desire to clothe him, as it were, in gold and silver. There is a proprietary feeling about him, a fierce protectiveness all the stronger at a time when Islam itself is under such intense scrutiny in the West.

But the law of unintended consequences applies. To idealize someone is also, in a way, to dehumanize them, so that despite the millions if not billions of words written about Muhammad, it can be hard to get any real sense of the man himself. The more you read, the more liable you are to come away with the feeling that while you may know a lot *about* Muhammad, you still don't know who he was. It's as though he has been all but smothered by the accumulated mass of so many words.

Though the reverential legends about him are often magnificent, they work as perhaps all legends do: they obscure more than they reveal, and he becomes more a symbol than a human being. Even as Islam is rapidly closing on Christianity as the world's largest religion, we thus have little real sense of the man told three times in the Quran to call himself "the first Muslim." His is without doubt one of the most consequential lives ever lived, yet for all the iconic power of his name alone—or perhaps because of it—it is a life still to be explored.

How did this man shunted as a child to the margins of his own society ("a man of no importance," as his opponents call him in the Quran) come to revolutionize his world? How did the infant sent away from his family grow up to redefine the whole concept of family and tribe into something far larger: the *umma*, the people or the community of Islam? How did a merchant become a radical re-thinker of both God and society, directly challenging the established social and political order? How did the man hounded out of Mecca turn exile into a new and victorious beginning, to be welcomed back just eight years later as a national hero? How did he succeed against such odds?

To answer such questions requires exerting the biographer's privilege and real purpose, which is not merely to follow what happened but to uncover the meaning and relevance within the welter of events. It means weaving together the complex elements of Muhammad's life, creating a three-dimensional portrait not so much at odds with the "authorized" version as expanding it.

The great British philosopher and historian R. G. Collingwood maintained in *The Idea of History* that to write well about a historical figure, you need both empathy and imagination. By this he did not mean spinning tales out of thin air, but taking what is known and examining it in the full context of time and place, following the strands of the story until they begin to intertwine and establish a thick braid of reality. If we want to understand the dynamics of what can only be described, with considerable understatement, as a remarkable life—one that would radically change his world, and is still shaping ours—we must allow Muhammad the integrity of reality, and see him whole.

His story is an extraordinary confluence of man, time, and culture, and it begs a deceptively simple question: Why him? Why Muhammad, in the seventh century, in Arabia?

Just to think in such terms is both exciting and daunting. On the one hand, these questions lead straight into a virtual minefield of deeply held beliefs, unwitting preconceptions, and cultural assumptions. On the other, they allow us to see Muhammad clearly, and to understand how he accomplished his journey from powerlessness to power, from anonymity to renown, from insignificance to lasting significance.

The constant guides through his life are two early Islamic histories: the lengthy biography of him written in eighth-century Damascus by ibn-Ishaq, on which every subsequent biography at least claims to be based, and the more politically focused history of early Islam by al-Tabari, written in late-ninth-century Baghdad, which comes to a magisterial thirty-nine volumes in translation, four of them devoted to Muhammad's lifetime.

These early historians are conscientious. Their authoritativeness lies in their inclusiveness. They wrote after the fact, working with oral history in the full awareness of how both time and piety tend to warp memory, blurring the line between what was and what should have been. If they erred, it was deliberately on the side of thoroughness rather than judgment. Reading them, one senses their awareness that they are walking a fine line between their responsibility to history on the one side and tradition on the other. This delicate balancing act between history and faith goes hand in hand with their acknowledgment of the elusiveness of definitive fact—a quality as slippery in the hyper-documented world of today as it was in the oral tradition of theirs. Instead of aspiring to omniscience, then, they included conflicting accounts and left it to their readers to decide for themselves, though they did indicate their point of view. Throughout ibn-Ishaq's work, for instance, there are phrases such as "it is alleged that" and "so I have been told." In fact when several eyewitness accounts seem to contradict one another, he often sums up with "As to which of these is correct, only God knows for sure"—a statement that verges on a helpless "God knows!"

Perhaps the only other life that has been written about so much and has yet remained such a mystery is that of Jesus. But thanks to the efforts of scholarly groups like the Jesus Seminar, new studies in the past few decades have explored beyond the letter of the Gospel accounts to create not only a more human portrait of him, but also deeper insight into his impact. These scholars delved beyond theology into history, political science, comparative religion, and psychology, highlighting the radical political relevance of Jesus' message. By looking at him in the full context of his time, they made him not less but more relevant to our own.

The parallels between Muhammad and Jesus are striking. Both were impelled by a strong sense of social justice; both emphasized unmediated access to the divine; both challenged the established power structure of their times. As with Jesus, theology and history travel side by side in any account of Muhammad's life, sometimes as closely as train tracks, at others widely divergent. Miracle stories abound in an accretion of sacred lore built up by those treasuring what should have happened even if it didn't. Despite the Quran's insistent disavowal of the miraculous, there seems to be a very human need for it, and for theology to demand faith in the improbable—the impossible—as a test of commitment.

Conservative Islamic tradition thus maintains that Muhammad was destined from the start to be the messenger of God. But if that is so, then there is no story of his life. That is, it becomes a matter of the inevitable unfolding of divine will, and thus devoid of all conflict or tension. To some pious believers, this will more than suffice; the prophet's innate exceptionalism is a given, and any biography is irrelevant. But to many others, what is compelling is not the miraculous but the humanly possible. Muhammad's is one of those rare lives that is more dramatic in reality than in legend. In fact the less one invokes the miraculous, the more extraordinary his life becomes. What emerges is something grander precisely because it is human, to the extent that his actual life reveals itself worthy of the word "legendary."

His story follows the classic arc of what Joseph Campbell called "the hero's journey," from inauspicious beginnings to extraordinary success. But this journey is never an easy one. It involves struggle, danger, and conflict, within oneself as much as with others. So to elide the more controversial aspects of Muhammad's life does him no service. On the contrary, if we are to accord him the vitality and complexity of a man in full, we need to see him whole. This means taking what might be called an agnostic stance, laying aside piety and reverence on the one hand along with stereotype and judgmentalism on the other, let alone the deadening pall of circumspection in the middle. It means finding the very human narrative of a man navigating between idealism and pragmatism, faith and politics, non-violence and violence, the pitfalls of acclaim as much as the perils of rejection.

The pivotal point of his life is undoubtedly that one night on Mount Hira. That was when he stepped into what many think of as his destiny, which is why Muslims call it *laylat al-qadr*, the Night of Power. It's certainly where he stepped into history, though that word too can be misleading. It implies that Muhammad's story belongs in the past, when in fact it continues to have such an impact that it has to be considered a matter as much of current events as of history. What happened "then" is an integral part of what is still happening, a major factor in the vast and often terrifying arena in which politics and religion intersect.

To begin to understand this man who wrestled with the angel on the mountaintop and came down seared by the encounter, however, we need to ask not only what happened that night on Mount Hira and what it would lead to, but what led him to it. Especially since from the start, despite the legends, the signs were not promising. Indeed, any objective observer might have concluded that Muhammad was a most unlikely candidate for prophethood, since whatever stars he was born under, they seemed anything but auspicious.

Two

If you believe in omens, the fact that Muhammad was born an orphan is not a good one. Most biographers make little of it, moving on quickly as though this were just a quirk of fate not worth dwelling on. Yet his orphanhood bears the psychological weight that often determines history. Especially since if the legend of his birth is to be believed, he was almost never born at all. Just hours before he was conceived, his grandfather nearly killed his father. And as though the father had been spared only long enough to fulfill his singular role, he would then die far from home, unaware that he even had a son.

The grandfather was Abd al-Muttalib, the venerable leader of the ruling Quraysh tribe and a central figure in the short but spectacular lore of Mecca. As a young man, he had excavated the Zamzam well, a freshwater spring hard by the Kaaba sanctuary, which attracted pilgrims from all over Arabia. Rumors of the spring's existence had existed for as long as anyone could remember. Some said that it had first been discovered by Hagar after she gave birth to Ishmael and that it had then been tapped by Abraham, only to be abandoned and filled in over the centuries, its location forgotten until Abd al-Muttalib rediscovered it. All sorts of miraculous things reportedly happened when he opened it up.

By some accounts, a snake guarded the entrance so fiercely that nobody dared approach until a giant eagle swooped down to snatch it up into the sky. Others maintain that masses of treasure were found in the spring, from exquisitely wrought jewel-studded swords to life-size gazelles made out of solid gold. But by far the most chilling account is one that will be hauntingly familiar to anyone who knows the biblical story of Abraham's near-sacrifice of his son.

Since it was he who'd rediscovered Zamzam, Abd al-Muttalib claimed that the profitable monopoly on providing its water to pilgrims belonged to his clan, the Hashims, one of the four primary extended families banded together to form the Quraysh tribe. There were other springs in Mecca of course, but none so centrally located, none with such sweet water, and none with such a powerful legend. So it was hardly a surprise when the other Quraysh clan leaders challenged his claim to control its waters, thus questioning both his motives and his honor. What did come as a surprise was his response. He silenced his critics with a terrifying vow. If he had ten sons who survived into maturity to protect him and to uphold the honor of the Hashims, he swore, he would sacrifice one of them right there in the open precinct surrounding the Kaaba, beside the spring.

The vow cowed his critics into silence. The idea of human sacrifice was terrifying, all the more since it had surely come to an end with that ancestral legend of Abraham and Ishmael. Wasn't that why the sole thing in the forbidden interior of the Kaaba was rumored to be the horns of the ram that had taken Ishmael's place in that foundational act of sacrifice? Besides, there was no doubt that ten sons would be an extraordinary sign of divine favor. No matter how many wives a man had, the frequency of infant mortality and maternal death in childbirth made such filial riches all but impossible. Yet by the year 570, ten sons of Abd al-Muttalib had indeed survived. And according to ibn-Ishaq, quite magnificently. "There were none more prominent and stately than they, nor of more noble profile, with noses so long that the nose drank before the lips," he would write, celebrating the feature so admired in a society that scorned snub noses, considering them as effeminate as the pale skin of Byzantine Greeks, referred to derisively as "yellow men."

It was time for Abd al-Muttalib to fulfill his vow. A man's word was his bond, and he had given his. He had no choice in the matter if he was to hold his head high. The only question was which son to sacrifice, and since this was an impossible choice for any father to make, the traditional way would decide for him. He would consult the totemic icon of the Quraysh tribe: the sacred stone of Hubal, which loomed alongside the Kaaba and acted as a kind of consecration stone. Oaths were made and deals sealed at its foot, vows of both friendship and vengeance solemnized in its shadow. And when hard decisions had to be made or intractable disputes settled, the stone served as an oracle. Approached the right way, Hubal expressed the will of God—of al-Lah, "the high one," the great lord of the sanctuary, who was so remote and mysterious that he could be consulted only through intermediaries.

Lest there be any doubt that these were matters of life and death, Hubal spoke through arrows. Each one would be inscribed with an option tailored to the specific occasion. If there was a question of when to act, for instance, three arrows might be used, marked "now," "later," or "never," or with specific times such as "today," "in seven days," "in a month." Invocations were then made and a sacrifice offered—a goat or even a camel—and finally Hubal's priestly custodian would bundle the arrows together, balance them on the ground pointing upward, and then, in much the same way as the ancient Chinese consulted the *I Ching* using yarrow stalks, let them fall. Whichever arrow fell pointing most directly at Hubal, the inscription on it would be the judgment.

This time there were ten arrows, each inscribed with the name of one of the ten sons. The whole city gathered to witness the ceremony, simultaneously excited and horrified by what was at stake. The murmur of anticipation swelled to a raucous clamor as the decisive moment neared, only to give way to abrupt silence as the custodian let the arrows fall. Everyone pressed in close, eager to be the first to hear which name was on the arrow pointing toward the huge stone, and when it was announced, a horrified gasp rippled back through the crowd. With the inevitability of Greek tragedy, the arrow pointing toward Hubal was the one marked with the name of Abd al-Muttalib's youngest and favorite son, Abdullah.

If the father's beard had not already been white with age, it would have turned white at that moment. But he had no choice. Not only was his own honor at stake, but so too was that of his clan, the Hashims. His other sons stood stock still as their father prepared to kill their brother. It was not for sons to question their father, after all, and besides, each may have been overwhelmed with relief that the choice had not fallen on him. If they still hoped for some sudden last-minute stay from Hubal, however, none came. They recovered their wits only when Abd al-Muttalib had already ordered Abdullah down on his knees in front of him and taken the knife in his hand. This may not have been what Hubal intended, they finally ventured. Its will might be more subtle than any of them was capable of grasping. Surely there could be nothing lost by consulting a *kahin*, one of the handful of priest-like seers—their title the Arabic equivalent of the Hebrew *cohen*—who could enter spirit trances and understand the mystery of their signs. And if so, who better than one of the most revered in all of Arabia?

The woman so famous that she was known simply as the *kahina*, the priestess, lived not in Mecca but in the oasis of Medina, two hundred miles to the north. The distance alone meant that Medina was to all intents and purposes another country, which was in itself an assurance of objectivity. The spirits that spoke through her were those of another people—not the Quraysh tribe but the Khazraj. Since only spirits could truly understand one another, hers might cast new light on Hubal's judgment and thus free Abd al-Muttalib from his terrible vow. "If the *kahina* commands you to sacrifice Abdullah, you will do so," the other sons persuaded him. "But if she commands something that offers relief, then you will be justified in accepting it."

Father and sons saddled their fastest camels and were in Medina within seven days, bearing gifts for the *kahina* and her spirits. They watched anxiously as her eyes fluttered closed and she went into her trance; waited as her body trembled and shuddered with the force of the invisible encounter; held their breath as incomprehensible whispers and inhuman moans escaped her lips. Then there was the long, tense silence as she finally became still. Her eyes opened and slowly regained their focus on this world instead of another, and at last the faculty of human speech came back to her. Not with the expected words of wisdom, however, but with a strangely practical question: What was the customary amount Meccans paid in blood money, the compensation for taking a man's life?

Ten camels, they replied, and she nodded as though she'd known it all along. "Go back to your country," she said, "bring out the young man and ten camels in front of your sacred stone, and cast the arrows anew. If they fall a second time against the young man, add ten more camels to your pledge and do it again. If they fall against him a third time, then add more camels and do it yet again. Keep adding camels in this manner until your god is satisfied and accepts the camels in lieu of the young man."

They did as she had said, adding ten camels with every throw of the arrows against Abdullah. Time and again, the oracle ruled against him, finally accepting the substitution only when one hundred camels had been offered—an extraordinary number that had the whole city abuzz, not just with the news of Abdullah's salvation, but with the idea that his life was worth ten times that of any other man.

That evening, Abd al-Muttalib celebrated. He had no need of a Freud to remind him of the deep connection between Eros and Thanatos, the life force and the death force, and moved instantly to mark his favorite son's new lease on life by ensuring that it be passed on. Within hours of the camels' being slaughtered, he presided over the wedding of Muhammad's father and mother, Abdullah and Amina.

Some people would swear that there was a blaze of white light on Abdullah's forehead as he went to his new bride that night, and that when he emerged in the morning, it was no longer there. Blaze of light or no, Muhammad was conceived either that night or on one of the following two, because three days later Abdullah left on a trade caravan to Damascus, only to die in Medina on the way back, ten days short of home. If anyone thought it an ironic turn of the spirit world that he should die near the *kahina* who had saved his life, none would comment on it. After all, arduous caravan treks over hundreds of miles of desert took a regular toll on human life. Accident, infection, scorpion sting, snakebite, disease—any of these and more were common on such journeys, so exactly what killed Abdullah is not recorded. All we are told is that he was buried in an unmarked grave, leaving his bride a widow and his only child an orphan in the womb.

But like so many stories of the births of heroes, this one cuts two ways. The logic of legend is rarely kind, so even as this one gives Muhammad noble status, it deprives him of it. It insists that he was born into the very center of Meccan society, with a deep blood tie through his father and grandfather to the central events in the making of the city. Yet by the same token, it relegates him to the margins. Intended to establish a miraculous aspect to his birth, it instead singles out what may well be the central existential aspect of his life: in a society that venerated fathers, he was born without one. And sixth-century Mecca was not kind to either widows or orphans.

To be born without a father was to be born without an inheritance, or any hope of one. A son could not inherit until he had reached maturity; if his father died before that, everything he possessed went to an adult male relative, who would then assume the responsibility for the family left behind. In traditional tribal society, this had worked well. On the assumption that there was no such thing as personal wealth, only the good of the tribe, it assured that no member of the tribe was abandoned and that everyone was cared for. But in boom-era Mecca, newly wealthy from the caravan trade and management of the pilgrimage to the Kaaba sanctuary, the old values had been seriously eroded. In just a few decades, wealth had become concentrated in the hands of a few. It was every man for himself, and an orphaned infant, no matter how well-born, was more burden than blessing.

At least the child's gender offered some protection. If Muhammad had been born female, he might have been left out in the desert for the elements or predators to dispose of, or even quietly smothered at birth, since the focus on male heirs meant that female infanticide was as high in Mecca as in Constantinople, Athens, and Rome—a practice the Quran was to address directly and condemn repeatedly. As it was, Muhammad seemed destined to be what his Meccan opponents would later call him: "a nobody." And this destiny seemed only to be confirmed by the fact that for the first five years of his life, he would be raised by what the Quraysh elite regarded as another kind of nobody: a Beduin foster mother, far from Mecca and what was thought of as civilized society.

It was a drought year, and strange as it may sound, this was Muhammad's good fortune, since the lack of rain brought a young woman called Halima into Mecca in search of an infant to foster. Without her, he might well not have survived infancy.

To speak of drought in the desert may strike many people as redundant, but few areas within the world's deserts receive no rain at all. Most, like the upland steppes of north and central Arabia, get a few inches a year. Sudden winter downpours, however brief, turn the parched desert pavement into a sea of green fuzz within hours, dormant seeds seizing on the moisture to spring to life and provide fodder for livestock. But some years, like this one, those brief winter rains never came. No matter how far afield the Beduin herded their goats and camels, there was no grazing to be had and nothing to do but watch as the animals became gaunt, their udders shriveling and their milk drying up. In the worst droughts, when the rains skipped two or even three years in a row, the animals died, and the nomads were forced toward the outskirts of settled areas like Mecca. There they became an underclass of cheap labor, proud people reduced to begging for work. You might even say that they were reduced to the level of slaves, except that slaves were at least under the protection of their owners.

Like many Beduin women, Halima avoided this fate by hiring herself out as a wet nurse. This is what poor women did for the rich everywhere in the world at the time. They did it until well into the twentieth century, when the widespread availability of baby formula and the breakdown of traditional rural life made wet-nursing obsolete in most societies, to be replaced by nannies and boarding schools. But until then, from early biblical times on through the Greek and Roman empires, the Dark Ages, the Renaissance, and the Enlightenment, urban children born to well-to-do families were regularly sent to wet nurses in the country until weaning. This was partly a matter of status—"what one does"—but it also served the interests of the wealthy in a very specific way.

The prime role of an aristocratic wife was to produce male heirs, but with infant mortality so high that barely half of all infants born alive survived into adulthood, this was not easy. Obviously the chances were improved the more often a wife became pregnant, so it was important that she be fertile again as quickly as possible after giving birth. Since nursing inhibits ovulation, the best way to ensure this was for someone else to breast-feed her infant. (The obverse was that the peasant and nomad women who served as wet nurses had far fewer pregnancies. The ugly upper-class stereotype of the lower class "breeding like rabbits" was in fact quite the reverse: the upper class were the breeders, and the lower class the feeders.)

By her own account, Halima was one of the hardest hit of the Beduin women trying to find a foster infant in the late spring of the year 570. She was from one of the semi-nomadic clans eking out a subsistence living in the arid steppelands over the mountains from Mecca. Like all those living on the edge, her clan was fighting for survival. Even the donkey she rode was weak and emaciated. There was hardly any milk in her breasts, so that her own infant cried through the night for hunger. She knew she presented a poor prospect to elite Meccans looking for a good healthy wet nurse but she tried nonetheless, only to watch enviously as others she had come with found infants to foster, and the available market dwindled. Soon "every woman who came into Mecca with me had gotten a suckling except for me," she'd remember. There was just one child left, but "each of us refused when she was told he was an orphan, because we wanted to get payment from the child's father. We said 'An orphan? With no father to pay us?' And so we rejected him."

Halima had clearly heard nothing of the things people would later swear to: the flash of white light on Abdullah's forehead as he went to Amina on their wedding night, or the way her pregnant belly was said to glow so brightly that "you could see by its light as far as the castles of Syria." It would be at least a hundred years until such stories became widely circulated. So far as she and the other wet nurses were concerned, this was just an infant nobody wanted. Not even his grandfather. Though in principle Amina and her newborn son were under his protection as head of the Hashim clan, the aging Abd al-Muttalib evidently considered the fate of yet another grandson, and an orphaned one at that, no business of his, certainly not worth the payment for the customary two years of fostering until he was weaned.

Neither Amina nor Halima had statistics at their fingertips, of course, but they both knew that in the city, any child's chances of surviving into adulthood were not good unless he could be sent away to a wet nurse. In fact to survive infancy at all before the age of modern medicine was itself an achievement. At the height of Rome's power, for instance, only one third of those born in that city made it to their fifth birthday, while records for eighteenth-century London show that well over half of those born were dead by age sixteen. Whether in Paris or in Mecca, something as simple as a rotten tooth or an infected cut could kill you. Between disease, malnutrition, street violence, accidents, childbirth, bad water, and spoiled food, not to mention warfare, only ten percent made it beyond age forty-five. It wasn't until the early twentieth century, when the role of germs became clear and antibiotics were first developed, that life spans began to increase to what we now take for granted.

One statistic stands out from this dismal record, however: throughout the world, infant survival was higher in rural areas than in cities. If the specific reasons weren't understood, the concept of fresh air was. Cities were not healthy places to be, and for all its new prosperity, sixth-century Mecca was no different. At the height of summer, when daytime temperatures regularly reached well over a hundred degrees Fahrenheit, the air was barely breathable. Fumes from cooking fires were held in by the ring of mountains around the city, and vultures wheeled above the dung heap on the edge of town, a noxious dump where refuse rotted and fermented, earning it the name "mountain of smoke." Hyenas snuffled and scavenged there by night, and the narrow alleys echoed with their howls. With no sewage system or running water, infections spread rapidly. Earlier that same year of Muhammad's birth, there'd been one of the localized outbreaks of the smallpox that ravaged the Middle East as though by whim, disappearing as suddenly as it had arrived. Cities were thus dangerous places for vulnerable newborns, and Amina must have been desperate to find a wet nurse who'd take her only son to the safety of the high desert. Why else would she settle on so poor a prospect as a woman who had barely enough milk for her own child, let alone someone else's? And equally to the point, why did Halima settle for an orphan child?

Perhaps she caved in and took Muhammad simply because she didn't want to be the only one of her group to return across the mountains without a foster child. Perhaps she took him out of pity, or in open-hearted good faith, or impelled by a certain peasant pride: she had come to find an infant to nurse and was stubborn enough not to leave without one. She certainly claimed no special foresight. Instead, as she'd tell it, "When we decided to depart, I said to my husband, 'By God, I do not like the idea of returning without a suckling; I will go and take that orphan.' He replied, 'Do as you please. Perhaps God will bless us on his account.' So I went back and took him for the sole reason that I could not find any other infant."

The story reverberates with echoes of the Christian nativity story. Halima and her husband are the humble shepherds, and if there are no tales of wise men bringing gifts or of comets streaking across the night sky or of paranoid retaliation by a vicious king, popular belief demands its share of omens nonetheless. So the moment Halima decides to take Muhammad, the whole tone of her speech as relayed by ibn-Ishaq changes. The chatty style, the exchanges with her husband, the donkey's pathetic gauntness all disappear, and her story becomes a miracle one. Her breasts fill with milk, as do the udders of a she-camel they had brought with them, so that Halima and her family now drink all they want. The donkey is suddenly strong and fast, and when they arrive back at their encampment in the high desert, their sheep and goats are thriving, producing unprecedented amounts of milk even as the drought persists. It is clear to Halima that her decision to adopt Muhammad has brought her family divine good fortune. Or at least it was clear in retrospect, by the time she told the story—or by the time it was elaborated in the re-telling by others, turned into the apocryphal tale that piety and reverence demanded, much as the miracle stories of the infancy of Jesus were and still are treasured items of popular belief.

Something in us still believes that far more than nutrition and antibodies are involved in the act of breast-feeding. In ancient Rome, for instance, it was believed that a baby with a Greek wet nurse would drink in her language along with her milk and thus grow up speaking Greek as well as Latin (which was often the case, since the child was surrounded by the sounds of Greek for its first two years of life). Today we talk of the physiology and psychology of mother-child bonding, but we also tend to think of breast-feeding as somehow more authentic than using baby formula, giving it moral value as more honest and more natural. In this respect, sixth-century Meccans may not have been so very different. They believed that there was a kind of rudimentary, earthy vitality in the milk of Beduin wet nurses, and that this vitality went far beyond the physical. As Amina saw it, what her son would drink in with Halima's milk was authenticity: the essence of what it was to be a son of the desert, or as the Meccans called the Beduin, *arabiya*, Arab.

Honor, pride, loyalty, independence, defiance of hardship—these were the core values of Beduin culture, celebrated in the long narrative poems that were the most prized form of entertainment throughout the Arabian peninsula, everywhere from royal courts where cosseted bards were handed purses of gold in payment, to camel-hair tents where children would fall asleep to the rhythmic lullaby of an elder's chanted verses. If most people could neither read nor write, that did not mean they were insensitive to words. On the contrary, oral culture had a passion for language, for the music and majesty of it in the hands of a master. And what people lacked in literacy, they more than made up for in memory. Hours-long poems were recited by heart—an apt phrase for memory when it went to the heart of culture. Bards mourned ancestral tribes that had all but disappeared in the proverbial mists of time. They celebrated the great battles fought in the constellations of the night sky, and the ones fought on earth just beyond living memory. They immortalized warrior legends of courage and self-sacrifice for the greater good, and in the process created a literary tradition so strong that the best-known of their work, "the seven golden odes," are classics of Arabic literature to this day, epic tales alive with the particulars of sexual bravado, death-defying adventure, the pain of lost greatness, and the ache of lost love. And if the sense of loss was a recurring one, that made their work all the more hauntingly memorable.

To the urban elite of Mecca, Beduin poetry spoke to everything they wished to be and were uneasily aware that they were not. Their passion for it was fueled by nostalgia: a longing for a highly romanticized idea of a purity that once was, for a strong moral code uncontaminated by the exigencies of trade and profit. The Beduin warrior was a simpler, more honorable man for a simpler, more honorable time. Much as eighteenth-century Europe romanticized the presumed simple life of shepherds and shepherdesses, and twentieth-century America idealized the strength and flinty honor of the John Wayne cowboy, so sixth-century Meccans saw the Beduin as the human bedrock of Arabia.

But actual shepherds and shepherdesses, like actual cowboys, were something else. However pure and noble their past, real flesh-and-blood Beduin were considered primitive in the present. The phrases "boorish Beduin" and "Beduin rabble" appear often in the early Islamic histories, always spoken by privileged urbanites who saw those still living in tents as unsophisticated rubes, mere goat and camel herders good enough for child care and as caravan guides, but not much more. For most of the Meccan aristocracy, the Beduin were an uncomfortable reminder that for all their urbanized airs, they themselves were only five generations "off the farm," as it were.

Yet Mecca could not have existed without them. It relied on them not only for purebred horses and riding camels but for the mules and pack camels without which the trade caravans could never have crossed hundreds of arid miles at a time to make the city a major mercantile hub. And the Beduin produced the animal products so essential to everyday life: everything from harnesses and saddles to clothing and blankets, preserved dairy and meat staples, sandals and water-skins. Townspeople and nomads were caught in a symbiotic relationship that was valued and resented in equal measure by both sides. On the part of the Meccans, it was not unlike the way American political oratory still celebrates "the heartland" even while considering it relevant only at election times, when it is beholden on all candidates for political office, if they can, to hark back to their grandfathers living a hardscrabble life in middle America, thus celebrating the presumed virtues of hard work, perseverance, and thrift. If Meccans valued the Beduin past even as they abandoned its values, they were no more ambivalent in this respect than their modern Western counterparts.

In a way, then, it was perfect that Muhammad should spend the first five years of his life with the Beduin. Like him, they were valued and yet ignored, central and yet marginalized. Like those Roman infants hearing Greek and then speaking it, he absorbed Beduin values as naturally as that legendary mother's milk. A respect for the power and mystery of the natural world; the idea of communal property where personal wealth was meaningless; the music and grandeur of poetry and history echoing in his dreams—all these and more would form the core of the man he would become, and would inevitably place him at odds with the city of his birth.

Three

Halima had taken Muhammad despite the fact that he was an orphan, yet this was also precisely the reason he would stay with her not just the customary two years, but far longer. This is not the accepted explanation, however. That is the one given by Halima herself: her family saw the child as a kind of good-luck charm, allowing them to thrive despite the ongoing drought. "We recognized this as a bounty from God for two years, until I weaned him," she'd say. "Then we brought him to his mother in Mecca, though we were most anxious to keep him with us because of the good fortune he brought us. I said to her: 'It would be best if you were to leave your little boy with us until he is older, safe from diseases here in Mecca,' and we persisted until she agreed."

If it's easy to imagine the peasant woman cannily crafting her argument that the boy would be safer with her, it's equally tempting to imagine the tearful mother reaching her arms out to her toddler and hugging him close, torn between the desire to have him with her and concern for his well-being. But there is no record of any such scene, which is almost certainly more twenty-first-century sentiment than sixth-century reality. Amina had more than her son's physical health in mind when she accepted the offer to extend his fostering and sent him back with Halima to the high desert.

The stark fact is that she had not married again. Traditionally, a newly widowed woman, especially one in her early twenties with a newborn infant, would have remarried very quickly. If need be, one of her husband's brothers would have stepped up. Even as a second or third wife, she'd thus be ensuring both her own protection and the child's status. But in newly prosperous Mecca, the old rules were breaking down. In principle, Amina was under the protection of her father-in-law, Abd al-Muttalib, but after the trauma of having nearly killed his own son, that legendary leader of Mecca was aging fast. With his decline, his Hashim clan was also beginning to wane in influence and wealth. The Umayyad clan was in ascendance, and though the Hashims were hardly reduced to the status of poor cousins, at least not yet, there was no advantage for anyone in marrying Amina and adopting a son with no inheritance. She was destined to remain a widow, and her son an only child without even half-brothers and half-sisters, cut off from the dense tangle of family relationships that defined Meccan society. She must have felt she had no option but to leave him with his foster family, especially since they were still willing to postpone that matter of a fee.

Muhammad was taken back over the mountains, and Beduin life would become deeply ingrained in him. "Give me a child until he is seven, and I will give you the man," said Francis Xavier, the co-founder of the Jesuits, anticipating modern psychology by several centuries, and so it was with Muhammad. His Beduin childhood would play a major role in making him who he was.

The much-touted purity of desert life was essentially the purity of near-poverty, with no room for indulgence. Once weaned, he'd eat the regular Beduin fare of camel milk along with grains and pulses grown in winter pastures—a sparse diet for a sparse way of life, with an animal slaughtered for meat only for a big celebration or to honor a visiting dignitary. There were no luxuries, not even the sweetness of honey and dates. But if it was a sparse life, it was also a healthy one, spent almost entirely outdoors.

The high-desert steppe was an early education in the power of nature and the art of living with it: how to gauge the right time to move from winter to summer grazing and back again; how to find water where there seemed to be none; how to adjust the long black camel-hair tents to give shade in summer and create warmth on winter nights. Every child did whatever work he or she was capable of. As soon as he could walk, Muhammad was sent out to herd the flocks under the protective wing of one of his foster sisters, Shayma. As older children do with youngsters in large families, she carried him on her adolescent hip when his legs gave out, and kept a watchful eye on him. He in turn watched her, learning how to handle the goats and camels and becoming to all intents and purposes a Beduin boy except that he was always called "the Qurayshi," the one from the Quraysh tribe.

The name was a constant reminder that though he was living with Halima's clan, he was not one of them; he belonged somewhere else, on the other side of the forbiddingly jagged mountain chain aptly called the Hijaz, "the barrier." Though Mecca was only fifty miles away, it could as well have been a thousand. The Beduin talked of the place with a shudder. All those people hemmed in by walls with no space to roam? Even something as basic as the open horizon blocked by mountains all around? How could anyone live that way? Yet there was an undertone of grudging respect in acknowledgment of their economic reliance on the townspeople—a reliance of which Muhammad himself was a daily reminder.

By the time he was five, he could handle the animals by himself. He'd wait by a well while the camels drank seemingly endlessly, their humps fattening as the red blood cells in them hydrated; fight sleep as he stood night watch, guarding the flocks against hyenas howling at the scent of prey; listen for the rustle of desert foxes in the brush or the restless anxiety of his charges as a mountain lion prowled silently nearby, its tracks clear in the dust the next morning. He didn't need to be told that the desert was a lesson in humility, stripping away all pretense and ambition. He knew in his body how large and alive the world was, and how small a human being within it.

Even the sun-seared desert rock seemed to breathe as it released the accumulated heat of day into the cold night air. The vast canopy of stars moved overhead, each constellation playing out its story, impervious to the boy below. It was a world inhabited by spirits, palpable presences all around. How else explain a solitary tree defying all probability to stand tall in an otherwise barren valley? Or the landmark of a singular stone monolith standing out as though dropped from above by a giant hand? Or the way a spring hidden deep in the cleft of a rock wall suddenly came to life, bubbling as you bent down to drink from it as though it were speaking to you? The spirits of these places, the *jinns*, were unpredictable, capriciously capable of either good or evil. Either way, they demanded respect. In much the same way as Christians might cross themselves to ward off evil, travelers camping for the night would chant an incantation: "Tonight I take refuge in the lord of this valley of the *jinn* from any evil that may lie here." And if you were ever tempted to take this world for granted, there were times when the ground itself would remind you of your folly and the rock you thought so solid would began to shake and tremble, even to groan, leaving you no place to hide or take cover from what felt like the wrath of God.

In the desert, nobody needed to preach that there was a higher power than the human. Whether you think of it as natural or supernatural—and in the sixth century there was no difference between the two—anyone unaware of it did not survive. But how, then, was Muhammad to survive when this whole world was abruptly taken from him? Without warning, the five-year-old was separated from the only brothers and sisters he'd ever have, taken over the mountains to a city that seemed an unutterably foreign country, and handed over by the only mother he'd ever known. It would be fifty-five years until he saw any of his foster family again.

The traditional story of why Halima brought Muhammad back to Mecca tells of a kind of divine open-heart surgery. Ibn-Ishaq narrates it first in Halima's voice: "He and his foster brother were with the lambs behind the tents when his brother came running to us and said, 'Two men clothed in white have seized that Qurayshi brother of mine and thrown him down and opened up his belly, and are stirring it up.' We ran toward him and found him standing up, his face bright red. We took hold of him and asked him what was the matter. He said 'Two men came and threw me down and opened my belly and searched in it for I don't know what.'"

Two later versions of the same story are told in the adult Muhammad's own reported words. In the first, he doesn't say how old he was when it happened: "Two men came to me with a gold basin full of snow. Then they seized me, opened up my belly, extracted my heart, and opened it up. They took a black drop from it and threw that drop away, and then they washed my heart with the snow until it was thoroughly clean."

In the second and more ornate of these later versions, however, Muhammad places the angelic visitation not in childhood but in adulthood, after he'd left Mecca for Medina. "Two angels came to me while I was somewhere in the valley of Medina," he said. "One of them came down to earth, while the other remained between heaven and earth. The one said to the other, 'Open his breast,' and then, 'Remove his heart.' He did so, and took a clot of blood which was the pollution of Satan out of my heart, and threw it away. Then the first said, 'Wash his heart as you would a receptacle, and his breast as you would a covering.' Then he summoned the *sakina*, the spirit of the divine, which had the face of a white cat, and it was placed on my heart. Then the other said, 'Sew up his breast.' So they sewed up my breast and placed the seal of prophecy between my shoulders, and then turned away from me. While this was happening, I was watching it all as though I were a bystander."

As the detail accretes with each repetition—the snow in the desert, the white face of the divine spirit, the dialogue between the angels—you can see the story taking shape. It becomes less specifically Arabian as it develops, calling on elements of hero legends worldwide: on Greek and Egyptian god legends (the golden bowl, the cat face); on the Christian idea of Satan lodged like a black clot in the heart; on Jewish mysticism (the *sakina* being the Arabic counterpart of the Kabbalistic *shekhina*); and on Buddhist tradition (the mysterious seal of prophecy between the shoulder blades). In fact it becomes almost dream-like.

Whether as boy or man, Muhammad's calmness and the almost serene beauty of the scene have none of the terror he would experience on Mount Hira. This was part of the biography he *should* have had—one created by later believers who, despite the Quran's insistent abstention from miracles and omens, had the very human desire for miracles to be performed and omens to be fulfilled. They needed faith bolstered by physical evidence, and thus insisted that Muhammad conform to popular expectations of a man blessed by the divine. However un-Quranically, they called on the tradition of miracle to create a physical image of Muhammad's purity of heart, a miraculous apparition that people could grasp and hold on to. In a world where mystery was tangible, this was something familiar. It was what was expected, of a piece with other stories like the blaze of white light on Abdullah's forehead the night Muhammad was conceived, or the glow from Amina's pregnant belly, or the sudden abundance of Halima's milk.

In Halima's version, however—or at least the one attributed to her—neither she nor her husband saw the episode this way. They paid no attention to their own son's tale of having seen two men clothed in white, doubtless attributing it, as any sensible parent might, to a child's overactive imagination. Being practical people, they put the episode down to illness. "We took Muhammad back to the tent," Halima would remember, "and my husband said, 'I am afraid that this child has had some kind of fit, so we should return him to Mecca before it happens again.'" What they really feared, she added, was that he was possessed by a *jinn* and that "ill will befall him."

It seems absurd to play armchair diagnostician on the basis of such evidence and use what is clearly a miracle story to argue, as some have done, that Muhammad suffered from epilepsy. Especially since whatever this was, it was evidently a one-time event. If he were in fact subject to epileptic fits, his many opponents in Mecca would certainly have made much of his condition, yet even though they would use every argument they could muster against his preaching— he was a fabulist, they'd say, a dreamer, a liar, a sorcerer—they would never use this one.

In the end, the most important function of this angelic intervention is probably quite mundane: it serves as a narrative device. It's a means of transporting Muhammad back to Mecca, and one that provides a more satisfying explanation for the Muslim believer than the more likely reason for his return: since there had been no improvement in Amina's fortunes, Halima and her husband saw no possibility of ever being paid for their trouble. Muhammad at age five had become just one more mouth to feed, and for a family living on the edge, one mouth too many.

The child Halima delivered back to his mother was more Beduin than Quraysh: a lean, hardy boy, with none of the chubbiness usually associated with his age. The desert was written on his hands, criss-crossed with a fine tracery of dust worked deep into the pores; in his eyes, narrowed against sun and blowing sand; on his hard-soled feet, with widespread toes and deeply cracked heels. Riding into Mecca on that well-used donkey, he was unmistakably the country boy in the big city, overwhelmed by the rush of sensation, by the smells, the noise, the sounds, the colors, the press of people, the finery of their clothes, the smoothness of their skin. One imagines him shrinking back and clinging to his foster mother's skirts as they entered Amina's house, though more likely he stood straight and tight-lipped in a young boy's imitation of the stoicism so admired in the desert.

Now he'd sleep within hard stone walls instead of the animal warmth and softness of a camel-hair tent, alone on a pallet with a stranger-mother instead of in the familiar huddle of foster brothers and sisters. He has to have felt hemmed in by those walls, as Beduin always have, and hemmed in too by the mountains that practically encircled the city, creating "the hollow of Mecca." The stars that had seemed so close in the high desert were suddenly far away, dimmed by the stale haze of cooking smoke. Longing for the pure air and open spaces he was used to, he must have experienced a loneliness he had never known possible. He was familiar with the solitude of the desert, but this was different: not solitude—there was no such thing with so many people packed so closely together—but a sense of isolation. Among the people who were supposed to be his own tribe, he found himself a stranger.

Just the way he talked marked him as an outsider, his Beduin accent and gestures mocked by other boys until he learned to adapt to the Qurayshi ones, eager as any child to be accepted. A certain wariness crept into the corners of his eyes, and his smile became tentative and cautious; even decades later, hailed as the hero of his people, he'd rarely be seen to laugh. He was Quraysh, and Hashim within the Quraysh, but his existence did not appear to count. In a society where you were defined by who had sired you, he seemed fated to be haunted by his father's absence. Even if he had no words for it as yet, he must have sensed that he would have to prove himself again and again, always wondering on what terms he existed, and by whose grace.

This was what it meant to be an orphan: the ordinary childhood freedom of being without care would never be his. He would never have that blithe ability to take things for granted. Yet this was precisely the key to the man he would become. Those who are comfortably established in life tend to have no need to ask what it means. They are the insiders, and for them, how things are is how they should be. The status quo is so much a given that it goes not just unquestioned but unseen, and the blind eye is always turned. It is those whose place is uncertain, and who are thus uneasy in their existence, who need to ask why. And who often come up with radically new answers.

Psychologists have pointed to the remarkably long list of "high-achievement" figures orphaned young. They include Confucius, Marcus Aurelius, William the Conqueror, Cardinal Richelieu, the metaphysical poet John Donne, Lord Byron, Isaac Newton, and Friedrich Nietzsche, to name just a few, and possibly also Jesus, since Joseph disappears from the Gospel narratives almost the moment he is born. Against all expectation, it seems, early loss can be a stimulus to achievement. As one researcher puts it, the awareness of vulnerability can have a paradoxical strengthening effect: "The question of morality and conscience, a hallmark of creativity, enters with the sense of injustice that the orphaned child feels and continues to feel into adulthood," and eventually develops into "a thirst for identity, a need to imprint oneself on the world."

If such a thirst could indeed be said to exist in Muhammad, it would very quickly be doubled. We can only speculate as to why Amina had left her child for so long with his Beduin foster family, because she would not live long enough to tell her own story. And this may have been why she took him on the two-hundred-mile trek north to Medina just a few months after he had been returned to her.

For a woman of the time, this was not a journey to be made lightly, least of all with a child in tow, so one has to ask why she would undertake it. Did she know she was going to die? Had she been frail ever since her son's birth, which might have been another reason she had not remarried? If she was indeed already sick, the journey would have been all the more arduous, so she must have had a compelling reason.

As things stood, her child's future in Mecca did not look bright, but Medina might offer an alternative. Muhammad's great-grandmother had been Medinan, and his grandfather Abd al-Muttalib had been born there, so Amina may have made the journey in the desperate hope of a sick woman to find a secure home for her child before she died. But the visit apparently made little if any impression on Muhammad's distant Medinan relatives. When he did finally find refuge there, forty-six years later, there is no mention of any special welcome from kin, merely a note registering his partial local ancestry. Any meaningful blood connection, it seems, had been lost.

We have no details of what illness Amina suffered. All we know is that on the way back from Medina, at the caravan halt of Abwa, halfway between the two cities, the boy born without a father would watch his mother die. The small caravan they'd traveled with delivered him back to Mecca, to his grandfather's house. At age six, he was now doubly orphaned, his sole inheritance a radical insecurity as to his place in the world.

Four

The traditional accounts maintain that Muhammad was his grandfather's favorite. This is, after all, what emotional logic demands. For believing Muslims, the idea of such a treasured figure ignored and neglected hurts, so the reality of sixth-century Mecca would be subsumed to a more comforting one: the doubly orphaned boy discovering his identity at his grandfather's feet, hearing the legends of clan and tribe from the lips of the man who had played such a central role in those same legends.

Abd al-Muttalib had become so infirm that even walking with a cane was painful. Each day he was carried to the Kaaba precinct on a rug-covered litter, there to lie in the shade of a palm canopy and be deferred to and consulted, longevity rewarded with honor. It's tempting to imagine his eyes lighting up as his favorite grandson climbs onto the litter beside him and listens wide-eyed while the old man tells him of his heritage, one as rich and complex as the patterns in the rugs they lie on. This was his ancestry—in Meccan terms, his pride. Who you were was determined by your forefathers, so much so that there was practically a cult of ancestors, their tombs venerated close to the point of worship, as is still done throughout North Africa and the Middle

East, from Abraham's tomb in Hebron to those of famed rabbis and imams.

But exactly what comfort could the young Muhammad have derived from an ancestry such as his? What was he to make, for example, of the dramatic tale of how he had come into being? Of the fact that this old man had nearly murdered his own son, Muhammad's father, in front of a mere block of stone? Did he take it as a mark of his specialness, as the early historians assume? Did it give the boy who had never laid eyes on his father a sense of pride in who he was, a kind of genetic memory of greatness? This was surely what was intended, but one can't help thinking that a child with neither father nor mother may have heard it another way altogether, his eyes gone wide not with pride but with horror. For all he knew, the old man could kill him as easily.

In fact the whole issue is probably moot, since it's unlikely that Muhammad ever heard the story from his grandfather. Before what Philippe Ariès would call "the invention of childhood" in eighteenth-century Europe, children were seen simply as small adults. With such high mortality rates, there was no room for sentiment. Especially not for orphans. If Abd al-Muttalib even registered the boy's existence, it was doubtless as just another child scurrying around. And if Muhammad saw his grandfather at all, it was probably only from a distance, a remote figure too highly placed to pay attention, and one with plenty more progeny with far more promising futures. He would not have dared approach the old man, knowing he'd be shooed away, called a pest, a day-dreamer, a good-for-nothing. "Make yourself useful," he'd be told. "Go gather fuel, draw some water. Scram, away with you." And a slap about the head for good measure.

He'd have been grateful in the end to simply be ignored and

given room to learn, as the marginalized always must, how to adapt and survive. A boy without a birthright, his existence was conditional, dependent on making himself unobtrusive, keeping to the background. Yet this was precisely what would enable him to see his own society with such clear eyes. Treated by his own people as one of them yet not one of them, he couldn't help but be aware of the contradictions inherent in a society that was supposed to be his, but seemed to have no place for him.

What the six-year-old saw was a society in which the sacred and the profane mixed so easily that there was no saying where one left off and the other began. Mecca was not the backward, isolated enclave most modern Westerners seem to imagine. It was a thriving capitalist hub, a central point on the north–south trade route that ran the length of western Arabia from the ports of Yemen up to the Mediterranean, and to Damascus and beyond. The genius of the Quraysh was their canny combination of commerce with pilgrimage. Piety and profit were the twin engines of their city's prosperity.

It had been only five generations since the Quraysh had taken control of Mecca, refurbished its ancient shrine, and appointed themselves its new guardians. They had migrated north from Yemen, their movement impelled, like so many mass migrations throughout history, by disaster. In this case, the disaster was the collapse of the giant Marib dam, whose ruins can still be seen in the hills outside Sana, the biblical Sheba.

A quarter million acres of irrigated fields had been created thanks to the dam. Along with irrigation came a vibrant civilization, funded in large part by the cultivation of the native spindly thorn trees that looked utterly negligible to anyone who failed to realize the value of their sap: myrrh. But with wealth, as always, came greed. And with greed instability. Control of Yemen shifted from Byzantine-backed Christian Ethiopia to Zoroastrian Persia to independent kings (one of them, in the fifth century, Jewish) and then through the whole cycle again, each shift accomplished by force of arms. The chaos of warfare took its inevitable toll, and the upkeep of the Marib dam was neglected. In the end, its collapse was due to something ridiculously simple: moles had burrowed so deep into its huge clayey base that it gave way, and the land reverted to high desert. A northward exodus began, including several clans led by the legendary Qusayy, Abd al-Muttalib's great-grandfather. Banding into a single tribe, they adopted the name Quraysh, meaning "those gathered together," and turned their backs not only on Yemen but also on agriculture. When they settled in Mecca, they realized that if you controlled the sacred, you would never starve.

The sanctuary they adopted was soon to be known as the Kaaba, though it was not yet the tall cube-shaped structure (the word "cube" comes directly from the Arabic *kaaba*) that was to become the focal point of Islam. When Muhammad first laid eyes on it, it was a relatively modest affair, at least by modern standards. Its stone and clay walls were still only the height of a man, and its roof was merely palm fronds draped with cloth. To the boy fresh from the life of nomadic herders, it was reassuringly familiar since it was often referred to as the *arish*, the word used for a palm-covered sheepfold or livestock pen. But this term also had profound mystical significance throughout the Middle East. It was the ancient Semitic name for the tabernacle built in the wilderness by the Israelites under Moses, and indicated not just a protected place but a place of protection—a sanctuary and shelter for humans as well as animals, as in "The Lord is my shepherd." The shrine was thus the ultimate enclosure, holding the spirit of God within itself: the godhead al-Lah, literally "the high one" like its Hebrew equivalent Elohim or the still more ancient Mesopotamian El—the one supreme divinity reigning above all lesser tribal gods and totems.

In keeping with the age-old metaphors of height and grandeur, you might expect such a sanctuary to tower imposingly above its city as the Parthenon did above Athens or the Temple above ancient Jerusalem. But the early Kaaba defied the tradition of "high places" for communion with the divine. It was at the lowest point of Mecca, deep in the hollow carved out by intersecting wadis, the dry riverbeds created by flash floods. And somehow this only added to its sense of mystery. The small open precinct around it was hidden by houses so that you came on it suddenly, emerging from the warren of dusty alleys overhung with latticed balconies to the light of open space. It was as though the city were sheltering the Kaaba, folding in on it. In effect it was not the crown but the navel of Mecca—the core of its being, around which everything else revolved. Even literally so. When Meccans returned from a journey, they'd do as pilgrims did and circle the sanctuary seven times, left shoulder inward: a ritual circumambulation that was a kind of seal made with one's own body. "Here I am," it said. "Here is where I belong."

This sense of belonging was echoed by the tens of thousands who came from all over the Arabian peninsula during Dhu al-Hijja, "that of the *hajj*," the central of the three consecutive sacred months in which the whole of Mecca was considered a sanctuary city, with all fighting banned within its limits. Pilgrims tripled its population in these months, thronging the alleys and chanting invocations as they made their way to the Kaaba. *Labbayka allah-umma labbayka*, they intoned: "Here I am, oh God of all people, here I am." And *La sharika laka illa sharikun huaw laka*, "Thou hast no partner except such partner as thou hast"—a mysteriously ambiguous formulation that seemed to include and acknowledge all the other tribal divinities while still keeping them, as it were, in their place.

That place was not in the Kaaba itself, but in the open precinct surrounding it. How many of them there were, however, remains an open question. Three centuries later, one Damascus historian would assert that there were three hundred and sixty of these "idols," as he called them, a number much repeated by modern historians. But aside from the practical impossibility of so many in such a small space, the number itself is probably anachronistic, since it was the number of degrees in a circle as determined by the Islamic science of mathematics, which developed only in the ninth century. In reality there can have been no more than a dozen such idols, and they acted not as gods per se but as tribal totems. The fact that they were arrayed around the Kaaba, not inside it, made it clear that they were subordinate to the one god whose shrine this was. That, after all, was how polytheism worked. Despite the misleading modern idea of a cluster of gods duking it out with one another, all ancient polytheisms revered one high god above all others. These others were said to be "associated" with the supreme god, and this term, used in both the Hebrew bible and the Quran, makes it clear that they were of lesser rank: not "partners of God" so much as junior associates.

To call them idols is equally misleading, bringing to mind old-fashioned Hollywood images of garishly painted and gilded statues. The whole point was that they were *not* statues. The Hebrew bible had been insistent that the twelve stones for the altar were to be "unhewn," not shaped in any way by human hand. In the same way, the totem stones of Mecca were objects of mysterious power precisely because they had not been sculpted, at least not by humans. Some other, greater force had shaped them: the power of wind and time on sandstone, or the volcanic power behind quartz and feldspar and mica, or the other-worldly power of meteorites falling in fire from the heavens. They could be as small as the football-size Black Stone set into one corner of the Kaaba shrine, or as rounded and smooth as the three "daughters of God" known as Manat, Lat, and Uzza, or as large as Hubal, towering over the tallest man. Whether by virtue of size or shape or sheen, each had stood out so sharply in the desert landscape that even the most secular modern mind might sense some spirit force in the fact of their existence, and look for some way to bring them home.

These stones were venerated, garlanded, given offerings and animal sacrifices, but nobody bowed down to them or prayed to them. The stones themselves did not have power; the spirit they represented—the spirit that created them—did. But the stones were palpable; you could see them and touch them. They offered the reassurance of physical presence, expressions of the human yearning for a god made manifest, a god who spoke and could be spoken to. A personal god, you might say, functioning as a kind of user-friendly subordinate to the ineffable, invisible mystery of the force that animated the world.

Accounts of what was inside the Kaaba would become as exaggerated as what was outside. While some early Islamic historians favored comparative restraint, saying it contained only the horns from the ram sacrificed by Abraham in place of Ishmael, or just a single solid gold dove, others insisted it was full of statues representing all the many tribes of Arabia. And Christian paintings of Mary and Jesus. And hoards of treasure. And ancient swords. And still more ancient scrolls. Each version was sworn and attested to, each one seen with someone's own eyes or with the eyes of someone close to them, and each one contradicted by the next. But the most haunting possibility, as well as the most likely, is that as in the holy of holies of the Jewish temple that had once stood far to the north in Jerusalem, the Kaaba was empty. No physical object could possibly contain the essence of the one god, so that the emptiness constituted a much greater mystery than any number of idols or piles of treasure.

It's not hard to see why historians writing in the sophisticated urban milieux of later Damascus and Baghdad (a city that did not even exist in the sixth century) would insist that pre-Islamic Mecca was mired in idol worship. What guided them was the Quranic concept of *jahiliya*, variously translated as "idolatry," "barbarism," "darkness," or "ignorance," and taken as a kind of shorthand for the all-purpose idea of paganism—a word that evokes the idea of godless creatures living in benighted ignorance of all things holy.

But paganism was not godlessness. Quite the contrary, it was an over-abundance of gods: polytheism. The image of it as involving a total lack of morals and values, a chaotic infinity of competing deities, barbaric rituals, and erotically charged lasciviousness, was a product of emerging monotheism's need to claim the higher moral ground. The concept is thus more a political creation than historical fact. All the great thinkers of antiquity were pagan, yet they lacked neither soul nor a sense of the sacred. The last way any of the great Greek philosophers would have described themselves was pagan. Then as now, the word was used derogatively. It came from the same root as the English word "peasant" (*pagus* in Latin, meaning a rural district); to the Roman aristocrat, a peasant was by definition a pagan, and vice versa.

The Islamic image of pre-Islamic Mecca would closely parallel the image of Israel painted by the Hebrew prophets before monotheism prevailed. Isaiah, Jeremiah, and Ezekiel wrote metaphorically when they described all of Jerusalem, and indeed all of Israel, as "playing the harlot." They were accusing the ancient Israelites of selling not their bodies but their souls. And they knew what they were doing when they chose the word "harlotry." Then as now, sex sells; use a sexual metaphor and you have people's attention. Sooner or later, however, you're going to be taken literally.

The irony is that the early Islamic historians, like the Hebrew prophets before them, thus proved themselves as Orientalist as any of the nineteenth-century scholars and writers so effectively dissected by Edward Said in his classic critique *Orientalism*. Orientalism, that is, began in the Middle East itself, long before European imperialism, and for the same reason: intellectual snobbery. These supremely urban eighth- and ninth-century men took understandable pride in the cultural and intellectual achievements of the Muslim empire, from the splendor of Jerusalem's Dome of the Rock to the academies laying the foundation of modern medicine and science. They contrasted their own sophistication with the presumed primitivism of what had gone before, painting an Islamic picture of pre- and post-enlightenment. As we tend to do in the West today, they nurtured the fond idea that they and their contemporaries were the peak of civilization, the sophisticated heirs who had come so far since those days of darkness. Like us, they couldn't help seeing the past through the lens of their own accomplishments and thus distorting it in the process, as though looking through the wrong end of the telescope.

This is how they would come to interpret a single Quranic reference to "abominations" at the Kaaba to mean nakedness, which was exactly what they would expect of unenlightened pagans. But like those who read the Hebrew prophets' condemnation of harlotry literally, they grasped the image but missed the point. Pilgrims would indeed cast aside everyday clothes in acknowledgment of the presence of the sacred, but then they'd don the two seamless lengths of homespun unbleached linen still worn on the *hajj* today and known as *ihram*. By comparison with the usual billowing robes covering everything but the hands and feet, this was nakedness. The pilgrims made themselves deliberately vulnerable, assuming the simplest and humblest possible covering in order to allow no distinction of status or tribe, emphasizing that all were equal in the presence of the divine. All, that is, except those who supplied the homespun garments: the people who ran the business of pilgrimage, the Quraysh.

It is nothing new that there is a lot of money to be made in religion. The sixth-century Quraysh knew this as well as any modern televangelist. In the equivalent of a Wall Street bull market, the elite of Mecca ran the city as a kind of oligarchy, with power in the hands of the wealthy few. Access was always mediated, and always for a fee.

Selling the special *ihram* clothing was part of the business of pilgrimage, as was the provision of water and food for the pilgrims, and the sale of fodder for their camels and donkeys and horses. Which clans controlled which franchises was determined by the Quraysh leadership, who essentially parceled out monopolies (Muhammad's own clan, the Hashims, held the one on providing water, thanks to Abd al-Muttalib's ownership of the treasured Zamzam well). Every aspect of the pilgrimage had been carefully calculated down to the last gram of silver or gold or its equivalent in trade. Fees for the right to set up a tent, for entry to the Kaaba precinct, for the officials who cast arrows in front of Hubal or cut the throats of sacrificial animals and divided up the meat—all these and more were predetermined, and to the sole profit of the Quraysh. Their business was faith, and their faith was in business.

To a boy imbued with the rough egalitarianism of Beduin life, all this could only have come as a shock. His own people had co-opted faith, piously declaring it even as they contravened its most basic principles. From his perch on the sidelines, he saw the social injustice of what was happening all too clearly. Much like large urban areas in Africa and Asia today, the city offered both hope and despair, pulling people in from its hinterland but then condemning them to lives of poverty. Its success rode on the backs of an ever-growing underclass, drawn by dreams of wealth but condemned to the nightmare of poverty.

Muhammad was unable to close or avert his eyes as the wealthy had learned to do. He could not ignore the constant presence of the maimed reduced to begging or of once proud nomads selling themselves as indentured servants, let alone the lifelong dependence of slavery. As he lingered on the outskirts of the

Kaaba precinct, always alert for an errand to be run, he learned how the system worked. He noted how the powerful always seemed to come out ahead and the powerless behind. Saw the self-satisfaction of the wealthy, as though wealth were a virtue in and of itself, a sign that they had been favored by God. Listened carefully as arbiters settled disputes over property and privilege—urban arguments in another world from the Beduin one, where all property was held in common—and admired their skill at shaping the compromises by which both sides would come away satisfied. Watched as oaths were taken and business deals concluded, pacts made and agreements witnessed, prices fixed and franchises portioned out, all sealed and pledged in the name of the one god whose precinct this was.

If any doubt lingered in his mind as to how deep the connection between piety and profit had become, it was dispelled by the blatant mix of the two at the great trade fair held just outside the city each year, at Ukaz. As vital and rambunctious as American state fairs once were, it ran in parallel with the main pilgrimage, the profane twin to the sacred *hajj*. This was when Mecca became not merely a trade hub but a destination, and the Quraysh took full advantage of that fact. The designated area of Ukaz was carnival, bazaar, and trading floor combined, packed with stalls and tents, animal pens, and carpeted reception areas under palm-covered shades. Everything was for sale here, every purchase lubricated with copious amounts of potent date wine and the fermented mare's milk known as *kumys*.

Stalls sold potions and salves, concoctions and decoctions made from such ingredients as the livers of "decrepit camels," scorpion tails, and spider webs fermented in the sun and then buried in jars to just the right degree of mold and fusty spores. There were healing herbs for those who sought them, and quietly, under the table, poisonous ones for those who sought the opposite. Amulets were made from animal parts and hair, parchment and rare shrubs, pieces of gold thread and precious stones, and they could make you fertile or virile, protect you against evil or call it down on those you wished. Sideshows featured Indian fakirs walking over coals and African snake charmers, dancing monkeys and fighting roosters. Bards competed with one another in the sixth-century equivalent of poetry slams while soothsayers traded in the future, preachers in faith, and prostitutes in the flesh. Shamans went into their trances, rolling and writhing in the dust; exorcists reached deep into ailing bodies and pulled out diseased organs dripping with blood, miraculously leaving no sign of incision; wild-eyed visionaries proclaimed themselves prophets.

But there were already so many prophets. Muhammad heard about them from the Jews who came to Ukaz from the great palm oases of Medina and Khaybar to the north, as well as from the Christians who came from Yemen and the cathedral city of Najran to the south. They were known as the People of the Book, and the very idea of a book—of words having their own separate physical existence, not in the mouth or the ear but before one's eyes, inscribed on parchment scrolls—itself exerted a magical force on a boy who could neither read nor write. These were people with physical proof that their god had spoken to them, or at least to their prophets. But how then could this god have said such different things, and how could one people's prophet be denied by another? How could every tribe revere its own totem in the Kaaba precinct but not all the others? How could there be so many truths?

To a young boy uncertain of his place in the world, this

THE FIRST MUSLIM · 53

hubbub of voices has to have been as bewildering as it was enchanting, arousing in him an inchoate longing for clarity, for a unitary
vision that would bring people together instead of dividing them.
But if he was even aware of such a longing, there was nothing a boy
like him could do about it—least of all when just two years after
his mother's death, his grandfather also died. With his nominal
protector gone, his life would be divided yet again.

Five

In effect, Muhammad was now triply orphaned. The eight-year-old was shunted between households once more, to become the responsibility of the new head of the Hashim clan: his uncle abu-Talib. On abu-Talib's part, taking in the youngster was a matter of filial obligation; he had assumed his newly deceased father's liabilities as well as his assets. In this he acted out of honor, and it was as a man of honor that he would play such an important role in his nephew's life in years to come. But how glad he could have been in the year 578 to find himself with yet another mouth to feed—one with no inheritance and seemingly no future—is quite another matter.

Muhammad appears to have been more an appendage to the extended abu-Talib household than an essential part of it. And he would have to earn his keep. So while wishful accounts would have it that the uncle took special care of his nephew from the beginning, the record is clear that Muhammad was put to work as a lowly camel boy, and that within two years he was working in that capacity on the Meccan trade caravans.

His years with the Beduin had served him well. He had a way with camels, among the most ornery of animals unless one knows how to cajole them: the particular clicks of the tongue, the exact tug on the lead rope, the hand on the flank with just the right amount of pressure to make them stand or kneel. Those who were bad with camels yelled at them and jerked the ropes, making the animals all the more stubborn and hard to control. Dealing with them was a skill, and the best handler was one whom nobody noticed because he never had to stamp and prod, and never yelled. The sounds he made to urge the camels on were so soft and sibilant, they were more like breath than noise.

At first Muhammad worked just with the milk camels. Only when he'd proven himself with them was he allowed to work with the castrated males that made Mecca's trade possible. These single-humped dromedaries had been introduced from Ethiopia in the third century, and turned out to be perfectly suited to the climate and terrain of Arabia. Not only could they vary their body temperature according to conditions, but they could store water in their red blood cells (legends of parched travelers slitting open the hump to drink from it may spark the imagination, but the hump actually stores fat, not water). This meant that they could go for days without drinking, spanning the distances between wells or springs. They were, that is, uniquely well adapted to the desert. But humans weren't, which is why so many caravan travelers, like Muhammad's father, never returned. It's a measure of how much they risked that of the four ancestors who had given their names to the main clans of the Quraysh, only one had died at home in Mecca; the other three, including Muhammad's forebear Hashim, had ended their lives far away in Gaza, in Iraq, and in the Yemen.

Besides sickness and accident, there was always the danger of bandits or of rogue Beduin raiders tempted by the drawn-out line of heavily laden beasts. Plus of course the sheer arduousness of travel in the scorching heat and light, magnified by the stone and packed dust of the desert pavement, which was seared to a crust. You needed to be hardy for such long treks. The heavily laden pack camels mostly carried goods, so only the wealthiest merchants rode. Those doing "Beduin work" like the young Muhammad walked alongside, and once they'd unloaded the camels, fed them, and hobbled them at the end of each day's stage—some thirty miles if the going was smooth and level, less than twenty if it was not—their work was still not done. They'd collect the oblong pellets of camel feces, so dry and densely fibrous that they gave off no odor even when broken open, and coax them into a slow burn for cooking fires; fetch water for their bosses from a well or a spring if there was one, or else from the bulging goat-bladders slung over the camels' flanks; make sure the merchants were well fed, taking for themselves only what was left; and then stand watch through the night against predators like wolves, hyenas, and mountain lions.

The caravans provided the safety of numbers. The lone traveler may have been a staple of the great Beduin odes, taking his pleasures where he could and stoically enduring the dangers of the road even as he boasted of them, but that was poetry, and this was real life, and only the young and inordinately idealistic would be so rash as to confuse the two. Any caravan consisted of at least a dozen camels, but twice a year the Meccan merchants organized huge camel trains up to two thousand strong, one heading north to Damascus in the spring, the other south to Yemen in the fall. And Muhammad had been newly assigned to work on the northbound one when one of the best-known events of his child-hood took place.

They had been following the high ground to the east of the Jordan River, on the ancient route known as "the kings' highway," and the caravan leader had already given the sign to halt for the night close by an abandoned Byzantine fortress in which a single Christian monk had taken up residence.

The ruins were a sign of the times: as political systems begin to collapse, so too does the infrastructure. The conflict between the Byzantine and the Persian empires was in effect an eight-hundred-year war that had gone on since the time of Alexander the Great, and by now it had thoroughly depleted the resources of both sides. To the east, the vast Persian-built irrigation systems of the Iraqi plain between the Euphrates and the Tigris rivers were deteriorating, much as upkeep on the Marib dam in Yemen had deteriorated under the stress of warfare over a century earlier. In the Byzantine province of Syria, which included all of what is now Syria, Jordan, Lebanon, Israel, and Palestine, troops had been withdrawn for lack of money, leaving many of the fortresses in the long north–south line of defense to be eroded by sand and dust storms. Occasionally Beduin nomads moved inside the crumbling walls, using them as winter shelter for themselves and their flocks, but monks also settled in them, sometimes in groups but more often as solitaries. Hermits, preachers, holy men, sometimes wild men, they were respected by local tribesmen, who'd leave food and water for them—offerings as much to the idea of holiness embod-ied in these men's one omnipotent god as to the men themselves.

The image of the monk in his desert cell "alone with the live-long night and its wearily lingering stars" became a romantic trope in pre-Islamic poetry, where the light from "the lamp of the hermit who pours o'er the twisted wicks the oil from his slender cruse" was a source of distant comfort to the solitary traveler or warrior. The pattern had been set as early as the fourth century in Egypt, when Saint Anthony, often called "the father of the desert fathers," spent twenty lone years in an abandoned Roman fortress on the Nile. Or maybe not so lone. His Alexandrian biographer Athanasius would write that his presence there attracted a steady stream of tourists, including Arabian traders who detoured to pass by his hermitage simply to be close to the presence of holiness. Anthony's example was so powerful, Athanasius claimed, that "monasteries flourishing like the flowers of springtime have been scattered throughout the whole earth, and the sign of the solitary ascetic rules from one end of it to the other."

The solitary ascetic who would now play such a vital role in the legend of Muhammad's childhood was known as Bahira, a strange name for a desert dweller since it comes from the Arabic *bahr*, sea. Perhaps he'd once been a seaman, or perhaps the name indicated that he had a sea of knowledge at his fingertips, specifically in the form of a book that was rumored to be old beyond knowing, handed down from one generation of monks to the next. At a time when few people could read or write, the very existence of this book was iconic. It was thought of as a kind of oracle, its power projected by osmosis into its guardian or possessor. In fact Bahira's book was most likely a parchment copy of the Bible in one of the many variants still current at the time, and since parchment was perishable, he was one of those who had devoted his life to the painstaking task of copying it, letter by letter, verse by verse, in order to preserve it.

As ibn-Ishaq tells it, with his usual sprinkling of caveats such as "it is alleged," Bahira had never before paid any attention to passing camel trains. But when abu-Talib's section of the Damascus-bound one approached, the hermit saw a single small cloud in the otherwise cloudless sky, hovering low over one particular point in the caravan. Recognizing it as an omen, he broke with his usual habit, went out, and invited everyone to be his guest and to come share what food he had. Abu-Talib and the others accepted, leaving the ten-year-old Muhammad behind to watch over the camels and the goods. But no sooner had they all entered the fortress walls than Bahira sensed that someone was missing. He questioned them closely, at which they acknowledged that, well, yes, there was always the camel boy. But surely the invitation didn't include him?

It did. Bahira insisted that the boy be brought in, then had him stand still while he examined his torso, searching for the "seal of prophethood" foretold in that mysterious tome of his—in varying accounts either a third nipple, as some say is found in each reincarnation of the Dalai Lama, or a birthmark between the shoulder blades "like the imprint of a cupping glass." Whichever it was, he found it, then turned to abu-Talib and announced: "A great future lies before this nephew of yours."

In a way, this is a perfect story, pregnant with signs and wonders. The aura of the hovering cloud and the code of the hidden seal are exactly what one might expect for a child with a heroic future. Yet once again a miracle story contains within itself the ironic counterplay of legend and reality. Even as it magnifies the young Muhammad's status, it also places him on the lowest rungs of the camel trade, so insignificant as to be thought automatically excluded from Bahira's invitation. If such an event did indeed take place, it can only have seemed risible at the time to abu-Talib and the others. They'd have understood it as the ravings of an old man who had spent far too much time alone, touched by solitude and the desert sun. *Majnun,* they'd have called him—under the influence of a *jinn,* a spirit of madness—and gone on their way to Damascus.

Still, the legend works as a classic illustration of predestination. Unknown and unrecognized among his own people, the hero is instantly recognized by the holy men of other peoples. And most significantly, in Byzantine Syria, by a Christian monk, thus establishing the future revelation of the Quran as the culmination of previous revelations foretold in the Bible itself. The point would be considered so important that a very similar version of the same story—the lone monk, the route to Damascus, the recognition of specialness—would eventually be placed fifteen years later, when Muhammad was twenty-five, by which time he had worked his way up through the ranks of the camel trains to become an independent agent representing the interests of others. But the transition from camel boy to a respected figure on the well-traveled trade routes was to be lengthy and hard-earned. He had much to learn, and a whole world to learn it from.

As a glance at the extent of foreign news coverage in *The Wall Street Journal* or the *Financial Times* still demonstrates, successful traders need information. Meccan merchants had to be politically and culturally well informed, with up-to-date information on what was happening both en route and at their destination. And they needed to be very skilled at diplomacy.

It began with the need to assure safe conduct across the territories of numerous tribes and tribal confederations. Such assurances had to be negotiated and paid for in a desert form of a toll, or basically, protection money. Permission was requested to use local springs or wells, arrangements made to buy provisions en route, gifts offered to the sheikhs and chieftains who could award such permission and make such arrangements. And all this entailed not only a widespread network of contacts but detailed knowledge of tribal politics: who had the authority to guarantee protection, who was in ascendance and whose power was fading, who was newly in alliance with whom, which alliance had recently fallen apart over issues of grazing or water rights. The caravan leaders needed to know whose word they could rely on, especially when a man's word truly was his bond. Agreements were signed not in writing but with hands clasped, forearm against forearm, constituting a solemn pledge on which rested the most important thing to any man of the time: his reputation. But some reputations were justified and others less so, and the difference could be that between life and death.

Once the caravan was under the formal protection of the local chieftain or sheikh, the merchants were guests in his territory, to be protected as though they were in his tent or his palace. Any attack on them by rogue elements like a raiding party from a rival tribe would be dealt with as though the sheikh himself had been attacked. He would assign guides to accompany the caravan through his territory, and these men could read the desert as you would a book. The seemingly endless expanse of stark rock, scrub steppe, and sharp-edged lava fields was neither empty nor monotonous to their experienced eyes, but as full of signs and recognizable landmarks as any city neighborhood today.

They needed no maps: the land was in their heads. They knew exactly which well held the freshest water in which season, and where to find winter pools—the depressions that collected runoff from winter rains and held it for a few weeks at a time. Much as sailboats tack with the prevailing wind, they led the caravans on routes that angled from one watering spot to the next, sometimes within a day's ride of each other, more often two or three. Usually they'd arrive at an encampment of nomads by an underground spring, or a few scraggly trees and a rough stone hut marking the presence of a brackish well. But occasionally there'd be the luxury of one of the oases strung like beads widely spaced on a chain necklace: permanent settlements like Medina, Khaybar, Tayma, and Tabuk on the northbound route from Mecca, where spring-fed date plantations stretched for miles, long ribbons of green hidden in deep valleys.

The profitability of these month-long treks more than compensated for their arduousness. By Muhammad's time, Meccan merchants had expanded their business through an area larger than Europe, reaching north and south in large sweeping arcs encompassing Syria and Iraq, Egypt, Yemen, and Ethiopia. And wherever they went, they were not strangers. They put down roots in the lands and cities they traded with, for to be a trader at that time was to be a traveler, and to be a traveler was to be a sojourner.

They did not travel eight hundred miles to do a kind of sixth-century version of a pilot's touch-and-go at Damascus airport. There was no dropping in, shaking hands on a deal, and heading right on out again. It took time to give and receive hospitality, to create and develop the face-to-face relationships that enabled trade, and to carry out the slow, elaborate ritual of negotiation. You settled in for the duration and made yourself at home, so much so that by the time Muhammad began work on the caravans, Meccan aristocrats owned estates in Egypt, mansions in Damascus, farms in Palestine, and date orchards in Iraq.

Like all property owners, they were keenly aware of everything that might affect the value of their holdings, especially the see-saw of dominance as the Byzantines and Persians pushed each other's boundaries of influence first one way, then the other. The geopolitical balance that had held for nearly eight hundred years was in question, and major cities like Damascus, where Byzantine control was becoming increasingly tenuous, were alive with rumor and speculation, conflicting claims and contradictory expectations.

For Muhammad, there could be no better education than Damascus, one far more expansive than that of any modern schoolchild confined to a computer screen and the four walls of a room. For the first time he realized that no matter how cosmopolitan Mecca might be in its own terms, it was provincial in terms of this greater world to the north. Just as he was simultaneously an insider and an outsider at home, so too his city was both inside and outside: relevant by virtue of its central position on the land route north from Yemen and the Indian Ocean, yet separated by that vast expanse of desert from the physical arena of Byzantine–Persian rivalry, in which Mecca played the role of a kind of giant, arid Switzerland unaligned with either side.

Damascus was an ancient city even then, its history stretching back over fifteen hundred years. It was the most important hub on the western portion of the famed Silk Road, and its streets teemed with people from as far north as the Caspian Sea and as far east as India. Greeks, Persians, Africans, Asians, light skins and dark, melodiously soft languages and harshly guttural ones— all came together here in a fertile intermingling not only of goods but of cultures, and of the religious traditions that framed those cultures.

Through the lingua franca of Aramaic, spoken throughout the Middle East in different but mutually comprehensible dialects, Muhammad was confronted with a kaleidoscope of sacredness. The stories treasured by those he encountered carried their history and their identity, and they were not shy about telling them. In the courtyards of synagogues and churches, in the markets and the great caravansaries, under the shade trees lining the canals that made Damascus especially enchanting to desert dwellers (the very idea of water in the streets!), these stories were told by soft-spoken elders, by young firebrand preachers, by poets and clerics, dreamers and philosophers. Their audiences sat rapt, nodding and swaying and joining in on the best-known lines as the heroic legends of Christians and Jews, Zoroastrians and Hindus—dramas of the human and the divine—played out across the backdrop of history. Everyone sought to explain the world in their own way, all of them full of the passionate conviction that they and only they knew the truth. Yet even among those of the same faith, truth differed.

The biblical stories told by the Jews of Medina, for instance, were not quite the same as those told by the Jews of Damascus. The Christian stories differed too, often with poignant variations. When Jesus defended the woman accused of adultery, one version had him saying: "Let he who is without sin cast the first stone." But another, still current in today's Middle East, had him physically protecting the woman by shielding her with his body and adding two crucial words: "Let he who is without sin cast the first stone *at me.*"

There were famed legends like that of the seven sleepers: seven boys walled up in a cave to die during the Roman persecutions of early Christians. But instead of dying, the boys (plus, in one version, a dog) miraculously fell into a deep slumber for two hundred years, when they were discovered and wakened to learn that Christianity had triumphed. (Ironically, Muslims now know the story better than most Christians, since it is cited in the Quran.) The seven sleepers were so popular that everyone, no matter where they came from, sought to claim them, placing the cave in their own part of the world with a kind of geographical possessiveness that still persists. In much the same way that modern pilgrims can find the place where John the Baptist's head is buried in at least three different locations in the Middle East, those wishing to visit the cave of the seven sleepers still have a choice: near Ephesus in Turkey, a few miles north of Damascus in Syria, or just outside Amman in Jordan.

The differences went deeper than legend, however. Christians and Jews both venerated the Bible, yet they held up different versions of it. And when it came to what these books might mean, there was intense argument not only between but within the two monotheisms. Jews were divided between the teachings of this rabbi or that, between the Jerusalem Talmud and the new Babylonian one, or between legalism and messianism. And the Christians were still more deeply divided, caught up in bitter and sometimes violent internecine rivalry. Seemingly abstruse questions as to whether Jesus was both God and man, or God in human form—whether he had one nature or two—had become highly politicized, creating such deep rifts that the Byzantine Empire was essentially at war with itself as various provinces sided with one theopolitical entity or another.

For an adolescent trying to cement a life from the shards of loss and displacement, the monotheistic idea has to have been immensely powerful. It resonated with what Muhammad knew of the stark purity of the desert, that sense of an animating force far greater than anything human. It spoke to his own yearning for unity, for a way to bridge the gap he experienced between belonging and not belonging. And it seemed to offer the grand ideal of all peoples coming together in acknowledgment of a force so beyond human comprehension that one could only stand in awe of it and acknowledge the pettiness of human differences. Yet everywhere he looked, what should surely bring people together only seemed to drive them apart. The more they preached what the prophets had said, from Moses down through Jesus, the less they seemed to hear those same prophets' words. How could the idea of divine unity result in such human disunity? How could monotheism create such sectarianism? Were humans destined to be divided by what should surely unite them?

Whether you credit the monk Bahira's mystical foresight or abu-Talib's sharp merchant's eye, it did not take long for the uncle to note that his nephew was both genuinely observant and quick to learn. Muhammad seemed somehow to anticipate abu-Talib's needs. He'd be there when wanted yet fade into the background when not; run an errand even before his uncle fully realized it needed to be run; check on deliveries and keep track of inventory. As the boy entered his teens, abu-Talib began to rely on him more, taking him with him as he went about his business. The caravans would now become Muhammad's professional education as well as his cultural and religious one.

He saw how his uncle was always the first to reach out and clasp the other's hands in his own: a politician's handshake, making the other feel honored, drawn in, special. He watched as the merchants followed the time-honored tradition of hospitality graciously given and graciously received, as they sipped tea and honey-sweetened milk and pomegranate juice, savored stuffed dates and piquant delicacies wrapped in vine leaves, and dipped their bread into a common dish in acknowledgment of the bond between those who break bread together. He listened through the seemingly endless rounds of negotiation, learning the slow and stately dance in which each participant held the other off even as he invited him in, judging the degree of welcome and distance, of give and take, until finally trust was established and the deal was sealed.

As he worked his way up to abu-Talib's side, Muhammad learned the value of the goods they carried from Mecca. There were the relatively mundane loads such as leather and wool, as well as small amounts of gold and silver mined in the Hijaz mountains, to be worked into daggers and jewelry by the famed craftsmen of Damascus. But the lightest, most compact, and by far the most profitable of all their cargo was still more precious: myrrh and frankincense. There were fortunes to be made in these aromatic resins. Painstakingly tapped from the seemingly inconspicuous thorny scrubs that grew only in the highlands of Yemen, Ethiopia, and Somalia, they were in high demand throughout the Byzantine and Persian empires. Urban sophisticates favored myrrh as a perfume and deodorant. Mourners massaged the bodies of the dead with it before wrapping them in their shrouds. Vast amounts of frankincense were burned in churches, the smoke perfuming the air and anointing the lungs of the faithful, and it was thrown by the handful onto the sacred Zoroastrian fires of Persia to make the flames leap and sparkle in a dramatic rainbow of colors. Carrying nine different species of frankincense, as well as myrrh in both oil and crystal form, a merchant like abu-Talib could triple or even quadruple his original investment. After expenses, that is.

The Meccan caravan trade was no ad hoc affair. It was organized as a cartel and run by a syndicate. This financing system redounded to the benefit of all, or at least all who were allowed in. In the years Muhammad worked for abu-Talib, the largest shares were held by the four main clans of the Quraysh, but many others had minority shares, including individuals. Tolls, protection money, customs duties, and sales taxes were all paid by the syndicate and factored in, with a share of each member's profits deducted to cover the costs of administration. Here too diplomacy was needed to defuse the inevitable arguments about the distribution of profits, and here too Muhammad learned quickly, becoming as skilled at calming ruffled egos as he was at negotiating differences. By the time he was in his early twenties, he'd become abu-Talib's trusted lieutenant on the long caravan journeys, and had risen so far in his uncle's estimation that he was treated almost as a son. But only almost.

If the two men had not been close, Muhammad would never have asked what he did. He'd never have felt he had the right to even broach the idea. So when he requested the hand of abu-Talib's daughter Fakhita in marriage, he certainly cannot have expected to be refused. Yet he was.

This was no tale of young star-crossed lovers, however. Marriage in the sixth century was a far more pragmatic arrangement. We know nothing of Fakhita aside from her name. Muhammad's proposal was made to the father, not the daughter. In effect, he was asking abu-Talib to publicly acknowledge their closeness by declaring him not just "like a son" but a full member of the family. He would no longer be merely a poor relation who had risen in the world, but a son-in-law.

Abu-Talib's decision had nothing to do with the fact that Muhammad and Fakhita were first cousins. Gregor Mendel and the science of genetics were still eleven hundred years in the future, and marriage between cousins was as common in the sixth century, both in Arabia and elsewhere, as it had been in biblical times. It was considered a means of strengthening the internal bonds of a clan, and indeed would remain so in the marriage patterns of European royalty well into the twentieth century. So there is only one possible reason for abu-Talib's denial of his nephew's request: he did not consider this an advantageous marriage for his daughter. No matter how much he trusted and relied on Muhammad, the father was not about to marry his daughter to an orphan with no independent means. He intended for her to marry into the Meccan elite, and quickly made a more suitably aristocratic match for her.

If Bahira had indeed foreseen a great future for Muhammad, abu-Talib had clearly not taken him seriously. And if Muhammad had imagined that he had overcome the limitations of his childhood, he was now harshly reminded that they still applied. Abu-Talib's denial of his request carried a clear message. "This far and no further," he was saying in effect. "Good but not good enough." In his uncle's mind, Muhammad was still "one of us, yet not one of us."

In time, abu-Talib would come to regret this rejection of Muhammad. The two men would eventually overcome the rift it caused between them and become closer than ever. But in a pattern that was to recur throughout Muhammad's life, rejection would work to his long-term advantage. Abu-Talib's denial of him as a son-in-law would turn out to be one of those ironic twists that determine history—or, if you wish to see things that way, fate. If Muhammad had married his cousin, nobody today might even know his name. Without the woman he did go on to marry, he might never have found the courage and determination to undertake the major role that waited for him.

Six

It was an unusual marriage. She was older than he, and while accounts vary as to exactly how much older, most settle on age forty for her, twenty-five for him. Not that this was what made the marriage unusual. Except, that is, to many Western scholars. Revealing more about themselves than about Muhammad, they'd assume it had to be a marriage of convenience. Specifically, financial convenience. He married her for her money, they'd say—the "wealthy widow" syndrome—since it seemed to them self-evident that there was no way he could have been attracted to her. One or two, of a more psychoanalytical bent, imagined that he saw her as a mother figure, the orphan seeking a substitute for the mother he had lost at age six. Few seem to have considered that he really did love her.

In fact the difference in age meant little in a culture where multiple marriage was common. Whether serial marriages due to death or divorce, or polygamous ones among the elite, the practice meant that an aunt might be younger than her nephew, one half-brother a generation older than another, and a first cousin the age we would now expect of an uncle or a niece. It is certainly true, however, that few of these marriages were love matches. The vast majority were political or financial arrangements, tying one clan or tribe to another. Which is not to say that romantic love did not exist. The pre-Islamic bards celebrated it in vivid detail, just not within the bounds of marriage, which was a pragmatic matter, not a romantic one.

Yet the relationship between Muhammad and Khadija seemed anything but pragmatic, and this is what has really so confounded scholars. The most cogent explanation for their long, monogamous marriage is also the simplest: they had a real bond of deep love and affection, one that lasted twenty-four years. She would be the one person most central to Muhammad's accepting his public role, but she would do so quietly, contributing little to the later myth-making about him, since she'd die before he began to attract large-scale support.

Long after her death, he would hold her up as far superior to any of his later wives, declaring that he would never find that kind of love again. How could he when he was already the leader of a burgeoning new faith—the revered prophet, the messenger of God, the one whom people vied to be close to, to have his ear? Khadija loved him for himself, not for who he would become, and he would never forget her in those later years, turning pale with grief at the sound of any voice that reminded him of hers.

What made the marriage unusual, then, was not the age difference but its closeness, especially given the difference in social status between husband and wife. And the fact that it was she who proposed to him.

Ibn-Ishaq describes her as "a merchant woman of dignity and wealth, a determined, noble, and intelligent woman." It's unusual to see the words "determined" and "intelligent" used about any woman of the time, but in Khadija's case they were entirely appropriate. Twice widowed, she had inherited her second husband's share in the Meccan caravan cartel, which meant that she was financially independent—not as wealthy as the leading Meccan merchants, but certainly comfortably situated. She now had a choice: she could sell her business to one of the powerful trading blocs or continue as an independent, in which case she'd need someone she could trust to represent her interests on the trade caravans. A business manager, essentially, who knew commerce well and would not put his own interests ahead of hers.

In the year 695, she hired Muhammad to be her agent on the Damascus-bound caravan, and by one account sent a trusted servant along with him with instructions to report back on how he handled her affairs. The servant, a slave called Maysara, returned with a story that echoes that of Bahira fifteen years earlier. Muhammad had sought shade beneath a tree near a monk's cell in Syria, he said, and the monk, seeing him there, had been amazed. "None has ever halted beneath this tree but a prophet," he told Maysara, who then upped the miraculous by claiming that as the heat grew intense toward noon on the homeward journey, he had seen two angels shading Muhammad.

It seems somewhat insulting to Khadija to conclude, as ibn-Ishaq does, that this report is what impelled her to propose marriage. That is the problem with miracle stories: if you look at them closely, they tend to boomerang. This one implies that without the monk and the angels, Khadija would never have considered marriage, though she hardly needed someone else to tell her either that Muhammad was a trustworthy manager or that there was far more to him.

He had already built an excellent reputation in his years working with abu-Talib. Instead of haggling endlessly, offering lower prices and demanding higher ones than he knew he would get, he offered fair prices from the start—and because he was known to be fair, was given better-quality merchandise in return. He never took an extra cut for himself under the table or fudged the expense reports (such practices being as old as trade itself), so after abu-Talib had rejected him as a son-in-law, he became a sought-after independent agent, working on commission. A man for hire, that is, with no interests of his own to promote, to the degree that he seemed almost to disdain the profit motive that ruled Mecca.

What commissions he earned, he gave away in alms to the poor. Other merchants undoubtedly thought him foolish for this. How did such a man expect to marry at all, let alone marry well? How did he expect to care for a family? To rise in society? They tried to use his lack of self-interest to their own advantage, which he certainly knew but did not care about. His values were elsewhere, though so long as they were not about money and self-advancement, few bothered to inquire exactly where. His disinterestedness set him apart, making him part of the culture but not of its values, and while this may have seemed odd to most people, Khadija saw it as admirable.

As a widow, and until Muhammad a childless one, she knew what it was to be uncertain of one's place in society, and how hard it had been for him to work his way up through the ranks from camel boy to owner's agent. She could see that in terms of maturity, he was far closer to middle age than to youth. So it's not hard to understand how these two people, both unusual in their time and place, could have reached out to each other. Or rather, how she reached out to him, and by marrying him, brought the outsider inside.

It was she who proposed, quite simply because he could not.

Especially after abu-Talib's rebuff, he would not have dared take the initiative. Khadija was from the powerful Asad clan, which made her eminently marriageable. Her suitors included the wealthiest merchants in Mecca, all of them offering large gifts to her father as a way of sweetening the deal. Except that Khadija, unlike abu-Talib's young daughter, refused to be auctioned off. She had no need for another conventional marriage; this time she would defy convention by marrying the man she chose, not the one chosen for her. So as ibn-Ishaq tells it, adding "so the story goes" in acknowledgment of the oddly stilted language, she said: "I like you, Muhammad, because of our relationship and your high reputation for trustworthiness and good character and truthfulness," and asked him to be her husband.

Still, the formalities had to be observed. Having rejected Muhammad as his own son-in-law, abu-Talib could hardly represent him to Khadija's father as custom demanded. Instead, another of the ten sons of Abd al-Muttalib, Muhammad's uncle Hamza, formally asked on his behalf. One version has it that Khadija's father willingly assented, though what he thought of his daughter marrying a "nobody" is something else, especially given the dowries being offered by other suitors and the probability that he was against the marriage, as another, racier version of events implies. Conscientiously included by ibn-Ishaq, this version has it that "Khadija called her father to her house, plied him with wine until he was drunk, anointed him with perfume, clothed him in a striped robe, and slaughtered a cow. Then she sent for Muhammad and his uncle, and when they came in, she had her father marry him to her." By the time her father had sobered up, the deed was already done.

Perhaps such attempts to explain the marriage are understandable, given that a relationship based on genuine love, caring, and respect was a rarity at the time. But this one ignores Muhammad's reputation for honesty, and from what we know of Khadija, she was no more likely than he to have taken part in a drunken deception. The story underrates her; she may have married down in terms of wealth and social status, but what she saw in Muhammad was more important than any of that.

Children arrived quickly, cementing the couple's bond. They had four daughters together, and one son, Qasim. But Qasim died before his second birthday, and while the Quranic revelations would later make a point of celebrating daughters, inveighing against those who measured wealth and status in terms only of sons, the loss of this one son must still have hurt deeply. It meant that Muhammad would remain what was known as *abtar*, literally curtailed, cut off, or severed. Without male offspring, that is.

The sorrow of Qasim's death would be assuaged to some degree by a boy already close to the household. Khadija had given Muhammad a young slave called Zayd as a marriage gift, but Muhammad treated him less as a slave than as a son, so much so that when the boy's north Arabian clan raised the money to buy him back, Zayd begged to be allowed to stay. Muhammad refused the money, freed the boy, and formally adopted him, setting the stage for the Quran's future encouragement of manumission. And there was another boy too: Muhammad's cousin Ali, abu-Talib's youngest son. His father's business had begun to falter without Muhammad working by his side, so Muhammad offered to help out by taking the boy into his own household. The man raised by his uncle would now raise that same uncle's son, and if Muhammad and Khadija did not formally adopt Ali, they considered him part of their family. Indeed he would eventually marry their youngest daughter, Fatima.

In his thirties, then, Muhammad seemed at last to be a happy man. With Khadija by his side, the respect of others, and a comfortable living, he seemed to have all a man could reasonably ask for. Despite the odds against him, he had thrived. But that did not mean he had put the awareness of those odds behind him. The experience of the boy could not simply be shucked off by the man; it was part of who he was, and part of what Khadija loved in him. She shared his values, and was as disturbed as he by the inequities of Meccan society. They lived their joint life accordingly, wearing homespun linen instead of the ostentatious silks of the elite, darning and mending clothes instead of purchasing new ones, and giving away most of their income in food and alms. And through Khadija's cousin Waraqa, they found a framework for their values in a small group of independent Meccan thinkers known as *hanifs*.

Linguists tend to hedge their bets by saying that the word *hanif* is "of obscure origin," but it probably came from the word for "bending" or "turning," as in someone who bends or turns to a greater power. We know of six of them by name, including Waraqa, who was reputed to have studied both the Hebrew and the Greek bibles deeply. By some accounts he was actually a Christian, by others a rabbi. More likely he was neither, the attribution being merely the result of the human need to categorize. The whole point, after all, was that the *hanifs* resisted categorization. Their search was for a purer form of monotheism, untainted by the sectarian divisiveness rife in the Middle East of the time. They were deliberately unaffiliated with any one sacred practice, instead recognizing the universality of the one high god, whether the name used was Elohim, al-Lah, or Ahura Mazda, the Zoroastrian "lord of light and wisdom." Still, the Hebrew bible spoke to their sense of roots, and they harked back to Abraham—"the father of all who believe," as Saint Paul had called him—as the founding ancestor of Mecca through his son Ishmael. It was to Mecca that Hagar had fled with her young son, they believed, and Abraham and Ishmael together who had built the Kaaba as the sanctuary of the *sakina*, the divine presence of God, thus establishing the true ancestral tradition, one far older and with far deeper meaning than the relatively recent tribal one of the Quraysh.

The word *hanif* would eventually be used in the Quran in praise of all those from Abraham on who acknowledged the one god and excluded all others. But in these pre-Quranic days, however respected the *hanif*s might be for their knowledge, they were tolerated rather than accepted—an essential difference, since in Mecca as in any modern society, the fact that something needed to be tolerated implied that it was still somehow distasteful. And as always, tolerance had its limits. When Muhammad was still a child, one *hanif*, Zayd ibn-Amr, was hounded out of the city by his own half-brother after he publicly challenged the power of the totem stones. Known as "the monk," he found solitary refuge in a stone hut at the foot of Mount Hira before leaving to pursue the life of a wandering dervish, seeking out the great spiritual masters of the day throughout the Middle East. Years later, he would make his way back to Mecca, eager to hear Muhammad's preaching, only to be killed by bandits just a few days from home.

Was Muhammad himself a *hanif*? Like them, he was part of

THE FIRST MUSLIM · 79

Mecca even as something in him remained apart. He saw his society too clearly for comfort: the contradictions, the hypocrisies and denials, the seemingly ever-widening gap between what people professed to honor and what they actually did. With his own immediate ancestry so embroiled in conflict, he may have been pulled toward this other, larger, and more ancient lineage embodied in the story of a child almost sacrificed, as his own father had nearly been, in submission to the one ultimate god. Even if he did not describe himself as a *hanif*, he must have felt a sense of kinship with this handful of men who had knowingly placed themselves outside the norm, responding to the purity of the idea of a god so great that he, if that pronoun could even be used, was beyond male or female, beyond any form of representation: a single, ineffable, universal idea of the divine.

The *hanifs* practiced a form of ascetic meditation in solitary vigil known as *tahannut*, and it seems clear that Muhammad adopted this practice in the mountains outside Mecca. There was a long tradition of such meditation, in the Hebrew and Greek bibles as much as in Indian and Chinese practice. Prophets, hermits, preachers, gurus, all sought the timeless vastness of the high desert for a clarity of vision, a sense of eternity uncluttered by everyday human concerns. What, after all, could be older and more long-lasting than stone? What could be cleaner and purer than a mountainside bare of all human habitation, even of trees and shrubs?

The red granite of the Hijaz mountains was no smooth Zen-like stone but jagged rock so harsh it would bloody your hands if you fell and clung to it. Yet there was also immense beauty in such harshness. Wrapped in his threadbare robe against the gathering chill of early evening, Muhammad would watch as the monotonous glare of day gave way to a rich light that mellowed the mountains into gold. There'd be a slight tremor inside him as the sun abruptly slipped from sight, leaving the western horizon to glow with color before fading as though someone were languorously drawing a heavy veil over it. A while yet, and moon-shadows would begin to silver the landscape, or there'd be the ethereal cold light of the star-studded sky at new moon, and then the quality of time itself seemed to change, as though he could sense it stretching into infinity until at last the merest hint of light paling the eastern sky brought with it a chill pre-dawn breeze—the signal that time had returned, and the night's vigil was almost done.

Did he practice breathing exercises on these night vigils, the kind of exercises only now being rediscovered in the West but widely used by mystics throughout history? What is prayer, after all, if not a form of breath control? The long, rhythmic incantation, the trance-like meter, the reverberation of sound in the mouth and throat and chest, the cyclical act of inhalation and exhalation—all these create an awareness of *ruh*, a word that means "wind" in Arabic, but also "breath" and "spirit," as though the spirit is borne on the wind, or in the breath. Did he repeat that pilgrim's chant—"Here I am, oh God, here I am"—or find a new one taking form in his mouth, *La ilaha illallah*, "There is no god but God"? Did sibilance take over his body, his breath slowing and deepening as the soft, musical chant enchanted the tongue, rolling from deep inside him out into the empty night? Alone here on the mountain, away from the swirl of competing claims and narratives, did he find the clarity he was seeking? Or at least a calm acceptance of his apartness—a certain peace?

We know that he spent nights on end in such vigils, with just the barest amount of food and water, and that each time he came down, he made first for the Kaaba to circle it seven times, left shoulder inward, in the familiar ritual of homecoming. It was a rite of transition, of coming back to the everyday human world, grounding him before he returned home to the bedrock of his life, Khadija. But coming back down was not always so easy.

In the harsh Hijaz landscape of rock and dust, there is no such thing as a gentle rain. It comes instead in rare spasms, violent downpours as capable of wreaking havoc as the most malevolent of *jinns*. With a kind of warped vengeance, water turns from blessing into curse, and the stuff of life becomes the agent of death. The sky might be clear, with no cloud in sight, so that the first sign of rain cascading off rock miles away could be nothing more than a barely perceptible scent carried on a passing breeze. If humans don't notice it, animals do. They stand still, ears alert, vaguely aware of something different. Minutes pass, even an hour, before the sand underfoot begins to dampen. It might be the merest trickle at first, as though someone had emptied a pail on the ground, but then the trickle builds, tugging gently at your ankles as a faint rumble echoes through the mountains. Before you quite know what is happening, you find you are stumbling in a current that seems to have come from nowhere. Thrown off balance, you flail and fall, trying to pick yourself up only to be knocked down again by the gathering weight of tumbling sand-laden water sweeping down through the wadi, hammering at your shins. The roar of it is on you now, the terrible sound of large stones grinding against rock. Branches of broom and acacia and saltbush and then whole bushes come hurtling at you, and there's the flailing bulk of a drowning animal, legs akimbo, and you can't hear your own voice crying for help as you fall again and again, caught up in the chaotic momentum of water and debris. If a stone hits your head and you lose consciousness, you can drown in just a few inches.

The worst place to be in Mecca in such a flood was at its lowest point, where all the wadis met, and that was exactly where the Kaaba stood. Most flash floods were relatively shallow, but as Muhammad began his retreat on Mount Hira in the year 605, a violent storm system to the south sent a foaming mass of water hurtling toward the sanctuary. Nobody in Mecca at the time could remember a flood of such magnitude. They had taken precautionary measures, of course, building a semi-circular wall upstream from the sanctuary to protect it. But against the fury of this much water, the wall gave way under the battering of boulders and debris. The torrent raced on into the Kaaba precinct, swirling around the totem stones and crashing into the sanctuary itself with such force that it washed away the clay mortar and loosened its stone walls until they collapsed. By the time it had abated, the Kaaba was rubble.

There was no question that it had to be rebuilt, and as quickly as possible, before word of its destruction spread through all of Arabia and it was taken as a bad omen, undermining the whole raison d'être of Mecca. The Quraysh council decided on a raised foundation so that the door would stand above the new peak flood level, and they took advantage of the opportunity to opt for a sturdier, more imposing design: a tall, almost cubic shape. As it happened, timbers had been salvaged from a Red Sea shipwreck caused by the same storm system that had produced the flood, and these were now hauled up to Mecca to serve as a solid infra-structure. Everyone in Mecca was involved. Since labor on the new sanctuary was clearly a privilege, not a chore, it was carefully portioned out between the various clans of the Quraysh, ensuring that no single clan could claim that it had been especially hon-ored. And indeed all went smoothly until the time came to place the famed Black Stone back in the northeast corner.

From a distance, you might take this stone for a large chunk of black onyx, though on close inspection (it's still set into the corner of the Kaaba today, almost overshadowed by a huge silver frame) it contains streaks of red, brown, and dark green, and appears to be meteoric in origin. Islamic tradition has it that it was placed in the wall of the original sanctuary by Abraham and Ishmael, and was then lost until it was rediscovered by Muham-mad's forefather Qusayy, the founder of the Quraysh tribe. For all its fame it is surprisingly small, barely larger than a football, so lifting it into place when the Kaaba was rebuilt in the year 605 was not the issue. One reasonably strong man could have done it easily enough, but now there was the question of who that man should be.

Everyone claimed the honor of replacing the stone, and none was willing to cede it. Within minutes the process that had been a model of cooperation between the various clans of the Quraysh broke down into such violent disagreement that it seemed actual violence was imminent. One clan even produced a bowl filled with animal blood, then thrust their hands into it and held their bloody palms high for all to see, swearing that they were willing to shed their own blood for the right of one of their own to lift the stone into its newly built niche. Fists were bunched and hands reaching for daggers when one of the elders, distressed at the prospect of bloodshed in this of all places, found a way to defuse the situation. They were all too exhausted with the effort of intensive labor to make such a weighty decision, he said. Instead, they should leave the decision to God by agreeing that the first man to enter the precinct from that point on, no matter which clan he belonged to, should decide whose hands would lift the stone. As it happened—or, depending on your point of view, as it was predestined—that man was Muhammad.

Newly returned from his retreat, he'd made for the precinct in order to circle the sanctuary the prescribed seven times, but instead of walking into the peaceful ritual of homecoming, he'd walked into conflict—and into an almost Solomonic role in resolving it. "This is the *amin*, the trustworthy one," they agreed when they saw him, "and we will be satisfied with his decision."

He was to be the arbiter: enough of an insider to know what would work yet at the same time enough of an outsider to be considered objective. It was a role Muhammad seemed made for. Precisely because he was not one of the movers and shakers of the city, he was the ideal man for the moment. And if it had been anyone else who had walked into the Kaaba precinct at that particular point? The question is moot to the early Islamic historians; as they saw it, it could only have been Muhammad.

"Bring me a cloak," he said, and when they did so, he had them lay it on the ground and place the Black Stone in its center. "Let the elders of each clan take hold of the edge of the cloak," he ordered, "and then lift it up together." This they did, and when they had raised it to the right level, Muhammad eased it into position himself.

It was acclaimed as the perfect solution. Everyone had had a hand in the process, and all had been equally honored. But for

Muhammad this small but poignant demonstration of the constructive power of unity can only have served as a distressing reminder of division. What would stay with him was not the praise for his judiciousness but the alacrity with which the Quraysh had resorted to threats of violence, and at the one place, the sanctuary of the Kaaba, where violence was forbidden. As he left the precinct that day, he has to have been more aware than ever of his strangely ambivalent position among the Quraysh, trusted only because he was one of them yet not one of them, only because he was not in a position to lead. Or so he thought.

Seven

Perhaps it could only have happened when he was forty, given the auspiciousness of that number throughout the Middle East. For the Beduin, for instance, it is a healing number—one that saves life. A common cure-all is called *al-arbain*, the forty, a blend of herbs in olive oil and clarified butter. Traditional healers say it takes forty days for a broken bone to mend (or as Western doctors will tell you, six weeks). And a man cannot be attacked within forty paces of his home or tent, or that of anyone who gives him shelter, no matter how just the cause.

Forty, that is, gives a new lease on life, and this is how the number consistently appears in the sacred books that came out of the Middle East. The duration of the great flood waited out in Noah's ark, the years of Israelite wandering in the desert after the exodus, the nights Moses spent on Mount Sinai, the days and nights Jesus spent in the wilderness—all forty, the number signifying a time of struggle and displacement in preparation for a new beginning. For anyone fortunate enough to live that long, forty years marked the fullness of time: the time to step into one's destiny.

And so in the month of Ramadan this year of 610, as he had the past few years, Muhammad sought the solitude of retreat up on Mount Hira, where everything human was stripped away and he could be part of the silence, letting the implacable vastness enter into him. As he climbed the familiar path, following tracks made by mountain goats, Mecca receded beneath him. He knew the mountain well by now, its hidden hollows and crevasses part of the landscape of retreat, and by dusk he was standing in his usual place.

He leaned forward as though into the wind, though there was barely a hint of a breeze as the last birds darted for home. As the darkness thickened, so too did the silence—the kind of absolute silence that rings in the ears, a high, perfect tone that comes from everywhere and nowhere. A vibration more than a sound, really, as though the whole landscape is sentient. The rock itself seems to be alive as it releases the accumulated warmth of daytime into the cool of night, and as the stars begin their slow revolution overhead, there comes that sense of being a human all alone and yet inexorably part of something larger, a sense of life and existence far older and deeper than the superficial ambitions and everyday cruelties of human affairs.

Was this meditation or was it vigil? Did Muhammad stand in simple gratitude for the ordinary human happiness that had been granted him against all expectation, or was there a certain watchfulness about him, as though he were waiting for something about to happen? We only know that if it was peace he was seeking, what he experienced that night would be anything but.

What actually happened on Mount Hira? We have what appear to be Muhammad's own words, but they come relayed through others, at several removes, with each narrator struggling to translate the ineffable into terms they could understand.

One account is credited to Aisha, the youngest and the most outspoken of the wives he would marry after Khadija's death: "He said: 'When the angel came to me, I had been standing, but I fell to my knees and crawled away, my shoulders trembling . . . I thought of hurling myself down from a mountain crag, but he appeared to me as I was thinking this and said, 'Muhammad, I am Gabriel and you are the messenger of God.' Then he said, 'Recite!' I said, 'What shall I recite?' He took me and pressed me tightly three times until I was nearly stifled and thought that I should die, and then he said, 'Recite in the name of thy Lord who created, created man from a clot of blood, that thy Lord is the most munificent, who teaches by the word, teaches man what he knew not.'"

The narrative continues in words credited to one of Muhammad's future followers, ibn-Zubayr, who again quotes him directly: "I recited it, and the angel desisted and departed. I woke up, and it was as though these words had been engraved on my heart. There was none of God's creation more hateful to me than a poet or a madman; I could not bear to look at either of them, yet I thought, 'I must be either a poet or a madman. But if so, Quraysh will never say this of me. I shall take myself to a mountain cliff, hurl myself down from it, and find respite in death.' But when I came near the top of the mountain I heard a voice from heaven saying 'Muhammad, you are the messenger of God.' I raised my head to see who was speaking and there Gabriel was in the form of a man with feet astride the horizon. I stood looking at him and this distracted me from what I had intended, and I could go neither forward nor back. I turned my face away from him to all points of the horizon, but wherever I looked I saw him in exactly the same form."

"This was a true vision," Aisha would say, but the form it took in her mouth and those of others is clumsily flat. These were well-intentioned people trying to find words for a state of being they had never experienced. In the process, they simplified it, turning the metaphysical into the merely physical as in that image of the angel Gabriel straddling the mountains. It is as though the moment itself were cloaked, as though too close an account of what happened that night were beyond human comprehension, which is in fact exactly how Muhammad experienced it. Where his reported words come to life is not in the angelic apparition but in the palpable feeling of terror—that panicked disorientation, that sundering of everything familiar, that feeling of being utterly overwhelmed to the point of near death by a force larger than anything the mind can comprehend. In short, a terrible awe.

This may be difficult to grasp today when the word "awesome" is used to describe a new app or a viral video and "God-awful" is casually attached to a rotten movie or a bad meal. With the exception perhaps of a massive earthquake, we are protected from real awe. Few people even know any longer what it's like to stand alone in a thunderstorm on the open plains, or to feel the shore vibrate beneath you as a gale sends millions of tons of water pounding in across thousands of miles of ocean. We close the doors and hunker down, convinced that we are in control, or at least hoping for control, and lose touch with what it is to be overwhelmed by a force much greater than ourselves.

How, then, to understand Muhammad's awe? Something that is literally metaphysical—beyond the physical—is by definition beyond rational explanation. Yet while the attempt to reconstruct mystical experience may well be absurd, one can at least be a fool for trying rather than a different kind of fool for not trying.

Rudolf Otto, the great scholar of comparative religion, may have come close in his book *The Idea of the Holy*, albeit in the rather overly impassioned language of the Victorian era. The fear of God in the Hebrew bible, he wrote, "seizes upon man with paralyzing effect." Job experienced "a terror fraught with an inward shuddering such as not even the most menacing and overpowering created thing can instill. It has something spectral in it." And he really meant spectral. In ghost stories, he continued, the sense of dread makes you shudder, going so deep that "it seems to penetrate to the very marrow, making a man's hair bristle and his limbs quake." Yet by comparison with what he called "numinous consciousness"—the awareness of divine will and power—this ghostly shudder is child's play. At its highest level, "dread reappears in a form ennobled beyond measure where the soul, held speechless, trembles inwardly to the farthest fiber of its being."

There is nothing remotely blissful about such an experience, Otto emphasized, throwing in a sly dig at those who cling to the idea of revelation as ecstatic by concluding that "the singularly daunting and awe-inspiring character of such a moment must be gravely disturbing to those who will recognize nothing in the divine nature but goodness, gentleness, love, and a sort of confidential intimacy."

But if we don't need to be as purple-prosed as Otto, neither do we have to be as literal as Aisha or ibn-Zubayr. We don't need to insist that Muhammad actually heard Gabriel speaking as though the angel were a human being, let alone reduce Muhammad to the status of a divinely appointed voice recorder playing back what was dictated to him. Since we are rational products of the twenty-first century, we might look instead to science for an explanation, calling on neuropsychiatry and the idea of "altered states of consciousness."

Was Muhammad in such an altered state that night on Mount Hira? Of course he was. But neurological research has only revealed what ascetics have always known: that practices such as fasting, sleep deprivation, and intense meditation can induce such states, which are accompanied by changes in the brain's chemical activity. The fact that an altered state of consciousness has a physical correlate should come as no surprise, since brain chemistry parallels experiential input. But to then imagine that everything is explained by chemistry is to fall into the reductive trap of what William James called "medical materialism," which dismisses experience in favor of mechanics. While science can chart the physical effects of such altered states, it cannot enter the experience of them.

In the end, the most practical way to pursue the question may be the one that at first glance might seem the least practical of all: by making the leap into poetry.

The essence of religious experience is at heart poetic. Ritual and dogma are merely the framework of organized religion—its girders, as it were; they do not touch on religious experience itself, which is the experience of mystery, of the indescribably enigmatic.

Poetry pivots on enigma, which naturally has not prevented many poets from trying to define it nonetheless. Walt Whitman called the beauty of poems "the tuft and final applause of science," which is a nicely phrased response to medical materialism. Coleridge talked of "the willing suspension of disbelief for the moment, which constitutes poetic faith," while Ralph Waldo Emerson called poetry "the endeavor to express the spirit of the thing." Note the words used: "faith," and "spirit." But the most apt definition of poetry may be the anonymous one: "saying something that cannot be said." Which again is no reason not to try. If we look at the metaphors in the account of Muhammad on the mountain, it may be possible to at least begin to understand.

Start, then, with the idea of inspiration: literally, the act of breathing in, or being breathed into. The Arabic word for both "breath" and "spirit" is *ruh*, close kin to the Hebrew *ruach*. The idea of having spirit breathed into you is thus built into the language, as it is in the second verse of Genesis, where "the breath of God," *ruach elohim*, "lay upon the waters." But while this may sound wonderful in principle, consider that a human being is not water. Imagine being breathed into—inspired—with such force that your body can hardly bear it. No gentle breath from heaven here, but air being impelled into your lungs under immense pressure, as though a giant were giving you mouth-to-mouth resuscitation. It feels like every cell of your body is overtaken by it, and you are entirely at its mercy. Even as it gives you life, it seems to be squashing the life out of you, suffocating you under its enormous weight until it's useless to even think of fighting against it.

And then consider the real meaning of that phrase of Muhammad's: "as though these words were engraved on my heart." If this is by now a cliché, consider it afresh, as he used it, and you begin to grasp its impact. If you have read Franz Kafka's story "In the Penal Colony," you will think instantly of the prisoner suffering the words of his penitence being carved letter by letter into his flesh.

Imagine, then, the unimaginable: the agonizing pain of a

THE FIRST MUSLIM · 93

sharp blade carving deep inside you as you lie beneath it, conscious but unable even to struggle against it. Here is the real experience of that childhood scene in which the two angels sliced into the five-year-old's rib cage to lift out his heart and wash it, and it has none of the unearthly calm of that earlier story. Instead, it contains all the violence of open-heart surgery: the wrenching apart of the chest, the baring of the heart, the unutterable pain— all in the name of a new lease on life.

Muhammad was left cowering on the ground, depleted. Covered in sweat yet shivering, he was inhabited by those words that were his and yet not his, the words he had repeated out loud into the thin, pure air of the mountain, into the emptiness and the darkness. Maybe he sensed somewhere inside him that these words could only come to life, could only achieve reality, when spoken into the face of—breathed in by—another human being, the one person he could run to for consolation in the face of this overwhelming force, who could perhaps save him from both the fear of madness and the fear of the divine: Khadija.

Or perhaps at first there were no words at all. Perhaps it took time for experience to form into something as human and tangible as words. We know that he came stumbling down the mountain, slipping and sliding on the loose scree, his breath hot and rasping, each inhalation needing to be struggled for until it felt like his chest would burst with the effort of it. His robe was torn, his arms and legs scratched and bruised by thorns and sharp-edged rocks in the path of his headlong flight for home.

"I have been in fear for my life," was the first thing he said. "I think I must have gone mad." Trembling, shuddering almost convulsively, he begged Khadija to hold him and hide him under her shawl. "Cover me, cover me," he pleaded, his head in her lap, like a small child seeking shelter from the terrors of the night. And that terror alone was enough to convince her that what her husband had experienced was real.

She held him, cradled him as the night sky began to grow pale in the east with the reassuring prospect of day. Slowly, haltingly, the words he had perhaps felt more than heard began to find physical shape in his mouth. Even as he still shook in Khadija's arms, Muhammad found his voice, and the first revelation of the Quran formed into words that another human being could hear. What had been breathed into him up on the mountain was now breathed out, to take its place in the world.

They had been man and wife for fifteen years, but she had never heard him speak with such beauty before. His speech was usually terse and restrained, as one might expect of a man who had learned the hard way from childhood to listen rather than talk. Yet even as the words entered her mind, she was aware of how extraordinary they were. Not just for the man she loved, but for her whole world. Whatever this was, she instantly grasped one thing: it was the end of the quiet, almost modest life they had lived until now. Nothing would ever be the same again.

Another woman would have thought it unfair, perhaps. She would have feared the upheaval that was bound to come, the scorn and derision that she could see looming. She would have tried to protect herself as much as him by denying the validity of what had happened, preferring to think that his first reaction was right and that he had indeed been possessed by a *jinn*. Would have tried to dissuade him, to smooth things over, to reassure him that all would be well if he just got some sleep, that there was nothing to fear, that this was just a passing trick of the mind, nothing to be concerned about, it would all be better in the morning.

Instead, Khadija reacted as though this was what she had been half expecting all along—as though she had seen in Muhammad what he had barely glimpsed in himself. When he said he feared he'd gone mad, she simply shook her head. "May God save you from madness, my dear," she said. "God would not do such a thing to you, since he knows your truthfulness, your trustworthiness and kindness. Such a thing cannot be." And once he told her everything that had happened, her calm conviction was reinforced. "By him in whose hand is my soul," she said, "I hope that you may be the prophet of this people."

She held him until sunrise, feeling his muscles relax as the shuddering fear subsided. His head became heavy in her lap and he slipped at last into the deep sleep of exhaustion. When she was sure he would not wake soon, she eased him onto the bedding, wrapped herself close in her shawl, and went out into the early morning, heading for her cousin Waraqa's house. She walked with calm determination through the narrow alleys as the first cock-crows echoed through them, past stray dogs scratching for scraps, donkeys braying for feed, the occasional muffled curse of someone trying for just a few more moments of sleep. Waraqa, the most senior of the *hanifs*, would confirm what she already knew: that Muhammad's fear of delusion was precisely what argued most powerfully for his not being deluded. He was no unworldly mystic floating above ordinary humans in a smug aura of holiness, but as the Quranic voice would soon tell him, "just a messenger," "just one of the people." Just a human being suddenly charged with what seemed an inhumanly huge task.

Her cousin's response was no less than she had expected: "If you have spoken the truth to me, Khadija, then what appeared to Muhammad was the great spirit that appeared to Moses in olden time, and he is indeed the prophet of this people. Bid him be of good heart."

But as she made her way back to her sleeping husband, she must have done so with a heavy heart of her own, aware of the seeming incongruity of a middle-aged man and a woman on the verge of old age who between them held the key to what could be a new age. Her child-bearing years were over, yet here she was at the birth of something so radically new and at the same time so old as to be utterly daunting.

She had no illusions about how hard it would be. As though the terror of his experience that night was not enough, she knew Muhammad faced yet another level of fear: the very human fear that this was too much to ask of him, and that he'd be unequal to the task. Because if she was right, and Waraqa too, then the respect that Muhammad had worked so long and hard for was now in jeopardy. He would be the outsider again, even the outcast. Not merely ignored but actively despised and derided, his honor impugned, his dignity transgressed. The small, modest peace he had achieved over the years would be torn away from him, and there was no knowing if he would ever find it again.

Part Two

EXILE

Eight

Then, for two years, nothing. Instead of the steady flow of revelation that one might expect—the familiar clichés of the floodgates opened, of the life-giving waters of inspiration pouring out of him—there were two years of silence, a frustratingly fallow period in which Muhammad struggled to come to terms with what had happened to him.

Inevitably, as a man doubly orphaned early in life, he experienced these two years as abandonment. The effects of such a childhood can never be conquered altogether. That sense of being cut off never disappears; it may be pushed deeper inside, but it is always there. A gate had been opened wide in the most momentous night of Muhammad's life, but had then slammed tightly shut again. What had been granted him was now being withheld, and he felt a terrible loneliness, a despair of ever being able to connect again with that voice.

This was his dark night of the soul—the phrase coined centuries later by Saint John of the Cross for the pain, loneliness, and doubt experienced by mystics yearning for union with the divine. Especially the doubt, which is in many ways essential to real faith. If this seems a startling idea at first blush, consider that religion risks becoming fanatically inhuman without it. As Graham Greene indicated in his novels of those struggling with faith, doubt is the heart of the matter; it is what keeps religion human. In a way, it is the annealing fire of faith. Without it, there is only a terrifying certainty, a blind and blinding refuge from both thought and humanity.

Certainty requires no leap of faith such as Kierkegaard talked of. To walk out on the limb of a tall tree believing that it won't break requires only a certain foolhardy credulity; to walk out on that same limb fully aware that it might indeed break requires placing one's faith or one's trust in God or fate or the law of averages. Where certainty is often a refusal to think, to question, to reason—a refusal to engage in the kind of Socratic dialogue with unbelief that the Quran urges—faith requires an awareness of the possibility of being wrong, which is why it is perhaps best defined in Hebrews 11:1 as "the substance of things hoped for, the evidence of things not seen."

In the lack of doubt, then, faith is moot. The certainty that you are right devolves into righteousness and dogmatism, and worse, an overweening pride in being so very right. "*If* what you say is true . . ." Waraqa had said. "I think you *may* be the prophet," Khadija had said. They'd spoken in the conditional, sure and yet unsure. Only more revelations could confirm that first one, but as weeks and then months passed and no more came, Muhammad alternated between hope and despair.

So too did many of the Meccan elite, though for very different reasons. To the north, the world was rapidly changing, and Muhammad's own uncertainty seemed mirrored in a new anxiety about what the future might bring. The always uneasy balance of power between the Byzantine and the Persian empires was shifting ominously. In the year 610, the general Heraclius ousted his predecessor and proclaimed himself the new Byzantine emperor, swearing to retake lands lost to the Persians only to have his bluff called by the Sassanid king of Persia, Khosroe II, better known as Parvez, "the ever victorious." The title seemed strikingly apt as Parvez racked up victory after victory: first Iraq and the Caucasus, then Syria and eastern Anatolia (present-day Turkey and Armenia). Traders and pilgrims to Mecca began to bring word that Persian armies were planning to advance on Jerusalem and even Damascus. If that happened, the whole network of Meccan business would be thrown into upheaval until they could establish working contacts among the new powers-that-be. The one thing essential to successful trade is political stability, yet this was the one thing that could no longer be taken for granted.

Muhammad was certainly aware of this growing uncertainty around him. It was the talk of the Kaaba precinct, and the focus of preparations for the next northbound caravan to Damascus. But those preparations no longer involved him. To keep working as a trader's agent after what had happened on Mount Hira was impossible; he had neither the energy nor the interest for it. Instead, he increased his vigils on the mountainside, seeking out the voice that had manifested itself in him and then gone silent. Yet the harder he searched, the farther away that presence seemed. With each dawn he again faced the disappointment, the gnawing awareness that he might have been as deluded as he had at first feared.

If he knew that this was a classic time of testing, a trial of his fortitude, he must have felt that he was failing the test. It was a test of his own fear, perhaps—the dark fear that this extraordinary vision would never be granted him again, and this one single glimpse was all there would be, an unimaginable gift proffered and then withdrawn. Or perhaps he felt he was being punished for having doubted the message in the first place, for having even considered that he was mad or possessed, just another raving poet or seer fit for nothing better than to shout out in the marketplace and receive in return the jeers and laughs of those seeking entertainment, or the coins of those who bothered to take pity on him. And even as he longed for the voice to return, he may have been terrified of the possibility. Was what he most desired also what he most feared? Could he even endure such pain again? "Never once did I receive a revelation without thinking that my soul had been torn away from me," he'd say toward the end of his life. Who could withstand that? "Tell him to be of strong heart," Waraqa had said, and the phrase was apt: the force of such experience could stress a middle-aged heart to the point of cardiac arrest.

He wrestled, then, with uncertainty. Had the words come from deep inside him, or had they indeed come from beyond him as he felt they had—words that he himself would never have been capable of? A boy who had learned to survive by silencing his voice had suddenly been given one, but was it his own voice he had been given, or the voice of God? Or was the voice of God within him, part of him? Had divine words really been planted inside him, or had his own words been an expression of the divine? Where did man end and God begin? What was this boundary so powerfully and briefly broken?

The conventional picture is the literal one: God speaks to Muhammad, or more precisely, speaks *through* Muhammad. But when you are the one being spoken through, you must inevitably ask if the voice you hear is your own transformed, or if that transformation is indeed the result of an agency outside you. Or is there, in the end, no difference? This is the basic insight of the

Gnostics, the one known to the great mystical thinkers of all traditions: the divine spark is within each human being. But if some might take this to mean that there is no boundary between human and divine, Muhammad was achingly aware of the concept of hubris, of the dangerously arrogant assumption of one's own powerfulness.

All this and more constituted Muhammad's personal struggle to accept what had happened. Until these questions were resolved within him, there could only be silence, because what he was now called on to be—prophet and messenger, bringing the word of the divine—went against his whole nature. The boy who had survived by blending into the background had to accept that he would now be thrust into the foreground, into the unrelenting eye of the world.

At last it came. It would be known as the Sura of the Morning, eleven tantalizingly brief verses which read in full: "By the morning light and the dark of night, your Lord has not forsaken you, Muhammad, nor does he abhor you. The end shall be better than the beginning, and you will be satisfied. Did he not find you an orphan and give you shelter? Did he not find you in error and guide you? Did he not find you poor and enrich you? Do not wrong the orphan, then, nor chide the beggar, but proclaim the goodness of your Lord."

He had not been abandoned, nor mistaken. And as though in compensation for those two dark, silent years, the Sura of the Morning heralded a spate of revelations building the early mystical foundation of the Quran. Brimming over with richness and lyricism, they were full of wonder and awe. The earth itself was a manifestation of the divine, and humans were mere stewards of God's creation.

The verses laid out an almost environmentalist approach to the natural world still unparalleled in any other holy book, as in this from Sura 91, The Sun: "By the sun and its morning brightness and by the moon which rises after, by the day that displays the glory of the sun and by the night that conceals it, by the heavens and he who built it and by the earth and he who laid it out, by the soul and he who molded it and inspired it with knowledge of good and evil—blessed shall be the one who keeps it pure, and ruined he who corrupts it." Or this from the mysteriously titled Ya Sin, Sura 36: "Let the once-dead earth be a sign for them. We gave it life, and produced grain for their sustenance. We planted it with the palm and vine and watered it with gushing springs so that you may feed on their fruit." And most famously, this from the shimmering vision of Sura 24, known as The Light: "God is the light of the heavens and the earth; the likeness of his light is as a niche wherein is a lamp—the lamp in a glass, the glass as it were a glittering star—kindled from a blessed tree, an olive of neither the west nor the east, whose oil all night would shine even if no fire touched it."

The mystery of creation was all around. Verse after verse celebrated the stark power of mountains and earthquakes, the bounty of rainfall and harvest, the seemingly simple sequence of night and day, sun and moon, plenty and drought. Or rather, not verse after verse, but sign after sign, since the Quranic word for a verse is *aya*, a sign. The verses themselves, that is, were signs of the active presence of the divine, and the Quran itself the only miracle necessary.

These early revelations were like exquisite poems, some so short and dense as to be almost haiku-like. Later, they'd become long and densely involved with the issues of the moment, and these longer revelations would form the suras, or chapters, that would be placed toward the beginning of the Quran when it was written down and compiled shortly after Muhammad's death, arranged not chronologically but more or less by length, from longest to shortest. This may have been decided on as a matter of aesthetics, or it may have been intended to give equal weight to every verse, no matter when it had first come into being. Whatever the reason, the arrangement means that any non-Arabic speaker looking for the mystical underpinnings of the Quran might find it best to start from the end and to read from right to left as though it were in Arabic.

In these first few years, Muhammad never knew when a revelation was about to come. One might follow hard on the heels of another, or there might be weeks or even months between them. But the unpredictability of the timing was itself part of the process. If revelation had come on a regular basis, the words piling up like those of a writer determined to fulfill a daily quota, one might suspect too much neatness for credibility, as though a direct line had been established between human and divine, one that could be dialed into on demand. Instead, the verses themselves taught him how to receive them. "Be not hasty in your recitation before the revelation of it is finished," he'd be told. Let it come in full, that is, before trying to repeat it. "Be patient," he was told again and again. It was a kind of ongoing lesson in how to surrender to the process. He was not to fight it nor attempt to hurry it, but allow it to take shape.

In a sense Muhammad was less the messenger than the translator, struggling to give human form—words—to the ineffable. The revelations left him equal parts humbled and determined, exhausted and energized, dazed and clear-headed. Sometimes he'd be covered with sweat even in cold weather; at others, he'd shiver and shake. There were times when he'd sit slumped with his head between his knees "as though a great heaviness had fallen on him," his eyes narrowed in what seemed to be intense pain or grief, and others when he'd shudder violently. Whichever way it happened, he was left helplessly weak as the words formed inside him, waiting to be recited into the world. The pain was an essential part of it, part of the birthing process, for this is what he was doing: verse by verse, he was giving birth to the Quran.

At first, only Khadija heard Muhammad recite these early verses, as though they needed to be incubated in a safe place before they could be recited to the wider world. It would be another full year until the sign came to go public with them. According to ibn-Ishaq, the go-ahead came from the angel Gabriel, who appeared to Muhammad with precise instructions. He was to prepare a meal of wheat, mutton, and milk, invite his Hashim kinsmen to dine, and when they had eaten their fill, recite the verses he had so far received.

Some forty men came, among them all the surviving sons of Abd al-Muttalib, including abu-Talib and his half-brother abu-Lahab, whose name means "father of flame." Some would say that he had earned this name by virtue, as it were, of his quick red-faced temper; others that it marked his eventual destination in the fires of hell. Whichever, abu-Lahab would justify the name at this meal.

They had all eaten with appetite, and had leaned back satiated against their pillows when their host calmly began to recite in the heightened rhyming prose known as *saj*, which was the accepted form for poetry and oracular utterance. The word literally means "cooing," because this was the effect of what linguists call the desinential inflection: an extra vowel often added to the ends of words so that they linger on the breath and in the ear, with al-Lah, for instance, becoming *allaha*. The usage would be gradually abandoned over the next century or so as poetry fell victim to practicality and Arabic replaced Aramaic as the lingua franca of the Middle East, but in seventh-century Mecca it was still highly regarded, and all the more when it came with such gentle majesty as was now heard from Muhammad's lips. Yet even as the others sat entranced, astonished at hearing such eloquence in the mouth of this terse kinsman, abu-Lahab stood up, interrupting the recital in angry protest. "He has bewitched you all," he declared, and walked out.

To reject any form of hospitality, let alone from your own nephew, was more than an act of unspeakable rudeness; it was a declaration of enmity. The gathering broke up in a confused babble of shame and alarm, but Muhammad remained nonplussed. He simply invited everyone to return for the same meal the next day, when he again recited the Quranic verses, this time without interruption since abu-Lahab had conspicuously stayed away. Then he appealed directly to his kinsmen. "Sons of Abd al-Muttalib," he said, "I know of no man among the Arabs who has brought his people something better than what I have brought you. I bring you the best of this world and the next, for God has commanded me to summon you to him. Which of you will aid me in this matter?"

Only one, it seemed. The story continues in the voice of abu-Talib's adolescent son Ali, who was by now part of Muhammad and Khadija's household: "They all held back, and although I was the youngest and the most short-sighted, pot-bellied and spindly-legged, I said, 'I will be your helper, oh messenger of God.'" In response, "Muhammad put his hand on the back of my neck and said, 'This is my brother, my representative, and my successor among you, so listen to him and obey him.'"

This announcement broke the spell cast by the Quranic rec-itation. "They rose up laughing," Ali would remember, "and said to abu-Talib: 'Muhammad has commanded you to listen to your son and obey him!'" How could anyone possibly expect them to take this seriously? It was patently absurd to elevate a mere spindly-legged adolescent over his father. And to his father's face? Such a reversal of authority was unthinkable—a foolish challenge to the whole accepted order of things.

The kinsmen must have emerged from Muhammad's house shaking their heads in bemusement, wondering if his success as a trader's agent had not gone to his head and if he should not, per-haps, have remained a lowly camel boy after all. They had done him the common courtesy of listening, and had been moved by the verses he'd recited—until this. However much they may have abhorred abu-Lahab's deliberate insult of the previous day, they now wondered if perhaps he had been right. This was surely a delusion of grandeur, they told one another; Muhammad could only be *majnun*, possessed by a *jinn*. They tsked and tutted in dis-appointment, trying to reassure themselves that if they just gave him time, he'd return to his senses.

None would dream of saying it to abu-Talib's face, but they must also have pitied the man who had taken in Muhammad as an orphaned lad but somehow failed to instill in him the absolute respect for fathers and forefathers so central to Arabian society. And pitied him all the more for having compounded his mistake by giving Muhammad his own son Ali, a lad who had clearly emerged from the experience equally lacking in the respect due a father.

But while Muhammad's uncles and the other more established Hashims had been deaf to his appeal, a few of his younger kinsmen had not. Like Ali, they had been stirred by what they'd heard, and began to meet secretly with Muhammad in the wadis outside Mecca to perform what would soon become the established prayer ritual of Islam away from the public eye. This is what they were doing, it seems, when abu-Talib happened on them one day, stopped dead in his tracks in surprise, and asked, "Nephew, what is this?"

Muhammad invited his uncle to join them, begging him to disavow Uzza and Lat and Manat, the three totems known as the daughters of al-Lah, and to acknowledge the unitary power of the one god, "neither begotten nor begetter." But even if the older man had wanted, he could not. "Nephew, I cannot abandon the ways of my fathers," he replied.

The "ways of the fathers" were what held the Quraysh together, creating a tradition that was unbreakable so far as abu-Talib was concerned. The phrase invoked the faith and practice not only of his immediate fathers but of his forefathers, the venerated ancestors of the Quraysh. This was a matter of loyalty and identity, so that to abandon the tribal gods would be, in a sense, to abandon himself. Yet something in him must have responded nonetheless to Muhammad's appeal, as well as to the sincerity of this small group of young people, because he did not denounce what he had seen. Instead, he tempered his refusal by assuring Muhammad that no matter how far he seemed to stray from the ways of the fathers, he would remain under his uncle's protection as head of the Hashim clan. "Come what may, by God, you shall never meet with anything to distress you so long as I live," abu-Talib declared— a statement that in hindsight would only reveal to what extent he underestimated what was to come.

This is how both ibn-Ishaq and al-Tabari tell the story, and yet one wonders how abu-Talib really felt when he saw his son following a strange new ritual. He had sent Ali to live with Muhammad in good faith, but how would any father feel on real- izing that his son was going in a direction that seemed to place him far outside the norm? The ways of the fathers were too hal- lowed, too strongly entrenched in a society built on respect for ancestry and lineage, to be dismissed so quickly. Indeed they may have been all the stronger for abu-Talib as he struggled to rebuild his business, since a man reduced in external circumstance tends to treasure all the more the bedrock of tradition.

It has to have been immensely painful for him to realize that his son was in effect no longer his, but Muhammad's. Did he accept this with such apparent ease because he regretted his rejec- tion of Muhammad as a son-in-law years before? Or did he sim- ply not want to make too big a fuss about it all, assuming that "this too will pass"? There were all sorts of preachers and new ideas floating around town, after all—including those of the *hanifs*—and for the most part they were considered harmless, no threat to the powers-that-be of Mecca. Or perhaps abu-Talib made his accommodation as a father. He could see that if he insisted that Ali leave Muhammad, the boy would refuse, and all he'd achieve would be a total break with his own flesh and blood. As many fathers know, there is nobody more stubborn than an adolescent boy.

Still, he was immensely disturbed by what he had witnessed. These young people were not only reciting the Quranic verses; abu-Talib had come on them in the act of prayer. He had seen them bowing down low in *islam*, that supple word whose associated meanings in Arabic ripple out to include peace and wholeness, but which means above all submission. True, it was not a forced submission but a willed and willing acceptance. Yet the posture of prayer—forehead on the ground, arms outstretched, rump high in the air—was the classic one of captive before conqueror, still visible today on ancient Assyrian victory steles, where prisoners do precisely this at the feet of the victorious king. It was the posture of utter surrender to the mercy and grace of a far greater power, and thus a clear statement, felt in muscle and bone, of the literal meaning of *islam*. So abu-Talib had been shocked, as so many others would be. To a man of honor in a society that prided itself, as it were, on pride, nothing could be more un-Arabian.

Within the year, the Quranic revelations took on a more urgent tone: "Oh you shrouded in your robes, Muhammad, arise and warn!" The time for discretion was over. Muhammad was to start speaking out loud not only to his kinsmen but in the most public way possible, in the Kaaba precinct. And the new verses he'd recite there would go far beyond mystical praise. They would constitute a stinging critique of the greed and cynicism that had turned Mecca into a kind of seventh-century equivalent of a Wall Street bull market, relegating the majority of its residents to the status of an underclass.

These new verses would build into an impassioned protest against corruption and social inequity. They took the side of the poor and the marginalized, calling for advantaging the disadvantaged. They demanded a halt to the worship of the false gods of profit and power along with those of the totem stones. They condemned the concept of sons as wealth and the consequent practice of female infanticide. And above all, they indicted the arrogance of the wealthy—"those who amass and hoard wealth," who "love wealth with an ardent passion," who "are violent in their love of wealth" and "think their wealth will make them immortal," unaware that "it will not avail them when they perish."

"Know that the life of this world is but a sport and a pastime," said one verse, "a cause for mere vanity and for rivalry in riches and sons." Only "righteous deeds, not wealth or sons, will bring you closer to God," said another, for "the bounty of God and his mercy are better than any wealth you amass." And in what may well have been a deliberate echo of "Blessed are the meek, for they shall inherit the earth" in the Gospel of Matthew: "We desire to show favor to those oppressed on earth, to make them the leaders and the inheritors."

If this was not quite a call for revolution, it was certainly a potent call for reform. It was not too late to reverse the disastrous course Mecca had taken, the verses said. Its people had only to think. "Remind them" of what they once knew, Muhammad was told. "Tell them to consider" what happened to past cultures that had succumbed to corruption and ended up as half-buried ruins. "Tell them to remember" the values they so treasured in principle but flouted in practice, the real "ways of the fathers" that had been so distorted.

In a sense the verses were an invitation: an appeal to the Meccans' better selves and a warning of what would happen if they ignored this prophetic call. Because prophetic it definitely was, placing itself explicitly in the tradition of previous prophets from Moses down through the ages to Jesus. "Say: 'We believe in God and in that which has been revealed to us; in what was revealed to Abraham, Ishmael, Isaac, Jacob, and the tribes of Israel; to Moses and Jesus and the other prophets." This was a call to return to the real tradition of the forefathers. "Before this, the book of Moses was revealed, and this Quran confirms it," said one verse. "All this is written in earlier scriptures, the scriptures of Abraham and Moses."

And so it had been. The call for justice was a protest as fierce as those of the biblical prophets and of Jesus, and the similarity of the call was no coincidence. As with early Judaism and early Christianity, early Islam would be rooted in opposition to a corrupt status quo. Its protest of inequity would be an integral part of the demand for inclusiveness, for unity and equality under the umbrella of the one god regardless of lineage, wealth, age, or gender. This is what would make it so appealing to the disenfranchised, those who didn't matter in the grand Meccan scheme of things, like slaves and freedmen, widows and orphans, all those cut out of the elite by birth or circumstance. And it spoke equally to the young and idealistic, those who had not yet learned to knuckle under to the way things were and who responded to the deeply egalitarian strain of the verses. All were equal before God, the thirteen-year-old Ali as important as the most respected graybeard, the daughter as much as the son, the African slave as much as the highborn noble. It was a potent and potentially radical re-envisioning of society.

This was a matter of politics as much as of faith. The scriptures of all three of the great monotheisms show that they began similarly as popular movements in protest against the privilege and arrogance of power, whether that of kings as in the Hebrew bible, or the Roman Empire as in the Gospels, or a tribal elite as in the Quran. All three, that is, were originally driven by ideals of justice and egalitarianism, rejecting the inequities of human power in favor of a higher and more just one. No matter how far they might have strayed from their origins as they became institutionalized over time, the historical record clearly indicates that what we now call the drive for social justice was the idealistic underpinning of monotheistic faith.

But if the Quran was a confirmation of what had come before—a renewal of a timeless message—it was also one with a huge difference. This time, through Muhammad, the message was "in a clear Arabic tongue." Not in Hebrew as it had been for the Jews, nor in Greek as for the Christians, but in the Meccans' own language, an Arabic so musical that it made the work of even the most famed poets seem mundane by comparison. It announced itself as theirs. They need no longer feel inferior to the "People of the Book," for they were now a people with their own book newly in the making, one sent not just to confirm but to complete the existing ones. For those who accepted it, there was the excitement of being present at something new coming into being. Now it was they who had been chosen to receive the word of God. It was their turn to be addressed directly, not only in their own language, but in their own specific terms of reference.

All the great civilizations of the past had failed, the revelations said, because they had strayed from the core principles of justice laid down so long ago. Just as the Jews had derided and ignored their prophets and thus been exiled from their own land, and just as the Christians were now going against the teachings of Jesus only to see their empire divided and failing as the Persians pressed their advantage against the Byzantines, so too with the legendary ancestor tribes of Arabia. The peoples of Ad and Thamud—the great Nabatean civilization in northern Arabia and the Yemeni one in the south—had mocked and scorned their own prophets. They had been warned that their pride contained the seeds of their own destruction, just as the Quranic verses were now warning the Meccans, and the proof that they had rejected the warning was there for all to see, in the ruins of the Nabatean necropolis of Petra in today's southern Jordan and in the remnants of the great Marib dam near Sana.

Muhammad's message was far more than a personal awakening; it was an Arabian one. It called on the values and ethics that had once been the pride of Arabia, celebrating the past even as it looked to the future. It was a call to action—a spiritual call to address the social and economic problems of the time. In short, it was overtly political. And for those without power, empowering.

The corrupt would finally be called to account. On the Day of Judgment, "wealth shall not avail," said the opening verses of what would become Sura 81, The Darkening. "When the sun shall be darkened, when the stars shall be thrown down, when the mountains shall be set moving, when the pregnant camels shall be neglected, when the savage beasts shall be mustered, when the seas shall be set boiling, when the souls shall be coupled, when the buried infant shall ask for what sin she was slain, when the scrolls shall be unrolled, when heaven shall be stripped off, when hell shall be set blazing, when paradise shall be brought nigh—then shall a soul know what it has produced."

Impassioned, outraged, the message was a warning of the highest order. This was a radical call, and the Meccan elite recognized it as such.

Nine

It seems inconceivable to modern Muslims that the majority of Meccans would have done anything but flock to Muhammad the moment he began to preach his message. But that is not what happened. Then as now, the status quo was a powerful force for inaction; safer to stay with what you know than to go out on a limb with a radically new vision of society. By the end of the first year, Muhammad had no more than a few dozen followers, a seemingly ineffectual medley of young men, women, freedmen, and slaves. You would hardly have thought this new movement worth the trouble to oppose.

Yet opposition was the crucible in which Islam would be forged. If the Quraysh elite had not so virulently opposed Muhammad—if they had not organized a campaign of denigration and harassment, leading up to a concerted attempt on his life—he might have remained just another of the many preachers of the time claiming divine inspiration. His revelations might never have been memorized and Islam never taken shape as a distinct religion, instead fading into a footnote in the history of monotheism. After all, the revelations insistently instructed Muhammad to say that he was "just a messenger," "only a man like you," "a warner from among yourselves." It would be years before the Quranic voice would call him "the first Muslim." This was emphatically not about him, but about the message itself. Those who opposed it did make it about him, however. And in so doing, helped him.

Where Muhammad's struggle had formerly been against his own doubts, now the doubters were external. No matter how frustrating and anxious and dangerous the next few years, and however great the despair that sometimes tempted him, it was no longer despair with himself. The stronger the opposition, the more he took it as confirmation of the validity of his message.

So long as the revelations focused on the wonders of creation, the movers and shakers of Mecca could afford to ignore him. They saw such ideas as nothing to get excited about—quite harmless, in fact. Nor did they have any problem with the concept of one omnipotent God, since that was already implicitly accepted in a city centered on the sanctuary of the high god. The tribal totems were powerful as intercessors, their subservience clear in the collective name given to Lat, Manat, and Uzza: "the daughters of al-Lah." But no other gods at all? That was a direct attack on the whole tradition of tribal identity. An attack, that is, on "the ways of the fathers."

Just as people swore their sincerity in the name of God, as well as in the names of lesser deities, so too they swore by their fathers and forefathers. This may sound strange to the modern ear until you remember that people still swear—at least in movies—"on my mother's grave." But in Muhammad's Arabia, this went far beyond honoring one's parents. The importance of forefathers is one reason why the early Islamic texts can be so hard for a Westerner to follow: they make the multiple nomenclature used in classic Russian novels seem simple by comparison. In the Middle East, full identification involved naming not just

THE FIRST MUSLIM · 119

your father but your whole ancestry: your grandfather, and his father, and his father in turn, back to the patriarch of the clan and even further back to the founder of the tribe (thus the long list of antecedents that opens the Gospel of Matthew, identifying Jesus as a descendant of Abraham and David). History was an integral part of identity, a way of rising above the particulars of individual life to reach both backward and forward in time through lineage. And it was all the more important given the awareness of how history could be lost.

The theme of lost greatness was as central in the Quranic verses of this time as it had been in the great pre-Islamic odes. The ruins of the past were object lessons, reminders not only of what had happened, but of what still could. Whether by earthquake or drought, plague or conquest, any civilization could be wiped out in the blink of history's eye. The emphasis on lineage thus served as a kind of defense against this awareness, an extension of oneself through time. Ancestors were venerated, and the dead accorded powers to intercede in the present. The graves of the most power-ful were made into shrines, as those of great rabbis, saints, and imams still are today throughout North Africa and the Middle East, monotheism notwithstanding. For Jews, Christians, and Muslims alike, they satisfy a deep-seated human longing for the tangible, for stones to touch and kiss, walls to weep and pray beside, places to bring votives and flowers, gifts and letters.

So there was nothing too radical when the Quranic revela-tions first began to talk about the Day of Judgment, when all souls would rise up from the dead to be called to account for their actions. It was understood that this was a world full of spirits, containing not only those living in it but also all who had lived in it in the past. Even though Muhammad's critics took the idea of resurrection literally and jeered at it—"What, shall those rooted in the dirt be brought back to life?" they taunted. "Can you give a dry bone flesh again?"—this was not what really disturbed them. It was what they saw as the disrespect for their forefathers that was so intolerable.

The tribal forefathers had been ignorant, the revelations now said, part of the benighted time of *jahiliya*. Worse, it seemed they would have to pay for their ignorance. True monotheists like Abraham were called *hanifs* and honored as prophets, but those who had refused the idea of the one god would be consigned to be "companions of the fire" in hell instead of "companions of the garden" in paradise. And since there was no possibility of the dead accepting monotheism, Muhammad's opponents took this to mean that their fathers and forefathers were condemned, ipso facto, to be companions of the fire. They took it, that is, as the ultimate insult: literally, "Go to hell."

It might be said that a man orphaned before he was born would be more than willing to abandon "the ways of the fathers." However unintentionally, Muhammad's immediate ancestors had let him down, leaving him adrift when the whole point of his culture was to be well moored. But what he was preaching now went far beyond matters of personal identity. Like that other prophet six centuries earlier and far to the north in Galilee, he was calling on his people to transcend the traditional ties of family, clan, and tribe, and to unite in renewed loyalty to the one God.

"I am come to set a man at variance with his father," Jesus had said. "If any man come to me and hate not his father, and mother, and wife, and children, and brethren, and sisters, yea and his own life also, he cannot be my follower." And now Muhammad was saying essentially the same. The Meccans faced losing everything "if your fathers, your sons, your brothers, your wives, your clan, the possessions you have gained, the commerce you fear losing, the dwellings you love—if all these are dearer to you than to strive in the way of God." Those who accepted *islam* were the true brothers and sisters, a new family that superseded the old, crossing all established boundaries to find its identity in the real forefathers: not the tribal ones, but the original founding figures of monotheism, Abraham and Moses.

What had been the sticking point for abu-Talib now troubled the whole Meccan elite. In a society where honoring your father and forefathers was itself a point of honor, it sounded as though people were being asked to abandon their ancestors. But even this could have been tolerated and thus ignored if Muhammad's message had not constituted a far more immediate threat to their well-being. The real issue was not one of principle, but of self-interest. With traditional values subservient to the new drive for profits, the Quranic attack on the accumulation of wealth for wealth's sake was downright subversive. It placed in question what the elite wanted taken for granted, exposing the injustice of what seemed to them the rightful order of things.

They responded with the blind scorn of power. "Just look at Muhammad's companions!" said one aristocrat with snobbish disgust. "These are the ones God has chosen to show the right way and teach the truth? If what he brings were of any value, it's hardly likely such people would have gotten hold of it before us."

Muhammad was a mere rabble-rouser, other critics said, a petty demagogue preying on those who were weak-minded and easily influenced: younger sons with no hope of leadership status; members of minor clans without influence; the outsiders known as "confederates" who lived under the protection of a Quraysh clan; freedmen and slaves and women. Yet even some of their own seemed to have been swayed by the new message, none more significantly than Attiq ibn-Uthman, better known as abu-Bakr, the man who would eventually be famed in Islam as the first caliph, Muhammad's *khalifa* or successor.

Abu-Bakr was well liked, successful, and highly respected as a genealogist, an expertise of prime importance in a culture that placed such emphasis on lineage. This made him the leading historian of Mecca, the one who determined all-important ancestry and kinship ties. So when he formally accepted *islam* by reciting the declaration of faith, the *shahada*—"There is no god but God, and Muhammad is his prophet"—he very publicly gave the lie to the argument that Muhammad was dishonoring the fathers and forefathers. "After that," ibn-Ishaq reports, "*islam* became a general topic of conversation in Mecca and everyone talked of it."

Determined to tolerate no more defections such as that of abu-Bakr, the ruling elite began a concerted effort to ensure that Muhammad and his followers remain "a despised minority," and even an endangered one. Pressure began to mount on abu-Talib to disown his nephew: to expel him from the Hashim clan and thus leave him without protection. Nobody needed the meaning of this to be spelled out. Expulsion would make Muhammad a man whose "blood was licit," as the phrase went: a man who could be killed legally, without fear of retribution.

The law of retribution is otherwise known as blood vengeance, a term that sounds suitably barbaric, and not just to modern ears. It was exactly the kind of thing eighth- and ninth-century Islamic historians, writing from their studies in Damascus and Baghdad, would expect of pre-Islamic Mecca—part of the dark ages and darker practices of *jahiliya*. It had been rescinded, as they saw it, by Islamic enlightenment, since the Quran would specifically say that while "an eye for an eye" had been called for in the past, "whoever forgoes it out of charity, this will serve as atonement for his own bad deeds."

That "eye for an eye" is of course from the Hebrew bible, where it appears first in the book of Exodus, and is then repeated for good measure in Leviticus. But it was never uniquely biblical. It had been the basis of law throughout the ancient world, and had been encoded under the Latin name of *lex talionis*—a phrase that means "law of retaliation" and is associated in English, however incorrectly, with the sharp talon of a predatory bird: nature red in tooth and claw.

Both early Islamic historians and modern Western ones tend to paint a picture of seventh-century Arabia as mired in ceaseless inter-tribal warfare fueled by blood feuds in which every violent death demanded retaliation by other members of the clan or tribe, resulting in a self-perpetuating spiral of violence. It's a picture that might well lead one to ask how any such society could survive for very long. In fact the root cause of inter-tribal conflict, throughout history and into the modern era, was the competition not for revenge but for power. In Arabia this meant control of water sources, territorial grazing rights, and the authority to levy taxes and tolls on those living in and passing through tribal territory. If anything, the principle of blood vengeance worked to keep the peace more than to break it; in the absence of a strong central authority, it was a rough-and-ready but effective way of ensuring security. Rather than perpetuating violence, it served to deter it.

All groups recognized that there was only one way the *lex*

talionis could work, and that was if retaliation was a sure thing. If a member of a clan or tribe was killed, then his kin were obliged to seek revenge. Indeed if a man's slaying went unavenged, it was believed that an owl would emerge from his grave calling "Give me drink! Give me drink!" in demand for blood to slake its thirst. This obligation was directed as much inward as outward, reinforcing group solidarity within the clan or tribe since all could be held responsible for the actions of any member. And it applied in preventive as well as offensive mode: the certainty that killing someone from another group would place your own kin in danger meant that you were under strong social pressure to avoid fatal violence. While Beduin warriors regularly raided camel caravans, for instance, they tried to avoid killing anyone in the process lest they set in motion a blood feud. The raids were purely for goods, not lives. At least in principle.

Whether by intention or not, swords wielded in anger did fatal work, which is why the law of retaliation incorporated a system of compensation. Well established in both Babylonian and Roman legal systems, it was applied also in Arabia, where it was known as blood-wit: blood ransom or blood money. The amount, whether in gold or in goods, was usually established by a *hakam*, a wise man or arbitrator. It might be ten milk camels, for instance, or even, as in the ransom demanded by the totem Hubal for Muhammad's father, as many as a hundred. Thus when extremists wanted to taunt others with the accusation of cowardice, they'd charge them with being content with "milk instead of blood." Most people, however, being attached to life rather than death, preferred milk.

The whole system was predicated on a strong sense of community affiliation. Your clan or tribe protected you, and this protection extended also to slaves and freedmen, who were under the formal auspices of their owners and former owners. But if someone had no clan affiliation—if he had been expelled as the Quraysh elite now wanted for Muhammad—he would have no such protection. He would be literally an outlaw: beyond the law.

Abu-Talib was in a terrible position. Even as his respect for Muhammad had grown, his status and influence had diminished along with his wealth. But he still had his pride. As the head of the Hashims, it was his duty to extend his protection to everyone within the clan. This was an integral part of the ways of the fathers, and he was sworn to uphold it. So when the heads of the other clans confronted him as a group, they placed abu-Talib squarely between the proverbial rock and a hard place. He was indebted to Muhammad, who had helped him out and all but formally adopted his son Ali. If he could not personally accept everything his nephew was preaching, that was no matter; over the years, the two men had developed a deep bond of trust and affection, and such ties were all-important elements in a man's sense of honor. Yet this sense of honor was exactly what abu-Talib was now urged to forgo.

The delegation confronting him was led by the head of the Makhzum clan, who would turn out to be the most vociferous and most violent of Muhammad's opponents—so much so that his name, abu-Hakam, meaning "father of wisdom," would be jettisoned in the Islamic historical record in favor of abu-Jahl, "father of ignorance." He certainly wasted no time earning the distinction, serving abu-Talib with an ultimatum. "By God," he declared, "we can no longer endure this vilification of our forefathers, this derision of our traditional values, this abuse of our gods. Either you stop Muhammad yourself, abu-Talib, or you must let us stop him. Since you yourself take the same position we do, in opposition to what he's saying, we will rid you of him." Either abu-Talib persuaded his nephew into silence, that is, or Muhammad would be forced into permanent silence.

To a man like abu-Talib, the idea was abhorrent; he would not and could not do it. The principle involved went to the basis of social and political existence: kinship. If he were to expel Muhammad from the clan, he'd essentially be signing his death warrant, and thus betraying his duty as head of the clan to extend his protection to every member of it. No man of honor could do such a thing, and abu-Talib saw it as a sign of how low honor had sunk that abu-Jahl would even demand such a thing. But there was another factor too.

Even if abu-Talib had not formally accepted Muhammad's message, something in it resonated with him. He could, after all, have declared that his nephew's preaching was against the tradition of the clan itself; he could have commanded him to stop on penalty of expulsion. But he did not. Instead, he finessed the situation, safe in the knowledge that abu-Jahl's threat on Muhammad's life could not be carried out without his cooperation. This was just heated talk, he must have thought; there would be no blood spilled. So he deflected abu-Jahl and the others with, as ibn-Ishaq puts it, "a soft answer and a conciliatory reply."

Surely Muhammad would be open to reason. Surely abu-Talib could persuade him to tone down his message, if only as a personal favor to himself. We know he tried, pleading with his nephew at least to be more discreet in his preaching. But however torn Muhammad may have been between seeing his uncle under such pressure on the one hand and the mandate of his message on the other, there was no doubt in his mind as to which had to prevail.

The record of their exchange is fraught with tension. "Uncle, by God," said Muhammad, "if they put the sun in my right hand and the moon in my left on condition that I abandon this path, I would not abandon it, even if I perish in the course of it." And having practically given abu-Talib permission to expel him and thus sanction his execution, he broke down in tears and made for the door, only to hear abu-Talib, himself now in tears, call him to stop: "Come back, nephew. Say whatever you want, for by God, I will never give you up on any account."

If abu-Jahl was unaware of exactly what had transpired between abu-Talib and Muhammad, the sight of Muhammad continuing to preach at the Kaaba precinct was enough to tell him the upshot of it, and his fury now focused as much on abu-Talib as on Muhammad himself. He began to talk openly about collective punishment of the Hashims for harboring this subversive in their midst, even hinting at outright warfare. But the other clan leaders still sought more judicious ways to deal with the dilemma posed by Muhammad. They were agreed that he had to be silenced, and that to do this they would need abu-Talib to expel him; but to declare open war would only be to roil the whole city in mayhem, and that was the last thing they needed. They decided instead on another tactic: go back to abu-Talib and offer him a new son instead.

This time the delegation was led not by abu-Jahl but by abu-Sufyan, the head of the Abd Shams clan, and it included Umara, "the strongest, brightest, and most handsome" scion of the Quraysh elite. With his arm around Umara's shoulders, abu-Sufyan addressed abu-Talib. "We hereby offer you a man for a man," he said. "Take Umara as your own, and you will have the benefit of his intelligence and support. Adopt him as your own son and in return give us this nephew of yours, the one who has opposed your tradition and the tradition of your fathers, who has severed the unity of our people and mocked our way of life, so that we may kill him."

Abu-Talib's response was as shocked and outraged as one might expect. "This is an evil thing that you would put upon me," he said. "You want to give me your son so that I can feed him and nurture him for you, while I give you my nephew so that you can kill him? By God, this shall never be."

That was the end of soft-spoken deflection from abu-Talib. In disgust at the level the other clan leaders had descended to, he called his clan and their allies together to take a united stand against the demand for Muhammad's expulsion. With the Hashims refusing to bend to the decision of the other clan leaders, the internecine warfare abu-Jahl had been advocating began to seem less unthinkable. People talked about it with alarm in the alleys and the markets, in private courtyards and in the Kaaba precinct, and though most condemned the idea, the fact that they were even discussing it brought it within the realm of possibility.

As the whole city debated the issue, the Meccan leadership made one last attempt at behind-the-scenes negotiation. They sent a third delegation, this time directly to Muhammad, and made what they evidently thought was an irresistible proposal: to buy him off. All he had to do was stop insulting the tribal gods and declaring that the tribal ancestors were unbelievers, they said, and the world would be his. "If what you want is money, we will gather for you of our property so that you may be the richest of us. If you want honor, we will make you our chief so that nothing can be decided without your agreement. And if this ghost which comes to you is such that you cannot get rid of it, we will find a physician for you and exhaust our means in getting you cured."

The proposal smacked of desperation, of course, let alone deceit. They intended to give Muhammad neither money nor power, hoping instead to tempt him into agreeing so that they could then claim that he was nothing but a hypocrite, a man who said one thing in public while accepting quite another under the table. There is no record of him laughing in response—he reportedly replied only with a Quranic verse about disbelievers "veiling their hearts"—but one suspects at least an inward smile at the culpable naïveté that could produce so blatantly bogus an offer. Unable to conceive that what drove Muhammad was anything other than self-interest, the Meccan leaders had merely emphasized the extent of their own.

It's not hard to understand their mounting frustration. Their aim was to silence Muhammad, yet everything they had tried so far only made him—and his message—all the more talked about. Now their problem assumed greater urgency as the date of the annual *hajj* neared, with tens of thousands due to descend on Mecca and on the annual Ukaz fair just outside town. Word was that the amped-up debate over Muhammad's preaching would bring even more pilgrims than usual, allowing him to "infect" the visitors with his radical ideas. How could the ruling elite contain his influence? How could they counter Muhammad without making him seem more important?

At a meeting recorded by ibn-Ishaq, one clan leader suggested, "We should say he's a *kahin*"—a soothsayer, that is, given to trances and possession by spirits. No, said ibn-Mughira, the man whose son Umara had been offered in exchange for Muhammad, that wouldn't work: "He doesn't speak like a *kahin*, with wild mutterings and incoherent rhymes."

"Then we should say he's possessed by a *jinn*," said another, but ibn-Mughira shot this one down too: "He's not that. We've seen plenty of possessed people, and with him there's none of that choking, no spasms, no incomprehensible muttering."

"So we'll say he's just another poet," came a further suggestion. But again, no: "We know poetry in all its forms, and his speech doesn't conform to that."

"A sorcerer?" Ibn-Mughira shook his head. "No spitting," he pointed out. "No magic charms, no chanted spells."

Finally they agreed: "These are just old wives' tales he spins, nothing but fantasies." That would be the line. Which turned out to be entirely counter-productive. The eagerness with which they insisted that Muhammad be paid no attention merely focused more attention on him. Anyone who could get the elite this riled up, after all, had to have something going for him.

Those in power are generally blithely unaware of how unpopular their exercise of that power can make them, and in this the Quraysh leaders were no exception. The hordes of visitors and pilgrims from other tribes were all too conscious of how they were being exploited. They had no choice but to pay the tolls and taxes, access and usage fees imposed by the city leaders, or to purchase over-priced food and water, but this did not mean they were happy about it. The Quraysh monopoly on power engendered resentment, and thus admiration for anyone who dared openly challenge it. What had been intended as a smear campaign turned out as such campaigns often do: it backfired on its authors. "The

Arabs went away from the Ukaz fair that year knowing about Muhammad," ibn-Ishaq would write, "and he was talked about in the whole of Arabia."

Angered by their failure, Mecca's leaders became less rational than they might otherwise have been. Abu-Talib's stubborn refusal to give up Muhammad had struck a nerve, since the principles on which he based his refusal were exactly the principles by which they too were supposed to be living. They had revealed themselves as shallow and hypocritical, and just as modern regimes tend to do in the face of such exposure, they over-reacted. Urged on by abu-Jahl, they declared a boycott of the whole Hashim clan.

Ten

The proclamation was inscribed on sheepskin vellum, sealed by the leaders of the two largest clans—abu-Jahl of the Makhzum and abu-Sufyan of the Umayyads— and nailed to the door of the Kaaba. It ordered that nobody was to have any commercial dealings of any kind with members of the Hashim clan, not even for basic foodstuffs. They were to be barred from the caravans, banned from the markets, excluded from all business deals and partnerships. No member of any other clan was to marry one of them. In a form of internal exile, they were to be shunned, treated as though they did not exist, made to feel like outsiders in their own home.

The intent was to force abu-Talib to hand over Muhammad, or if that could not be done, to squeeze the Hashims so hard that they'd oust abu-Talib and select another leader who would be either easier to intimidate or more amenable to doing as the power elite wanted. Whatever the rationale, however, it was collective punishment, unprecedented in Mecca.

An effective boycott is one that is widely observed, and for that to happen, its justice has to be acknowledged. But it escaped nobody's notice that only the two largest clan leaders had signed the declaration. Abu-Jahl's virulent rhetoric seemed to have swayed the usually more judicious abu-Sufyan, at least for now, but to what purpose? The real target was Muhammad and his followers, who at this stage called themselves simply *mu'uminin*, believers. But few Hashims were among them at this point. And whatever many Meccans thought about Muhammad, they still respected abu-Talib's principled stance as leader of the Hashim clan. Like every other clan, the Hashims did not exist in isolation, no matter how much abu-Jahl wished them to. Marriage ties had created a deliberately dense network of kinship across clan lines so that to boycott any one clan was, in a sense, to boycott oneself.

Throughout Mecca, group loyalty was already being stretched to the breaking point as dissent over Muhammad's message began to split families apart. After the respected abu-Bakr had accepted *islam*, for instance, his wife and two of his adult children followed his example, but one son remained vehemently opposed. And even as Khadija's half-brother was one of Muhammad's most bitter opponents, his own two sons were divided. One was an ardent believer while the other held back, despite having married Muhammad and Khadija's eldest daughter; now, under pressure from his clan, he divorced her.

Not even Hashim solidarity was complete. The most vehement exception was abu-Talib's half-brother abu-Lahab, the "father of flame" who had walked out when Muhammad first recited the Quranic verses to his kinsmen. Abu-Lahab strongly supported the boycott of his own clan, evidently expecting the Hashims to knuckle under to the pressure, oust abu-Talib, and select him as their chief instead—a stance that was to help earn him the unenviable distinction of being the one person singled out by name for condemnation in the Quran.

The boycott would become a perfect illustration of the degree to which traditional Meccan values had been distorted, and in this it only served to emphasize what Muhammad had been preaching. So while those who backed it blamed him for dividing families against each other, those who opposed it now blamed the boycotters instead, and organized to quietly defy them. They smuggled food into the Hashim quarter by night, and began to act as "fronts" to represent the clan's interests in the markets and on the caravans. But wary of reprisal, they remained careful to give any Hashim the cold shoulder whenever others could see them. Nobody yet dared stand up in public denunciation of what was happening.

Everyday life for the Hashims became a struggle, and one that extended beyond the effort to secure food and meet other basic needs. Being shunned ate at their self-respect. The respectful pleasantries of casual encounters in the street, the leisurely give-and-take of buying and selling in the market, the camaraderie of discussion and consultation in the Kaaba precinct—all the small things that made up the feeling of being an integral part of the larger community—were suddenly gone, and the insult was immense, especially to abu-Talib.

He was in his sixties by now, an old man for the time, yet even as his health suffered under the pressure, his determination to resist only increased. He issued a stinging rebuke of the Quraysh leaders in poetic form, and the rhymes he wrote went viral as they made the rounds of alleys and markets, private courtyards and public precincts. If this is what it meant to be Quraysh, he wrote, their honor was worthless. Who would want the protection of cowards like them? "Rather than your protection, give me a young camel, / Weak, grumbling, and murmuring, / Sprinkling its flanks with urine, / Lagging behind the herd and not keeping up. / When it climbs the desert ridges, you'd call it a weasel."

He called out those of his own clan, like abu-Lahab, who had sided against their kinsmen: "I see our brothers, sons of our mother and father, / When asked for help, they say, 'It's none of our business'. . . / You have flung us aside like a burning coal, / You have slandered your brothers among the people." And he excoriated the Umayyad leader abu-Sufyan, whom he'd considered a friend and ally: "He averted his face from me as he passed, / Sweeping along as though he were one of the great ones of the earth. / He tells us that he is sorry for us like a good friend, / But hides evil designs in his heart."

This boycott was "a heinous offense" against all accepted ethics and values, abu-Talib concluded, and he called on tribal solidarity, warning that "if we perish, you too will perish."

Abu-Jahl fought back, doing his utmost to bolster the boycott by pressuring other leaders to enforce clan discipline and bring any of Muhammad's followers within their ranks into line. In response, a small group of believers left Mecca for Ethiopia, determined to stay there until such time as tempers calmed in Mecca and the boycott was called off. Eleven men and four women, they were led by Muhammad's eldest daughter and her new husband, Uthman, one of Muhammad's few wealthy followers, who had married her the moment her first husband had succumbed to the pressure to divorce her. Ethiopia offered them not only refuge, but as ibn-Ishaq put it, "an ample living, security, and a good market" as well as "a righteous ruler," the Negus—the Geez title for the king.

In time, this Ethiopian sojourn, bolstered by the arrival of a second small group of believers, would become a major rhetorical factor in the history of early Islam. The argument was that while the pagan Meccans were persecuting early Muslims, Christian Ethiopians recognized and welcomed them, much as the hermit monk Bahira had done when Muhammad was still a boy on the camel caravans. Some reports maintain that the Negus gave the small group of believers special personal protection. It's said that he wept at the injustice of the boycott, summoned his bishops to confirm that Muhammad's message was also that of Jesus, and indignantly refused offers of gold from a Meccan delegation demanding that the refugees be sent back. But all of this errs on the side of too good to be true. More likely, any official protection was accorded the believers simply as foreign merchants, with permission to do business as temporary residents. Certainly, the Negus remained resolutely Christian.

Realizing that some of Muhammad's most loyal followers had slipped his net, a vengeful abu-Jahl decided on intimidation of those who remained. Under his direction, a campaign of harassment by the more thuggish elements of Mecca now verged on a kind of open season on believers. If they could not be persuaded into common sense, it would be beaten into them.

Ibn-Ishaq and al-Tabari both include several reports on the violence, such as an attack on a group of believers praying in one of the wadis outside Mecca. In the fracas, one of them was apparently struck and wounded with a camel's jawbone—a picaresque detail that sounds very much like a later stereotype of pre-Islamic Arabia. Assuming that seventh-century Mecca was mired in the pre-enlightenment darkness of *jahiliya*, a sophisticated ninth-century Baghdadi intellectual might easily imagine the area strewn with camel skeletons in much the same way as visitors under the influence of Georgia O'Keeffe might expect to see bleached cattle skulls littering the landscape of northern New Mexico. If only as a matter of practicality, a camel's femur would surely have served as a more effective weapon.

An oddly convenient camel jaw appears again in another report, this time placed even more strangely in a Meccan alley. A nephew of Khadija's had been smuggling flour into the Hashim quarter when abu-Jahl grabbed hold of him, leading a passer-by to intervene: "Are you trying to prevent him taking food to his own aunt? Let him go." When abu-Jahl refused, the nephew picked up the jawbone, knocked him down, and kicked him—a story that would certainly give great comfort to later believers, but that seems unlikely considering abu-Jahl's eminence.

Yet despite such retrospective embellishment, the harassment was all too real. Abu-Jahl himself openly threatened believers. If they were well connected, the threat was of shame: "You have forsaken the ways of your fathers who were better than you. We'll declare you weak-minded, brand you a fool, and destroy your reputation." If they were merchants, the threat was exclusion: "We will boycott your goods and reduce you to beggary." And if they were "people of no importance," as ibn-Ishaq put it— those without strong clan protection, the slaves and freedmen, migrant artisans and the seventh-century equivalent of "guest workers"—abu-Jahl didn't even bother with verbal threats. He saw to it that they were physically assaulted, as happened to the son of a freed slave who had volunteered to be the first after Muhammad to recite the Quranic verses in the Kaaba precinct. The moment he began, with the invocation "In the name of God, the compassionate, the merciful, who taught the Quran," he was set upon with blows and curses: "What on earth is this son of a slave woman saying? How dare he?"

Slaves were starved and freedmen deprived of work. Inevitably, some gave in to the pressure. It got so bad, one later remembered, that if the thugs had pointed to a beetle and asked the victim if this was God, he would have said yes just to stop the beating. Others withstood ill treatment to the point of torture, most famously Bilal, a tall, gaunt Ethiopian slave whose owner, a kinsman of abu-Bakr's, had him staked out in the open sun with a huge stone on his chest to slowly suffocate him. "You will stay here until you die," he was told, "or deny Muhammad and worship Lat and Uzza."

Abu-Bakr pleaded with his kinsman to let Bilal go: "Have you no fear of God that you treat him like this? How long is it to go on?"

"You are the one who corrupted him," came the retort. "It is up to you to save him if you want."

Finally, ibn-Ishaq reports, they agreed to exchange "a tougher and stronger slave, and a heathen" for Bilal. Abu-Bakr then declared him a freedman, and ten years later the former slave would become the first muezzin of Islam, his deep bass voice ringing out from the highest rooftop with the call to prayer.

Soon abu-Jahl had difficulty imposing his will even inside his own clan. Much as he wanted to knock some sense into one young Makhzum believer, he was wary of the notoriously violent temper of the youth's older brother, so he asked the brother for permission to "teach this young man a lesson."

"Very well," came the answer, "teach him a lesson, but have care of his life. I swear, by God, if you kill him, I will kill your family to the last man." That was enough to curb the teaching impulse.

Muhammad himself was spared the worst, since abu-Talib's protection still held sway, boycott or no. Most of the attacks on him remained at the level of insults as he walked by, though when a group of jeering thugs surrounded him and grabbed at his robe in the Kaaba precinct, abu-Bakr intervened and got beaten up instead; his daughter Aisha would remember him coming home that day "with the hair of his head and beard torn."

The danger forced the believers to meet secretly. A dissenting kinsman of abu-Jahl's offered his home as a safe house, so they gathered, as it were, right under the nose of their main antagonist. They had been forced into the role of a small persecuted minority, but this sense of threat served only to strengthen the feeling of solidarity among them. Taking their cue from Muhammad himself, they met violence with non-violence, a tactic that began to impress others with the injustice of the whole situation. In fact it was this sense of manifest injustice that now brought two famed warriors into the early Muslim fold.

The first was Muhammad's uncle Hamza. Another of the ten sons of Abd al-Muttalib, he was known as "the strongest man of the Quraysh, and the most unyielding"—never a man to cross. Just back from several days out in the mountains hunting game for the beleaguered Hashims, his bow still slung over his shoulder, he had come to circumambulate the Kaaba in the traditional ritual of thanksgiving and homecoming. That done, he passed by a group of people talking about an astonishing scene that had just taken place: Muhammad sitting absolutely still as abu-Jahl stood over him, ranting and cursing, all while "Muhammad answered not a word."

Passive resistance was not Hamza's style. Enraged by such flagrant abuse of his nephew, he strode on up to abu-Jahl and, in full view of everyone in the precinct, struck him with the edge of his bow. And then, possibly as much to his own amazement as anyone else's, he heard himself saying: "Will you revile Muhammad when I too am one of his followers and say what he says? Hit me back if you dare!"

It was the strongest endorsement yet of Muhammad, coming as it did with muscle and brawn to back it up. Even abu-Jahl backed down for the moment. As some of his Makhzum kinsmen made to come to his aid, he waved them off in apparent contrition, saying, "Let Hamza alone, for I insulted his nephew deeply." Or perhaps he was simply astonished that he himself had been the instrument of Hamza's accepting *islam*.

A different kind of dramatic conversion took place in the case of the second famed warrior, Omar, whose height alone made him fearsome: he was said to "tower above everyone else as though he were on horseback." Still in his twenties, he was known for his quickness with a whip and for his volatility, made worse by a fondness for potent date wine. He would mature into the most famed military commander of Islam, succeeding abu-Bakr as the second caliph, though if you'd told this to anyone when the boycott began, they'd have laughed you out of town. Omar was a nephew of abu-Jahl's, after all, and it was his father who years earlier had hounded his own half-brother Zayd the *hanif* out of Mecca. If there was one man abu-Jahl could rely on to tolerate no monotheistic nonsense, it was his nephew. Or so he thought.

Ibn-Ishaq recounts how one evening, musing on the split caused by the boycott and filled with the righteous anger of the thoroughly drunk, Omar strapped on his sword and declared, "I am going to Muhammad the traitor, who has divided the Quraysh and mocked and insulted us. I am going to kill him."

"You deceive yourself, Omar," a friend said, and invoked the law of retaliation: "Do you think the Hashims would allow you to keep walking this earth if you kill Muhammad? Better you should go back to your own family and set their affairs in order."

His own family? Why yes, replied the friend. Didn't Omar know that his sister, his brother-in-law, and his nephew had all accepted *islam*?

Since his sister had wisely neglected to inform him of this, he'd had no idea. In a fury, he went storming into her house, ready to lay about him with fists and whip, only to find a small group sitting peaceably on the floor, chanting verses from the Quran. They continued calmly despite Omar's bursting in, disconcerting him enough to make him stand still. The musicality of the verses began to reach through the fog of rage and alcohol, and he sat down to listen. "How fine and noble are these words," he said when they had finished, and asked to be taken to Muhammad to make the *shahada*, the formal pledge of belief. He'd never touch alcohol again.

These are classic "seeing the light" stories of the type familiar to any student of early Christianity. But however they came about, high-profile conversions such as those of Hamza and Omar led to more. And just as they boosted the strength and spirit of the beleaguered believers, so too they increased doubts among the Meccan leadership as to the wisdom of boycott and harassment. Yet again, their tactics seemed to be backfiring.

Voices were raised in favor of taking a less adversarial approach. "Let Muhammad alone," argued one elder. "He is only a man with no sons, so when he dies, his memory will perish, and you will have rest from him." Others tried for compromise, suggesting that they propose to Muhammad that "we will worship what you worship if you worship what we worship. If what you worship is better, then we will accept it, and if what we worship is better, than you will accept it." But a few took the Quranic message far more seriously, implicitly recognizing its power to radically change Mecca.

"Oh Quraysh, this is a situation you cannot deal with," said one of the more perceptive clan leaders. Neither ridicule nor force would work. "You liked Muhammad well enough until he brought you his message. It's time to look to your own affairs, by God, for a serious thing has befallen you."

Helpless to intervene as his kinsmen suffered deprivation and his followers were either forced into exile or threatened and beaten, Muhammad felt intensely responsible. He was buoyed by the faith of the believers and the stoic integrity of the Hashims, but haunted by the fact that if not for him, none of this would be happening. Yet the greater the turmoil inside him, the more the revelations responded to it. It was as though the Quranic voice was able to see deep inside him and address questions he was barely aware he was asking.

Steadily and repeatedly, new verses arrived to console and encourage him as the taunts and derision increased by the day. The need for patience and fortitude became a constant drumbeat throughout the revelations from this period, creating an almost Gandhian stance of non-violent resistance.

Again and again, he was told that he was not the only one to have undergone such treatment. "Many messengers before you were mocked, Muhammad," the voice said. Like him, they had been disbelieved, and called "sorcerers and madmen." From Moses to Jesus, they had brought the same divine message of warning, calling people back to a life of real values and ethics, only to be taunted and derided.

"We are well aware that your heart is weighed down by what the idolators say," he was told, but he was to ignore them. "Do not let their words grieve you," the voice said. "Do not let your heart be oppressed." "Do not be saddened." "Do not be distressed." "Do not let them discourage you."

His task was merely to warn his fellow Meccans, not to save them. "You cannot make the dead hear, nor the deaf listen to your call." The cynics have "hearts they do not understand with, eyes they do not see with, ears they do not hear with." Much as Muhammad may have wished it, "you cannot guide the blind out of their error . . . Even if they saw a piece of heaven falling down on them, they would say 'just a heap of clouds,' so leave them, messenger, until they face the Day of Judgment." This was hard to do, the revelations acknowledged, but "do not waste away your soul with regret for them."

At times the Quranic voice sounded almost like that of a protective parent or spouse: "Will you worry yourself to death because they do not believe?" Muhammad should pay no attention to the derision: "Leave them to flounder in their obstinacy." "Leave them to their own inventions." "Leave to themselves those who take their religion merely as a sport and a pastime."

"Turn away from them and wait," he was told. Or in the words of an earlier messenger, turn the other cheek. "Ignore them; you are not to blame. Be tolerant and command what is right; pay no attention to the foolish." And almost impatiently, the voice urged patience: "Endure what they say, ignore them politely, and leave those who live in luxury and deny the truth to me."

Yet by its sheer insistence on ignoring mockery, the Quran would ensure that the sting of it lasted long into the future. Here, in the foundation text of Islam, is the source of the modern Muslim sensitivity to insult that has taken so many by surprise. Where satire may be thought relatively harmless in the non-Muslim West, a matter more of entertainment than injury, the memory of the constant Meccan taunting of Muhammad and the harassment of his early followers would lie behind the worldwide outbreak of anger at the well-informed satire of Salman Rushdie's 1988 novel *The Satanic Verses* and at the 2005 publication in a Danish newspaper of crude cartoons of Muhammad. Since the wiser course in both instances would have been precisely the one advocated by the Quran—to pay no attention to such provocations—the fact that it was ignored has to be yet another of the many indelible ironies of history and faith.

To find himself the cause of such divisiveness among his own people was intensely painful for a man who had struggled through childhood to be included. The impulse to reconciliation had always been strong in him. It was part of what had made him so effective as a negotiator on the trade caravans, and it was what lay behind the perfect compromise he'd fashioned when he'd resolved the argument over who would replace the Black Stone in the rebuilt Kaaba. Surely now that the argument centered on him, he could find a way for everyone to live and work together again.

While men like abu-Jahl were clearly driven to extremes by hatred and ambition, Muhammad could see that most of the Quraysh leadership, like abu-Sufyan, were sincerely concerned that his message threatened what they held sacred. The Quran would call them *kufr*, a word that literally means "ungrateful," as in ungrateful for all that God had created, but is usually taken to mean unbelievers or faithless infidels. In their own way, however— "the tradition of the fathers"—these men were in fact deeply faithful. They did not deny God; the Kaaba was the divine sanctuary, and they took their role as its custodians in good faith as much as good profit. This faith demanded loyalty not only to al-Lah, but also to all the lesser gods such as the "three daughters" Uzza, Lat, and Manat. The Quraysh were not so much faithless as spreading their faith too thin. If they were misguided, there had to be an acceptable way for Muhammad to guide them in the right direction.

He resumed his long nights of prayerful vigil and meditation, hoping for the voice to give direction on how to resolve the divisiveness swirling around him. Surely there was some means to include rather than exclude the Meccan traditions. Surely the solution would be revealed to him. And in an all too human way, it was.

Ibn-Ishaq tells how it happened: "When Muhammad saw that his own people turned their backs on him, he was pained by their estrangement from what he brought them from God, and longed for a message that would reconcile him with his own people. He would gladly have seen those things that bore down harshly on them softened, so much so that he kept saying it to himself, fervently wishing for such an outcome. Then God revealed Sura 53, beginning with 'By the star when it sets, your comrade does not err, nor is he deceived, nor does he speak out of his own caprice.' But when Muhammad reached the words 'Have you thought on Lat and Uzza, and the third one, Manat?' Satan added this upon his tongue: 'These are the three great exalted birds, and their intercession is desired indeed.'"

And here they were: the infamous Satanic Verses. The three "daughters of God" were no longer false gods, but giant high-flying birds covering the earth with their wingspans, graced with the power to intercede for those who worshipped them.

The moment Muhammad recited these newly revealed verses in the Kaaba precinct, the response was overwhelmingly positive. "When they heard them, people rejoiced and were delighted," ibn-Ishaq reports. "They said: 'Muhammad has mentioned our gods the daughters in the most favorable way possible. We recognize that it is God, al-Lah, who gives life and death, who creates us and who provides sustenance, but if the daughters can still intercede for us, and if Muhammad gives them their share of worship, then we accept what he says.'"

At one stroke, the rift appeared to have been healed. But that verse praising the "three great exalted birds" would never appear in the Quran.

The following night, says ibn-Ishaq, the angel Gabriel came to Muhammad and berated him. "What have you done? You have recited something I did not bring you from God, and you have said what he did not say to you." In that moment, Muhammad realized that he had been misled by his own desire for reconciliation; he had taken the easier path rather than the hard one laid down for him. There was no god but God. There could be no partners with God, no daughters or sons. God was neither begotten nor begetter. What indeed had he done?

He was devastated—"bitterly grieved, and greatly in fear of God," as ibn-Ishaq puts it. "So God sent down another revelation to comfort and ease him, assuring him this: 'Never have we sent a messenger or a prophet before you but that when he longed for something, Satan cast words into his mouth. But God annuls what Satan does, and establishes the real verses. God is all-knowing, all-wise.'"

That assurance would find its place in the Quran, as would another verse sent to replace the Satanic ones. It began the same way, but went in quite another direction: "Have you thought on Lat and Uzza, and the third one, Manat? What, as men have sons, so God has daughters? This is indeed wrong. They are naught but names which you and your fathers have invented. God has sent them no authority."

It was the most radical rejection yet of the local Meccan divinities. They were just names, nothing more. They had no authority, no power; they were mere figments of the imagination.

Theopolitics would make the story of the Satanic Verses both famous and infamous. It has been rejected as apocryphal if not blasphemous by many Islamic clerics, especially after the nineteenth-century Orientalist William Muir used it to argue that Muhammad had been satanically inspired all along (an argument that led even *The Times* of London to criticize him for "Christian propagandistic writing"). Such clerics deem the whole thing impossible, since it runs counter to the tenet that Muhammad was divinely protected from error. Yet this idea appears nowhere in the Quran. To the contrary, human fallibility seems to be explicitly acknowledged in that verse stating that every messenger and prophet had had words "cast into his mouth" by Satan. Nonetheless, there are still conservative Muslim scholars who suspect that the whole episode was invented by enemies of Islam in order to undercut the credibility of Muhammad and of the Quran itself.

To an outside eye, however, the story of the Satanic Verses seems if anything to reinforce Muhammad's credibility. It casts light on the process of revelation, showing it less as a miraculous *coup de foudre* and more as a kind of collaboration between human and divine—an ongoing conversation, as it were, in which one side speaks for both. It allows us to see the depth of Muhammad's pain and of his desire for reconciliation. It reveals him as movingly vulnerable, given to the very human habit of projecting his own deepest desire onto divine will. And it shows him succumbing to a moment of weakness, imagining he heard what he wanted to hear.

It is precisely this fallibility that makes the whole incident so believable. That, and Muhammad's intense distress when even as the verses had their desired effect and the Quraysh opened their arms wide to welcome him back into the fold and embrace his message, he realized that he had deceived himself into betraying that message. As the Quran would order him to say again and again, he was only human: "a man like you" and "one of your own." Only God could be infallible.

It has to have taken a great deal of courage for Muhammad to acknowledge his mistake so publicly, all the more since it was clear how it would be used against him. Seventh-century Meccans were no more able to recognize the integrity of someone who could publicly correct himself than twenty-first-century Americans. To acknowledge error is still mistaken for a sign of weakness instead of strength. As Kathryn Schulz writes in *Being Wrong*, the "idea of error . . . is our meta-mistake: we are wrong about what it means to be wrong. Far from being a sign of intellectual inferiority, the capacity to err is crucial to human cognition. Far from being a moral flaw, it is inextricable from some of our most humane and honorable qualities: empathy, optimism, imagination, conviction, and courage."

The Quraysh elite, of course, did not see things this way. They were all the more incensed since so far as they were concerned, Muhammad had gone back on his word—the ultimate sin in a society where a man's word was his bond, an oath and a handclasp better than a written contract. While Muhammad knew that he had deceived himself, Mecca's leaders instead felt that it was they who had been deceived. And that was unforgivable. He had given his opponents exactly the weapon they had wanted all along. Where he had tried to meet them halfway, driven by the impulse to unity, now they could turn around and call him a liar. "All he says is clearly nothing but a tissue of lies. It is all of his own invention," they declared. He had tried to bridge the divide, and instead made it deeper than ever.

Yet however much conservative Muslims may disagree, it could be said that the whole episode was necessary. It was the means of making it clear that no matter how painful, Muhammad needed to be true to himself, to his voice and to that of God. That was the meaning behind the revelation of Sura 109, which reads in full: "Muhammad, say: 'Disbelievers, I serve not what you serve, and you serve not what I serve. I will never serve what you serve, and you will never serve what I serve. To you your religion, and to me mine.'" The Satanic Verses had forced the issue once and for all. There would be no going back.

Eleven

By the time the boycott was formally annulled, sun and wind had almost shredded the declaration nailed to the door of the Kaaba. It had taken nearly two years for the Quraysh leadership to concede the obvious, by which time the only words still legible on the tattered parchment were the customary opening ones: "In your name, oh God . . ." But no sooner had life returned to something approaching normal for Muhammad than personal tragedy struck: Khadija died.

It happened suddenly. There was no long illness, so the cause may well have been a heart attack brought about by the stress of living through the boycott, or simply the fact that she was in her sixties by then, a good old age for the seventh century. Quite possibly it was a combination of the two: the effect of stress on an aging heart. But to the end, a loving one.

For twenty-four years, she had been Muhammad's polestar—his refuge, his rock, his confidante, his solace. From the beginning, she had seen what was in him more accurately and more presciently than anyone else. She had defied social norms to marry him, lifting him out of insecurity into respectability. Together they had raised four daughters and two sons, one formally adopted and the other in effect adopted, both of whom had become as close as birth sons. It had been in her arms that he had sought shelter from the terror of that night on Mount Hira, and her voice that had reassured him. Together they had faced hardship and boycott, scorn and derision. They had persevered. And now, just when it seemed there might again be some measure of peace for them, she was gone, and Muhammad was utterly bereft.

No matter how many more times he married, he would never find that quality of love again. Many years later, Aisha, the youngest and most outspoken of the nine wives to come, would say, "I was never jealous of any of the prophet's wives except for Khadija, even though I came after her death." And though this was clearly not so—she'd bristle when there was so much as a mention of another wife's beauty—Khadija was certainly the focus of her jealousy. Muhammad's first wife was the one woman who was unassailable, and he would make this crystal clear to the teenage Aisha when she dared turn her sharp tongue on her predecessor.

Teasingly, Aisha would ask him how he could possibly remain so devoted to the memory of "that toothless old woman whom God has replaced with a better." The language is unmistakably hers; nobody else would have dared be so startlingly direct. It was the kind of question only a teenager could ask, and only a much older woman could regret as she related the incident many years later—words spoken with the casual disregard of the young and vivacious for the old and dead. But if Aisha thought for a moment she could gain precedence over Khadija this way, Muhammad's response would stop her in her tracks.

"Indeed no, God has not replaced her with a better," he'd say. And the man who though multiply married would never have any children after Khadija then drove the point home: "God granted me her children while withholding those of other women."

As he buried and mourned Khadija, however, Muhammad had no thought of marrying again. The ones who supported him through this time were his young cousin Ali, his close companions abu-Bakr, Omar, and Uthman, and two of his uncles, the fierce Hamza and the honor-driven abu-Talib, who continued to stand by his nephew out of loyalty to the cherished values of both clan and tradition. But the effort had taken its toll on him. Even as Muhammad was still reeling from Khadija's death, abu-Talib fell ill, and never recovered.

As it became clear that his sickbed would be his deathbed, other clan leaders came to pay their last respects—and to push once more for a negotiated solution to the problems his nephew's activities posed for them. Even abu-Jahl took a more moderate stance for the time being; whether because of the failure of the boycott or the imminence of death, he let abu-Sufyan do the speaking.

"You know we honor your standing, abu-Talib," said the Umayyad leader, "and now that you are on the brink of death, we are deeply concerned on account of what will happen to it after you are gone. So let us call your nephew and make an agreement that he will leave us alone and we will leave him alone; let him have his religion and we will have ours." Perhaps deliberately, abu-Sufyan's words were almost exactly those Muhammad had used after he'd acknowledged the error of the Satanic Verses. But what might have worked then would not work any longer.

Muhammad was called in, and stood by his uncle's bedside. "Nephew," said abu-Talib, "these notables have come to you that they may give you something and take something from you." Ill though he was, he had chosen his words carefully; even as he seemed impartial, he made it clear that there would be a price to pay, and implied that Muhammad would be the lesser for it if he accepted abu-Sufyan's proposal. After the reaction to his retraction of the Satanic Verses, Muhammad needed no further prompting. He stood firm, insisting that the Quraysh leaders acknowledge no god but God and abandon all the totems and lesser gods. By way of reply, abu-Sufyan and the others simply threw their hands up in frustration and stalked out of the sickroom, leaving Muhammad alone with his dying uncle.

What abu-Talib said then is still a matter of debate. In one account he whispered, "Nephew, why did you go too far with them?" But in another he said, "Nephew, you did not ask them for too much," and it is this second version that reflects the hope of many pious Muslims that the man who had led his clan through hardship to protect Muhammad did in the end die a believer. Certainly both accounts agree that Muhammad took his uncle's hand as the life began to fade from his eyes and urged him to say the *shahada*, to accept *islam* and testify that there was no god but God: "Say it, uncle, and then I shall be able to witness for you on the Day of Judgment."

But abu-Talib remained faithful to Meccan tradition to the last. "Were it not that they would consider this shameful and say that I was afraid of death, I would say it if only to give you pleasure, nephew. But I must remain in the ways of my fathers."

And just like that, within a few weeks of each other, Khadija and abu-Talib were both gone. Muhammad's two main bastions of support, the one impelled by love, the other by clan and honor, had been ripped away from him.

Death echoes in the mind. For those who mourn, no death takes place in isolation. Each one reverberates with memories, conscious or not, of earlier loss, and with the almost physical ache of abandonment that comes with such loss. So severe a blow as the double deaths of a beloved spouse and a firm protector would be devastating for anyone, but for a man whose father had died before he was born and who had known his mother for less than a year before she too died, it was all but overwhelming. Especially since this time, he was left even more vulnerable.

With abu-Talib gone, the Hashims had to select a new clan leader, and their choice did not bode well for Muhammad. Though they had not ousted abu-Talib during the boycott as his half-brother abu-Lahab had hoped, they now looked to the "father of flame" as the next in line, thus replacing Muhammad's protector with one of his most vehement opponents.

Even then, things might have worked out, since it seemed at first that their mutual grief over abu-Talib's death might bind the two men together. In honor of the dead man's memory, abu-Lahab assured his nephew that he would protect him as abu-Talib had done, but his assurance was short-lived. Alarmed at his apparent change of heart, the other clan leaders argued that far from upholding the honor of the Hashims by protecting Muhammad, abu-Lahab was in fact dishonoring it. Muhammad was shaming his clan, they maintained, since his message meant that the clan fathers, from Hashim through al-Muttalib down to abu-Talib himself, were all suffering the fires of hell in the afterlife because they had not accepted *islam*.

By the time they were finished, abu-Lahab was newly incensed at the idea of any Hashim pronouncing such a fate on the fathers and besmirching their memory in this way. He withdrew his protection, in essence expelling his nephew from the clan. Any physical attack on Muhammad would no longer be taken by the Hashims as cause for blood revenge. In the language of the time, "his blood was licit." He was beyond the protection of the law.

In the great pre-Islamic odes, this might have been presented in a romanticized manner, as was the legend of the fugitive "wandering king" Imr al-Qais, who lived proudly by his wits and his guts, defying rejection. But Muhammad was no admirer of this classic meme. Even as a boy thrust to the margins, he had never thought of himself as alone against his own people. On the contrary, he had done all he could to be one of them, and was now striving to change them from within, to save Mecca from its own worst self. His vision was not the subversive one of the rebel but the reformer's one of society remade. He thought of himself as Meccan to the core, deeply loyal to his place and his people, and thus all the more pained by the direction in which they were going. Yet the gulf between them had only widened. What he saw as reform, they took to mean overthrow. And in so doing, they may have grasped the revolutionary aspect of his message more acutely than he himself had yet done.

Muhammad was no longer merely mad or possessed, his opponents argued. He was far more dangerous than that. By trying to turn Mecca away from "the ways of the fathers," he was trying to undermine and overthrow the whole society. To the abu-Lahabs and abu-Jahls of Mecca, this was treason.

The political psychology involved here is dispiritingly familiar to the modern ear. In autocracies especially, but also in democracies under threat, those who speak out against injustice are still accused of subversion and branded as traitors. They take their stand as deeply loyal citizens, but are condemned by demagogues either as wantonly destructive, or as motivated by hatred or self-hatred. Character assassination comes with this territory, all too often followed by arrest, torture, and physical assassination.

· · ·

As news spread of abu-Lahab's withdrawal of protection, the attacks on Muhammad became more pointed. Pails of dust were emptied over his head as he walked to the Kaaba precinct, and stones thrown at him when he tried to preach there. Even at home, he was at risk. As he sat in his own courtyard, someone threw sheep's offal at him, splattering him with blood and gore. The specific organ hurled was the one distinctly female part of the animal, the uterus, making the insult all the more flagrant in a society based so strongly on male pride. It was clear that if Muhammad was not to live under virtual house arrest—in fact, if he was to survive—it was of paramount importance that he find the protection of a clan leader.

Some accounts say he looked first to Taif, a small city in the mountains a day's journey southeast of Mecca. But Taif was a major cultic center of Lat, one of the goddesses Muhammad had denigrated as false, and was closely connected with the Meccan elite. Many had built summer homes there, taking advantage of the ample springs and greenery that made it cool and pleasant by comparison with the stifling heat of Mecca. It seems like the last place Muhammad would look for support, but he reportedly ventured there nonetheless.

The reaction of Taif's leading citizens was wryly predictable. "If you were sent by God as you claim, then your state is too lofty for me to speak with you," came one sardonic response to his plea. "And if you are taking the name of God in vain, then it's not fit that I should speak with you."

Another simply looked at him and said, "Could God send only a nobody like you?"

Within a few days, stone-throwing thugs had hounded him out of Taif, but since it was unsafe for him to return to Mecca without official protection, he stopped a few miles short of the city and sent message after message to several minor clan leaders, begging for their help. Finally one agreed. The aging al-Mutim was one of the few who had never supported the boycott, and now he sent a small armed escort to accompany Muhammad back into the city.

Abu-Jahl, the "father of ignorance," watched warily as they arrived in the Kaaba precinct. "Is this protection or a call to arms?" he asked al-Mutim. "I am offering protection," came the reply, to which even abu-Jahl had no choice but to respond as any Quraysh was obliged to: "We shall protect whomever you protect."

It wasn't the strongest form of protection, since Muhammad was in the position of a "client" or dependent of al-Mutim rather than an equal, but it was as much as he could get for now. At least it gained him a temporary respite, some time in which to gain his bearings and figure out where to go from here. Yet it was at this point of utter insecurity, when it seemed he was forced to focus on the most down-to-earth matter of survival, that he would soar instead. The *isra*, the Night Journey, would become one of the most symbolically weighted events of his life.

In its simplest form, the Night Journey is a miracle story. Muhammad woke in the middle of the night and went to the Kaaba to pray in solitude. There he fell asleep, only to be woken by the angel Gabriel, who picked him up and lifted him onto a winged white horse. The horse took off and flew north through the night, in the same direction in which Muhammad and his followers turned when they prayed. Jerusalem was where the ancient Jewish temple had been built over the stone slab where Abraham, the first *hanif,* had raised his knife to sacrifice his son in obedience to the one god. By turning toward it in prayer, the early believers affirmed the primacy of Abraham as the founding monotheist in a tradition far more ancient and venerable than those of the Meccan fathers. Abraham was the original father, and thus the father of all. And now Muhammad would meet him.

Hordes of angels greeted him on his arrival, and as he dismounted, he was offered a choice of three goblets from which to drink. One contained wine, the second milk, the third water. He chose the milk as the middle way between asceticism and indulgence, and Gabriel was delighted: "You have been rightly guided, Muhammad, and so will your people be."

"Then," Muhammad is quoted as saying, "a ladder was brought to me finer than any I have ever seen. It was that to which the dying man looks when death approaches." Led by Gabriel, he climbed the ladder and ascended through seven circles of heaven presided over by, respectively, Adam, Jesus and John, Joseph, Enoch (called Idris in Muslim tradition), Aaron, Moses, and finally in the seventh and highest circle—at the threshold of the divine sphere—Abraham.

This is the essence of the Night Journey as given by ibn-Ishaq, who is quite clear that while he has been told one form or another of it by many people, he is unsure as to how reliable any of them are. Carefully choosing his words, he introduces the episode this way: "This account is pieced together, each piece contributing something of what that person was told about what happened." And to indicate that the story may be more a matter of faith than of fact, he makes ample use of such phrases as "I was told that in his story al-Hassan said . . ." or "One of abu-Bakr's family told me that Aisha used to say . . ." or "A traditionalist who had heard it from one who had heard it from Muhammad said that Muhammad said . . ."

The story is not told in the Quran, though the verse that begins Sura 17 is understood as a clear reference to it: "Glory be to God, who made his servant go by night from the sacred house to the far house, that we might show him some of our signs." From the sacred house of the Kaaba sanctuary, that is, to the far house of the Jerusalem one. In the light of this Quranic verse, ibn-Ishaq sums up his reportorial dilemma this way: "The matter of the place of the journey and what is said about it is a searching test and a matter of God's power and authority, wherein is a lesson for the intelligent, with guidance, mercy, and strengthening for those who believe."

It's a wisely phrased abstention from certainty. Whether the Night Journey was a dream, a vision, or lived experience, ibn-Ishaq's view is that what matters is not how it happened, but its significance. He steps carefully between his duty as a believer and his obligation as a biographer—a delicate balancing act that he carries out with considerable aplomb, finally threading the needle with this conclusion: "I have heard it said that the messenger used to say, 'My eyes sleep while my heart is awake.' Only God knows how revelation came and what he saw. But whether he was asleep or awake, it was all true."

Not every early Islamic historian would agree. Al-Tabari, writing a century later in the new Muslim capital city of Baghdad, was wary as always of miracle tales and far more focused on politics. Despite his repeatedly acknowledged debt to ibn-Ishaq, he would omit the episode altogether in his multi-volume history, and ignore the much-quoted dictum attributed to Aisha, speaking many years after Muhammad's death: "The messenger's body remained where it was, but God removed his spirit by night."

Was the Night Journey simply a dream, then? But there was no such thing as "simply a dream" at the time. Freud was far from the first to recognize the symbolic weight of dreams, nor did he invent dream interpretation; he invoked the new science of psychology to resuscitate an ancient practice in which sleep was understood not as a passive state, but with the right preparation as an active experience of the soul.

The ritual known as dream incubation was highly regarded in both Greek and Roman times, when people would purify themselves by fasting and meditating before sleeping in a temple precinct in order to receive divine guidance in a dream. And throughout the Bible, dreams are a manifestation of the divine. "If there be a prophet among you, I the Lord will make myself known to him in a vision, and will speak to him in a dream," Yahweh says to Aaron and Miriam. Joseph's skill at dream interpretation made him a senior counselor to Pharaoh, while Abraham, Jacob, Solomon, Saint Joseph, and Saint Paul were all visited by God as they slept.

The tradition continues in the Talmud, where dreams channel divine wisdom. According to one Midrash, "During sleep the soul departs and draws spiritual refreshment from on high"—a statement very close to the one attributed to Aisha. Later rabbinical tradition would prize the *she'elat halom*, literally the "dream question," or rather, a dream answer to a waking question. The mystical aspect of dreams would be incorporated into the thirteenth-century Zohar, the foundation book of Kabbala, which would identify the angel Gabriel as "the master of dreams" and the link between God and human, as he was for Muhammad. One story about the Kabbalist master Isaac Luria even has Gabriel appearing to him in a dream wielding the stylus of a scribe.

Muslim philosophers and mystics played an equally important part in the tradition. Two of the greatest, ibn-Arabi in the twelfth century and ibn-Khaldun in the fourteenth, wrote extensively about *alam al-mithal*, "the realm of images," in which dreams were the highest form of vision of divine truth. Ibn-Khaldun wrote that God created sleep as an opportunity to "lift the veil of the senses" and thus gain access to higher forms of knowledge. Several hadiths—traditional reports of Muhammad's sayings and practice—show him counseling his followers on the preparatory ritual of purification and prayer known as *istikhara*, which was to be used either when awake, in which case divine response would come in the form of "an inclination of the heart," or just before sleep, when it would come in a dream.

But in the days immediately after the Night Journey, even Muhammad's closest followers were nervous about how it would be understood. One of them begged him to keep quiet about it. His critics would deliberately take it as literally as possible, she said: "They will give you the lie and insult you." When Muhammad insisted nonetheless, the reaction was exactly as she'd predicted.

"This is patently absurd!" his opponents crowed, with all the glee of modern politicians exploiting an electoral rival's gaffe. "A caravan takes a month to go to Syria and a month to return, and Muhammad claims he made the journey to Jerusalem in one night?"

The journey is still the subject of disagreement between those Muslims who see it as mystical experience and those who take it more literally. Brightly colored posters of Buraq, the winged white mare whose name means "lightning," hang in many Muslim homes throughout Asia, North Africa, and the Middle East, the details of her saddle and trappings varying according to local folk-art traditions. Sometimes her wings are magnificently extended with peacock feathers, and despite the conservative Islamic ban on human representation, she's often shown with a beautiful woman's head, dark hair cascading down her long neck. Soaring against a star-studded sky, she spans the distance between the golden Dome of the Rock in Jerusalem and the minarets of Mecca, defying both geography and chronology, since neither the Dome of the Rock nor the minarets had yet been built.

But for the most part, this image of Buraq is not taken literally. It's a concretization of what cannot be made concrete—a translation of the metaphysical into the physical. And the same might be said for the account of the journey itself. The question has to be not whether Muhammad "really" flew overnight to Jerusalem and back, but what his experience of it meant.

As in Jacob's dream in the book of Genesis, a ladder led up to heaven. But where Jacob remained sleeping at the foot of the ladder, Muhammad saw it as "that to which a dying man looks," and climbed it. Did he feel as though he was dying, as he had during that first Quranic revelation on Mount Hira? Was this the death of the self that has been the goal of mystics of all faiths, the better to unite with the divine? Or did it seem as though he had taken leave of his body and hovered above it, looking down at his earthly self as some who survive near-death experiences report having done? Could there even have been some element of reaching beyond death to the wife and uncle he had so recently lost?

Certainly the Night Journey is deeply symbolic in psychological terms, coming as it did when Muhammad was at his most vulnerable, sure of his mission but deeply unsure as to where it would lead him or how. The images of flight and ascension are expressions of freedom and transcendence, of escaping the particulars of daily life to soar beyond them. In fact the journey could be seen as a kind of over-compensation for the double loss of Khadija and abu-Talib. Even as he was mired in the terrible loneliness of grief and made to feel more isolated in Mecca than ever, the episode acted as confirmation that Muhammad was not alone; he was welcomed within the community of angels and greeted by the great prophets of the past as one of them.

But just as a miraculous understanding of the journey ends up reducing it to a simple matter of yes or no, belief or disbelief, so this kind of psychological interpretation undermines its real significance. Because here is where it can be said that Muhammad fully assumes what the Hebrew bible calls "the mantle of prophecy." The man told earlier to say he was "just one of you" and "just an ordinary man" is now specially graced. "Just one of you" does not fly hundreds of miles through the night to consult with angels and prophets and ascend into the divine presence. Muhammad is no longer the passive recipient of revelation but an active participant: he flies, ascends, prays with the angels, and speaks with the prophets.

Whether physical or visionary, waking reality or dream reality, the Night Journey marks a radical change. This is where Muhammad first understands himself not merely as a messenger but as a leader. It is here, when his future in Mecca is most in doubt, that he sees himself projected into the future. "Thy seed shall be as the dust of the earth, and thou shalt spread abroad to the west and to the east, to the north and to the south," Yahweh told Jacob in his dream, and in a similar way, the Night Journey was the promise of the future for Muhammad. It represents a leap forward to a new level of determination and action, one that would give him the resolve to uproot himself from the bonds of clan and tribe, and fully commit himself to the radical implications of his message.

His closest ties had been irrevocably broken by death, but by the same token he was now free to step fully into the role assigned him and assume the authority of his vision. However cold-hearted the idea may be, perhaps the woman he most loved and the man on whom he most depended both had to die in order to release him from the ties of home and thus launch him on the journey out into the larger world.

Twelve

In much of the world today, the question "Where are you from?" is answered with either where you were born or where you grew up. To a greater or lesser extent, your childhood home still defines you. One way or another, whether gladly or resentfully, some part of you always belongs to that place. But in seventh-century Arabia, home was not merely part of identity; home determined it. Geography and identity were inextricably intertwined, each the foundation of the other. To be Meccan was not just to be *from* Mecca; it was to be *of* Mecca. For Muhammad, it was to be bound to both the place and the people whose place it was, the Quraysh, with a sense of belonging so deep it was imprinted in muscle memory through the ritual circling of the Kaaba.

Whenever the Quranic voice had spoken, it had told him what to say to his own people. The warning was specifically addressed to them. He had relayed the message as a Meccan, as "one of you." To stop being a Meccan was unthinkable. But now, as he neared fifty, Muhammad faced the prospect of doing just that. Home was no longer a safe place for him to be. Inconceivable as it was, he needed to leave.

Every immigrant knows that leaving home is not simply a matter of geography. Whether the move is from a rural to an urban area, from one city to another, or from one country or even one continent to another, it is often a wrenching experience. It means uprooting yourself—tearing out your roots and leaving yourself vulnerable. You abandon what is known and open yourself to the mercy of a new world, or the lack of it. Nothing is certain. Inevitably, questions of rejection and acceptance arise. What does it take to be accepted in a new place? Does it necessitate rejection of the old place? What if the place you move to does not accept you? Where does that leave you, especially if the place you always thought of as home has already rejected you?

For Muhammad, such questions were all but overwhelming. He had struggled for the acceptance and respect of his own people, earning his identity as a Meccan and as a Quraysh the hard way. But now everything he had struggled for had been placed in violent question. He faced an existential challenge to his most basic sense of identity. And the Night Journey was the key to his meeting that challenge. It had been an affirmation of a spiritual home beyond the physical confines of geography—a metaphysical experience that had its physical correlate in terms of a worldly home. It reoriented him in the world just at the time he was forced to think the unthinkable.

His message had had the potential all along to radically expand the sense of home, and thus of identity itself. Now that potential would be tested. Where Mecca had been the center of his life, would it now be only his point of departure? Could leaving it be the beginning of a new life, even a new world? But where?

There was no flash of inspiration, let alone revelation. Medina would be seen as the inevitable choice only in retrospect. But Muhammad was not entirely an outsider in that oasis settlement two hundred miles north of Mecca. There was an inside connection, at least in principle. His father had died there, and six years later his mother had died on the way back from a visit there. And if these connections seemed more a matter of fate and timing than anything else, there was also a deeper one. His great-grandfather, the eponymous founder of the Hashim clan, had married a Medinan woman. And fathered a son with her.

Hashim had been the chief Quraysh representative to Syria, which at the time included all of what is now Israel, Palestine, Jordan, and Lebanon, as well as the modern Syrian state. As such, he had often passed through Medina on his way north and south. During one such layover, he had married a woman from the majority Khazraj tribe, then continued on his mission, only to fall sick and die in Gaza without even being aware that he had sired a son. In a detail that certainly struck deep in the mind of the orphaned Muhammad, that son—the man who would become Muhammad's grandfather—was also born an orphan.

It's a measure of the psychological distance between Medina and Mecca that the existence of this son seems to have been unknown in Mecca for seven years. So far as the Meccans were concerned, Medina was the boondocks: a useful caravan stop, but really just a loose confederation of hamlets strung along the eight miles of a fertile spring-fed valley thick with date palms. Like most city dwellers even today, the Meccans considered themselves infinitely superior to what they saw as a bunch of provincials. So when news of the boy's existence finally reached Mecca, it was clear to his uncle, Hashim's brother al-Muttalib, that he had to be brought back to his father's flesh and blood.

It would turn into the sixth-century Arabian equivalent of a custody battle. Al-Muttalib had legal precedent on his side, since the paternal bloodline took priority over the maternal one, but this may not have been his primary motivation. What really drove him was more likely the prospect of this newly discovered nephew taking the place of the sons he himself had never had, since as with Muhammad three generations later, all his surviving children were daughters. At all events, he lost no time in riding to Medina, intent on persuading the boy's mother to hand him over.

In one version of what happened, the mother reluctantly agreed, worn down by al-Muttalib's persistence in arguing how much better life would be for the boy among the nobility of Mecca, where he belonged. But in another version she did not agree, and al-Muttalib lost patience and simply kidnapped his newfound nephew. That is, he placed the boy in front of him on his camel and rode off with him, leaving the mother to wail and sob helplessly when she realized her son was gone.

This second version is supported by the fact that al-Muttalib took pains to disguise the boy's identity on the journey back to Mecca. Wary of a possible rescue attempt by the mother's relatives, he identified him as his slave instead of his nephew. The seven-year-old was thus dubbed Abd al-Muttalib, the slave of al-Muttalib, and the name stuck. Five decades later, this was the man who would cast arrows in front of the oracle of Hubal to spare the life of his youngest son, Abdullah, who would then father Muhammad, only to die in Medina before his son was born.

Could the grandson establish a new home in his grandfather's birthplace? Put like that, it seems to have the power of narrative inevitability. But Muhammad's blood connection to Medina was not as strong as may seem at first. Nobody in sixth-century Arabia had openly challenged the idea that the seven-year-old Abd al-Muttalib belonged by right first to his father's family and only secondarily to his mother's. Muhammad's great-grandmother had been left to mourn her son's loss alone; there had been no repercussions, and nobody had tried to rescue him. The whole matter would have been almost a non-event in the collective memory of Medina if it had not involved a Meccan.

The idea of a Quraysh aristocrat swooping in to claim and kidnap a native boy was of a piece with Medina's awareness that it was relegated to second-string status compared with Mecca. Where Mecca was a flourishing center of both pilgrimage and commerce, Medina was a place to pass through, not a destination. It was an agricultural settlement, its date palms providing not only the fruits themselves but syrup and wine, oil from the sap, charcoal and animal feed from the ground pits, vegetables from the leaves, and everything from rope to roofing materials from the branches. There was a good living to be made in this fertile valley, at least for those who owned land.

While Mecca was controlled by a single tribe, the Quraysh, making for relative stability, Medina had become enmeshed in inter-tribal rivalry over issues of land ownership, which was why each of its hamlets was clustered around a small fortified stronghold serving as a defensible retreat in times of conflict. Indeed Medina's two largest tribes, the Khazraj and the Aws, had come to blows several times in recent years. Neither had managed to dominate the other, however, leaving the valley an uneasy tinderbox that could be reignited at any time. Perhaps the one thing that really united them was a simmering resentment of the Quraysh, who so clearly considered themselves far more sophisticated than those date farmers up north who couldn't even keep the peace among themselves.

∴

The move to Medina began quietly, almost imperceptibly. At first it was no more than an idea mooted during the *hajj* pilgrimage. As he had in previous years, Muhammad had been reciting the Quranic revelations among the pilgrims who set up their tents outside Mecca. Though none had been converted, most were willing enough to listen. They were tired after traveling hundreds of miles, and the preachers and poets, seers and diviners and soothsayers who wandered through their camping grounds were if nothing else a form of entertainment. Besides, there was never any harm in listening, especially not to the man they had heard so much about, thanks to the efforts of the Quraysh elite to undermine his message. Then as now, the adage that any publicity is good publicity held true.

This year, however, Muhammad had found a handful of more serious listeners. Six pilgrims from Medina paid especially close attention. In fact they seem to have sought him out. They were all from the Khazraj tribe, though it's unclear if they were even aware at this stage that Muhammad's great-grandmother had been one of theirs. They had heard about his preaching, and were especially intrigued by the way the Quraysh so adamantly vilified a man they had once unanimously respected as *amin*, trustworthy. The story of how Muhammad had resolved the dispute over who would lift the Black Stone into place in the rebuilt Kaaba had spread far and wide, and was cited and admired as an example of the wisdom of compromise. For Medinans enmeshed in bitter contention, such a well-crafted solution held out hope. Maybe Muhammad could resolve their disputes too. "No people is as divided by enmity and malice as we are in Medina," ibn-Ishaq quotes one of them as saying. "Perhaps God will reunite us through you."

This statement was most likely written back into history, not least because Medina—"the city," short for "the city of the prophet"— was still known by its pre-Islamic name, Yathrib. If there was any idea of Muhammad actually moving there at this point, it can have been little more than wishful thinking. Still, the six pilgrims were deeply moved by what they had heard from him. They accepted *islam*, arranged to meet him again during the following year's pilgrimage, and returned home to begin discreetly spreading the word.

The next pilgrimage fell in the early summer of 621. Since to meet in Mecca itself would have been foolhardy given the level of Quraysh harassment, the Medinans sat down with Muhammad three miles outside the city, in the wide valley of Mina. This time there were twelve of them, including three from the Aws tribe, which was a promising sign. If even a few Aws and Khazraj could come together in *islam*, perhaps many more could. But still more promising, each of the twelve represented a major clan of his tribe. This was a deputation.

Their idea was that Muhammad would come to Medina as an arbitrator, invited by both the Aws and the Khazraj to settle their disputes. But as the discussions deepened, he insisted that if Medina was to welcome him and accept his judgment, then it had to accept his followers too. By now some two hundred Meccan men and women had openly recited the *shahada* and declared themselves believers. But many of them were devoid of even such elementary protection as al-Mutim had given Muhammad, while others were under intense pressure from their own families to recant and return to the traditional fold. Many more were sympathizers, but afraid to openly declare themselves. After everything the believers had been through, Muhammad felt as intensely loyal to them as they did to him. There was no way he could leave Mecca and build a new life elsewhere unless they came with him, and no way he could ask them to do that unless he had solid assurance that this new life would be a better one. To be emigrants was bad enough; to become refugees was untenable. If they were to leave Mecca, it could not be as dependents or as "guests" of others. They needed strong protection, with guaranteed acceptance and security. It had to be a real home.

The problem was that there was no existing mechanism for such an arrangement. What Muhammad and the Medinan delegation were negotiating—equal status in Medina, independent of tribal affiliation—was something altogether new. The issue was still not fully resolved by the time the *hajj* was over, but it was clear that if Muhammad were indeed to move to Medina, it would be as more than simply an arbitrator. That was an outsider role, and the last thing he needed was to be the outsider all over again. If his judgment was to be respected, it would have to be because his authority as the messenger of God was widely recognized.

They parted with only a preliminary agreement, resolving to pursue the issue further during the following year's pilgrimage. For the time being, each of the twelve Medinans clasped Muhammad's hand close, forearm against forearm, and pledged himself as a believer to respect Muhammad's judgment. "We gave allegiance to the messenger that we would associate no others with God, nor steal, nor commit fornication, nor kill our offspring, nor disobey Muhammad in what was right," one of them recalled. "If we fulfilled this, paradise would be ours; if we committed any of these sins, it was for God to punish or forgive us as he pleased."

The phrasing marks a pivotal shift. They had sworn allegiance and obedience to Muhammad himself, as well as to God.
For the first time since the initial revelation on Mount Hira eleven
years earlier, Muhammad was acting as more than just a messenger. Now he was also acting as a leader, assuming the political role
that his Meccan opponents had feared all along. In his early fifties, he was growing into the politics of his mission.

The Medinan deputation returned home with an extra companion, Musab, hand-picked by Muhammad to teach and explain
the Quranic verses. Musab did his job well. Drawn by the sense
of unity in the Quranic message, which was all the more appealing in a settlement at odds with itself, several more of the Aws
and Khazraj accepted *islam*.

In a sense, Medina was ready, more so than Mecca. Like the
Meccans, most Medinans were already halfway to monotheism.
They recognized al-Lah as the high god even as many of them
followed the cult of Manat, one of the three "daughters of God,"
but since their economy was not built on traditional faith and pilgrimage as was that of Mecca, it would be easier for them to make
the leap away from the totem gods. And with no single "tradition
of the fathers" as there was in Quraysh-controlled Mecca, the
appeal of the more ancient tradition on which the Quran was
based was greater. All the more since it was already familiar in
Medina, where three of the smaller tribes were Jewish.

Modern Jews may be surprised by the fact that there were
Jewish tribes in seventh-century Arabia. From today's perspective, both political and religious, it seems impossible. But
then modern Christians in the West are often just as surprised at

the fact that Christianity was very much a Middle Eastern faith. The vast reach of the Byzantine Empire meant that with the exception of most of the Arabian peninsula, where distance and terrain deterred imperial influence, the majority of Middle Easterners of the time were Christian. At least nominally. Faith allegiance followed politics. It was always wise to declare the faith of whoever was in power, and the Byzantines under Heraclius had begun to push back against the Persians once more. Still, Judaism had persevered. Despite its lack of political power, it had flourished by dispersing far and wide.

Just as the Quraysh had originally migrated to Mecca after the collapse of Yemen's Marib dam and the consequent implosion of the economy, so the Aws and the Khazraj had come north in the same migration to take over Medina. But where Mecca had been all but abandoned before then, Medina had not. It was already home to descendants of Palestinian Jews who had spread throughout the Middle East in several waves, most notably after the dramatic but ill-fated rebellion against Roman rule led by Bar Kokhba in the second century. Some had settled in the chain of valley oases reaching down from what is now Jordan into northwest Arabia: Tabuk, Tayma, Khaybar, and the southernmost, Medina. Over the years they had integrated into the Arabian tribal system, to the extent that some historians describe them as "fully Arab." Like everyone else, they referred to God in everyday speech as al-Lah. Many had names such as Abdullah, a contraction of *abd al-Lah*, servant of God. They spoke the regional Hijazi Arabic, and while they could be distinguished by small differences in appearance such as the biblically mandated sidelocks still worn by ultra-Orthodox Jews, these differences were no greater than those that marked any other tribe. What made the Jews distinctive was less their concept of God than their claim that God had spoken specifically to them. After all, they had a book to prove it.

At a time when few people could read, a book was an iconic object. Words on parchment achieved an extra dimension of existence by virtue of their visibility. They were literally scripture, a word that comes from the Latin for writing. Each Jewish tribe had its own scroll of the Hebrew bible, which was treated with the utmost reverence, as is still done in synagogues today. Jews, and by extension Christians, were thus known as "the People of the Book"—the book in which God had spoken to them. But now God was speaking to everyone else in Arabia too. And this time he was doing it, as the Quran declared, "in your own tongue . . . in pure Arabic." Even better, the new book encompassed both the Jewish one and its younger Christian sibling. Eventually a full third of the Quran would reprise many of the biblical narratives and then go beyond them, declaring that it had come not only to renew but to perfect the previous revelations.

It made no difference that the ever-growing body of the Quran was not yet inscribed on parchment; with each recitation, it was inscribed in the memories of those who heard it. Writing had not yet replaced memory as it would after the invention of printing. Words lived in the mind, not on the page, and the assonance and alliteration of the Quranic voice, its lilting rhymes and doubling images, made it all the more memorable. "*Iqra!*"—Recite!—the voice had commanded Muhammad. The Quran, "the recitation," was made to be spoken out loud. Each time it was recited and heard and recited again, it achieved greater solidity. And in Medina, thanks to Musab's diligence, more and more people responded to its music and its message, recognizing its potential for unity.

By the time of the next *hajj*, in early June 622, the Medinan deputation to Muhammad had swelled to seventy-two clan leaders. The number alone testified to how serious they were. But both sides needed assurances. If the Medinans were to pledge full alliance and protection, they would have to be willing to back up their pledge with force if necessary. And as the leader of the Meccan believers, Muhammad would have to do the same. The pledge given the previous year had been a half measure. It would be known as "the pledge of women"—not because any women were involved, but because it fell short of the requirement to take up arms in mutual defense, an obligation assumed to fall only on men. The only way this could work was if both sides now committed themselves to the full "pledge of men."

Still unsure of the depth of Muhammad's commitment, the Medinans pressed. "If we do this and God gives you victory, will you then return to your people and leave us?" they asked. To which he solemnly replied: "You are of me, and I am of you. I shall fight whomever you fight and make peace with whomever you make peace." And so it was done. Muhammad was no longer bound to the Quraysh, or to Mecca. He had formally bound himself to Medina, and Medina to him. They had sworn themselves to full protection and help, *nasr* in Arabic. The Medinan believers would thus be known as the *ansar*, the "helpers," while the Meccans who came with Muhammad would become the *muhajirun*, the "emigrants."

One by one, the Medinan clan leaders clasped Muhammad's arm and pledged their bond. "We are of you and you are of us," they swore. "Whoever comes to us of your companions, or you yourself, we shall defend you as we defend ourselves." But in time, this pledge would come to mean far more. As one of the

Medinans would remember many years later: "We pledged ourselves to fight in complete obedience to the messenger, in weal
and in woe, in ease and in hardship, and in evil circumstances."

That summer of 622, the *hijra*—sometimes written in
English as "hegira"—began. The word is usually translated
as "emigration," but its Arabic root *hajar* carries greater psychological weight. It means to cut oneself off from something, with
all the wrenching pain that the term implies. Indeed the Quran
would eventually see the emigrants as having been expelled from
Mecca. The Quraysh disbelievers "have driven out the messenger
and yourselves from your homes," it would say. This would feel
more like exile than emigration.

For people with such a strong sense of place, the prospect has
to have been terrifying. They would almost literally cut the umbil-
ical cord. They would sever themselves from tribe, clan, and even
immediate family; from the Kaaba, the lode-star by which they
oriented themselves in the world; from everything that had made
them who they were. For every one of them, this took courage as
well as faith. Or perhaps the kind of courage that comes only
with faith.

At the word from Muhammad, they began to leave for
Medina ahead of him, in small groups so as to attract the least
attention. But in a city as crowded as Mecca, it was impossible to
leave unobserved. Fathers and mothers, brothers and sisters,
uncles and aunts and cousins quickly realized what their relatives
were planning, and moved to forestall them, sometimes by force.

"When we made up our minds to leave for Medina," one

emigrant would remember, "three of us arranged to meet in the morning at the thorn trees of Adat," about six miles outside Mecca. "We agreed that if one of us failed to appear, that would mean that he had been kept back by force, and the other two should go on without him." Only two of them reached Adat. The third was intercepted halfway there by one of his uncles, accompanied by abu-Jahl, who told him that his mother had vowed she would neither comb her hair nor take shelter from the sun until she had seen him again. On the way back, they pushed him to the ground, tied him up, and forced him to recant *islam*. This was how it should be done, the uncle declared: "Oh men of Mecca, deal with your fools as we have dealt with this fool of ours."

Women were not dealt with much more kindly. Umm Salama, who was later to become Muhammad's fourth wife after she was widowed, told how her kinsmen were enraged when they saw her setting out by camel with her then husband and their infant son. "You can do as you like," they told her husband, "but don't think we will let you take our kinswoman away."

"They snatched the camel's rope from my husband's hand and took me from him," she remembered. Then to make matters worse, her in-laws turned up, and a tussle developed over who would take custody of the child she was cradling in her arms— her family or her husband's family. "We cannot leave the boy with you now that you have torn his mother from our kinsman," her in-laws declared, and to her horror, both sides "dragged at my little boy between them until they dislocated his shoulder."

In the end, her husband's family took the child, Umm Salama's family took her, and her husband left alone for Medina. "Thus was I separated from both my husband and my son," she would say. There was nothing she could do but "sit in the valley every day and weep" until both families finally relented. "Then I saddled my camel and took my son in my arms, and set forth for my husband in Medina. Not a soul was with me."

This was what emigration meant: a young man beaten into submission by his own relatives, the lonely resolve of a young woman and her injured infant riding unaccompanied through the desert, the desperate attempts of family to hang on to them, and the echoing absence they would leave behind them, as though they had died. With each departure, the effect was magnified, all the more in the case of prominent believers like Omar and Uthman, who had been born into the Meccan elite and thus had higher public profiles. Throughout that summer of 622, one home after another was abandoned. People would pass by a house with "its doors blowing to and fro, empty of inhabitants," and realize that yet another family had left in the night. By early September, hundreds of men, women, and children had made the *hijra*.

Some leading Meccans like abu-Jahl tried to make light of it. "Nobody will weep over their leaving," he scoffed. But people did weep. It felt as though their close kin had been taken from them, and even as a pall of bereavement hung over the city, anger focused on Muhammad, the cause of all this pain. It might have been wiser for him to leave along with the first emigrants, but he was determined to stay in Mecca until he was sure that as many of his followers as possible had made it out safely. Concerned about the danger, two of his closest companions, his cousin Ali and the respected abu-Bakr, stayed with him. But then time ran out. As though to bring matters to a head, the elderly al-Mutim, Muhammad's interim protector, died. Until he reached Medina, Muhammad would have no protection at all.

· · ·

The Quraysh saw that the messenger had pledged allegiance not of their tribe and outside their territory, and that his followers had settled in a new home and gained protectors and were safe from attack," ibn-Ishaq would write. "Now they feared that Muhammad would join his followers in Medina in order to make war on Mecca. So they assembled their council, where all their important business was conducted, to deliberate on what they should do about the messenger, since they were now in fear of him." If Muhammad had inflicted so deep a wound in the fabric of Meccan society, who knew what he might do next?

Yet the fear of war seems exaggerated, and here again ibn-Ishaq may be writing the future back into history. The Meccans had never taken the Medinans seriously before; the Khazraj and the Aws were so divided that they posed no threat to anyone but themselves. The fact that Muhammad had pledged himself to take up arms in defense of Medina if necessary certainly did not mean that anyone considered war between Mecca and Medina likely. Though the total population of Medina was about the same as that of Mecca, some twenty-five thousand, the Medinans were farmers, not fighters. Besides, Muhammad himself had consistently met violence with non-violence, turning the other cheek whenever he could. If it was war the Meccans feared, it was a war of ideas, not of weapons.

Muhammad had subverted the whole concept of tribal loyalty and identity by appealing to a higher authority. But where his challenge had formerly been on the level of principle, he had now acted on it, and worse, induced others to act with him. It made no difference that the Quraysh had basically forced him into this. In their terms, his defense pact with Medina was an act of disloyalty to his own people, and they openly made the charge of treason.

One clan leader wanted Muhammad arrested and jailed. "Lock him up, keep him in fetters, and wait for death to overtake him," he urged. But others worried that this would only backfire. Muhammad still had sympathizers in Mecca, they pointed out, and if they were to attack the jail and release him, the authority of the council would be jeopardized.

Another advocated driving Muhammad not only out of Mecca but out of the whole of the Hijaz region. "Let us expel him from among us and banish him from our land. We don't care where he goes or where he settles; the harm he's been doing will disappear and we will restore our social harmony." But this was shot down as well: Muhammad was capable of winning over the nomadic tribes with his haunting verses, and Mecca could then come under Beduin attack. "He could lead them against us, crush us with them, seize power from our hands, and do with us as he wants."

It fell to abu-Jahl to come up with a plan of action they could all agree on, one that would achieve their aim while still preserving the public peace. "Take a young, strong, well-born man from each clan," he said, with the sole exception of the Hashims, "and have them strike him with their swords as one man, and kill him. If they do this as one, then the responsibility for his bloodshed will be divided among all the clans, and the Hashims will not be able to act in retaliation against the whole of the Quraysh."

With aptly Orientalist irony, this might be called the *Murder on the Orient Express* plot, the key to Agatha Christie's famous novel in which all turn out to have committed the murder and thus, legally, none. If they all participated in Muhammad's death, then no single one of them could be held responsible, and the principle of blood vengeance would be rendered moot. Not that the Hashims' new leader abu-Lahab, the "father of flame," would be likely to invoke it anyway. In fact he'd understand that the other clans were doing him a favor. He had already expelled Muhammad from the clan, and would be only too glad to accept monetary compensation for his death. All the other clans could then contribute to the blood-money purse. They would be rid of Muhammad, and there would be no consequences.

But the plot had a built-in flaw, and a major one: it depended on secrecy, and with so many people involved, somebody was bound to talk. Muhammad was warned that night—if not by a human, then as tradition has it by the angel Gabriel—and he sent word to the trusted abu-Bakr to meet up with him while his young cousin Ali volunteered to stay behind as a decoy. While the would-be assassins grouped together outside Muhammad's home, waiting for him to emerge as usual at dawn, their target slipped quietly out the back under cover of dark and made for his rendezvous with abu-Bakr.

At first light, Ali came out wrapped in Muhammad's cloak, only to pull back the hood as the attackers pounced. "Where is your companion?" they shouted.

"Do you expect me to keep watch over him?" Ali retorted. "You wanted him to leave, and he has left." However tempted they were to kill Ali instead, if only out of sheer frustration, they held off, knowing that this would definitely incur blood vengeance. Ali was roughed up but survived the face-off to stay on in Mecca a few more days, tying up Muhammad's business affairs before setting out to make his way to Medina alone, on foot.

The Quraysh council quickly organized a posse to go in pursuit of Muhammad, offering a bounty of a hundred she-camels for whoever caught him, dead or alive. But Muhammad and abu-Bakr had foreseen this. Knowing that the posse would look first on the route north out of Mecca, toward Medina, they headed some five miles in the opposite direction and hid out in a cave high on the side of Mount Thaur, overlooking the southbound caravan route to Yemen.

W hat happened in that cave would become a treasured part of Muslim lore. Caves have carried strong symbolic resonance for as long as there has been sacred legend. It might be tempting to say that it began with Plato's "allegory of the cave" in *The Republic*, which explores the interplay between shadows and reality (or in contemporary terms, perhaps, between virtual and actual reality). But legends involving caves are so widespread that they seem to be universal. If you are Freudianly inclined, you could see the cave as a symbolic womb. In more metaphysical terms, it becomes a safe place in which one sleeps, dreams, and grows before emerging back into the world. Either way, it's a place not merely of shelter, but of incubation.

For abu-Bakr, the cave on Mount Thaur would be a place of renewed faith as he worried that they would be discovered and Muhammad reassured him that God would protect them. For Muhammad, it would be a place of spiritual strengthening and further revelation. "They two were in the cave," the Quran would say, "and the messenger said to his companion, 'Sorrow not, for God is with us.' Then God sent down his spirit upon the messenger, and strengthened him with forces you cannot see." And with natural forces too.

Ibn-Ishaq relates how on the third day, when the bounty

hunters had widened their search and reached Mount Thaur, thousands of spiders appeared from nowhere and spun a thick maze of webs across the cave entrance. Seeing the dense network of filaments, the searchers concluded that nobody had entered that particular cave in years, and passed on by, leaving us with the image of Muhammad and abu-Bakr hidden by gossamer threads, nature itself conspiring to protect them.

Once the immediate danger was past, abu-Bakr sent word to a trusted freedman to bring camels and a guide, and the three men set off for Medina in an arcing roundabout route to evade capture: first, farther south, then west toward the Red Sea coast, then northward until finally heading up into the mountains. Even with fast riding camels, the journey took ten days, and it wasn't until September 24 that they reached the outskirts of Medina.

"The heat of the forenoon had grown intense and the sun had almost reached its midpoint in the sky," ibn-Ishaq writes. The emigrants who had been keeping watch, waiting for Muhammad, had given up for the day and gone back to the oasis to find shade, so the first Medinan to see Muhammad arrive was not one of his followers but a member of one of the Jewish tribes, who ran excitedly to spread the word. "Aws and Khazraj, your good fortune has arrived!" he shouted. They were words he might soon come to regret.

Thirteen

News of Muhammad's arrival spread fast. People ran out to greet him as he rode in, begging him to stop and accept their hospitality, but he turned everyone down. He would stop where his she-camel stopped, he said, and gave her free rein. She went on into the center of the oasis, where she wandered into a stony yard that had once been a burial ground and was now used only for drying dates. There she knelt, first her front legs buckling in that seemingly impossible way, then her hind legs, until finally she settled to the ground with a kind of sighing grunt as though to say, "This far and no further."

Like the spiders that had spun dense webs across the entrance to the cave on Mount Thaur, this camel would be seen as a sainted creature, divinely led. When she knelt and Muhammad dismounted, the *hijra* was complete. Mecca had been the birthplace of Islam, but its cradle, the place where it would grow and thrive, would be Medina, and it was from Muhammad's arrival in Medina that the Muslim era—After the Hijra, or AH—would eventually be dated. It would be seven years before he set foot in Mecca again.

The date-drying yard belonged to two young orphans from the same Khazraj clan to which Muhammad's great-grandmother had belonged, and the two boys were under the guardianship of an uncle. The similarities between their backgrounds and Muhammad's made the choice of locale seem inspired. Moreover since theirs was a small clan, a purchase of land from them was unlikely to make other, more powerful clans feel that they had been snubbed. In the event, the boys' guardian insisted that the land be a gift, promising that he'd pay his wards the purchase price himself (a promise Muhammad ensured was fulfilled), and so it was done. This unlikely patch would become the new center of the believers' world.

What they built here in the next few months was strikingly simple: an open compound inside a mud-brick wall, with a palm-thatched covered area in the center for shade and lean-tos built against the south and east walls as sleeping quarters. There was none of the ornate sacred space of the mosques that would be built after Islam had claimed an empire. As the earliest synagogues and churches had been, this was a gathering place as much as a prayer space (in fact the word "synagogue" is from the Greek for "coming together"). The secular and the sacred would take place side by side, blending easily into each other as they did in most of the world at the time. The single feature a modern Muslim would recognize was a niche in one wall to indicate the *qibla*, the direction to be faced in prayer. But this was not toward Mecca, not yet. It was toward the city of the Night Journey, Jerusalem—the same direction in which both Jews and Christians turned to pray.

That first year in Medina, the emigrants worked harder than most of them ever had before. They were city people, their muscles new to the demands of physical labor. They knew little about construction or agriculture, and had to learn the hard way. And while they tried to make light of it—one story has Ali covered in brick dust and Muhammad laughingly dubbing him abu-Turab, "father of dust"—many of them struggled with sickness, their resistance worn down by sheer physical exhaustion. It is one thing to bravely break old ties and commit oneself to a new way of being, but quite another to actually live that new life on a day-to-day basis, dealing with it in literally down-to-earth terms.

What buoyed them was a heady sense of idealism. They were not merely building the new compound, or even a new home. What they were building was a whole new society with a radically different concept of how people would relate to each other. However ironic it may sound in the context of modern politics, the closest parallel to these city people flexing muscles never used before is possibly the experience of the early Zionist pioneers in Palestine, who were also largely urban emigrants, in their case from Europe. That sense of close community, of physical hardship and shared purpose informed by communal and egalitarian ideals, produced an exciting esprit de corps, heightened further by a sense of historical self-awareness. Imbued with a vision of man and God in unison, these early Muslims threw themselves into what Kabbalists would later call *tikkun olam*, repairing the world. From the broken shards of life, they aimed to create a renewed whole.

The new community would become their new family. Muhammad insisted that each Meccan emigrant be "adopted" by a Medinan believer and regarded not as a guest but as a brother or sister, regardless of age or kinship or place of birth. What was being formed here was not another tribe but the kernel of a kind of supra-tribe. They did not yet call it Islam with a capital I, or themselves Muslims with a capital M. That usage would come later, after Muhammad's death, as Islam spread out into the whole of the Middle East and became institutionalized. They still called themselves simply *mu'uminin*, believers, and this is what held them together so powerfully: the fervent shining faith in being the advance guard of a new society.

Yet no exile ever really breaks the ties of home. Even someone who leaves by choice tends to focus on the place left behind. Emigrants turn first each day to the news from their country of origin. They search out places to buy familiar foods, and befriend fellow emigrants they would never have talked to "back home." This is more than simple nostalgia. It's as though by such actions they might lessen the degree of physical separation, even assuage a certain guilt at having left. If they are lucky, this will ease as they adapt. But when emigration is not chosen but forced, the place left behind assumes ever greater proportions in the mind.

"Exile is the unhealable rift forced between a human being and a native place, between the self and its true home," wrote Edward Said, referring to the modern Palestinian exile. The feeling of having suffered a great wrong does not fade with time, but increases and then crystallizes. Even as the exile establishes a new life, the place left behind remains the homeland, the focus of all hope for a perfect future. Only an exile could conceive of ancient Palestine as the land of milk and honey as did the writers of the Hebrew bible, turning rocky land fit mainly for thorns into a kind of paradise that should have existed even if it never had. In exile, they affirmed their belonging all the stronger. The lemon tree in the courtyard, the olive trees in the grove, the life that once was and no longer is—all these become idealized in memory, which is why the Jerusalem temple lovingly reconstructed in the minds of the second- and third-century rabbis who wrote the Mishna was far closer to perfection than the one that had been burned to rubble by the Romans.

In those early years in Medina, the sense of exile was kept alive in the distinction between the *muhajirun*, the "emigrants" who had left Mecca, and the Medinan "helpers" who had welcomed them—*ansar* in Arabic, the same word used in the Quran for the twelve apostles of Jesus. The nomenclature kept faith, as it were, with the idea of Mecca, and with the consciousness of exile.

"Exiles always feel their difference as a kind of orphanhood," wrote Said, and the metaphor is especially poignant when applied to Muhammad. While all the emigrants had in essence orphaned themselves, breaking ties with mothers and fathers, clan and tribe, the effect was magnified for a man born without a father. He had had to struggle for a sense of home in Mecca and, having gained it, had seen it wrenched away from him. Yet this loss may have been essential. To think creatively outside the habitual order of things, it helps to be placed outside it. Painful as it was, being hounded out of Mecca may have been the best thing that could have happened.

In Meccan terms, Muhammad was now the ultimate outsider. But if that city's elite thought that he had gone quietly into the dark night of exile, they would be proved very wrong. What seemed to be his weakness would prove to be his strength, and what appeared to be defeat would eventually turn into victory.

He was fifty-three now, his beard and braided hair flecked with gray. But if he felt his age, he gave no sign of it. He hardly seemed to need sleep, spending his days working side by side with the other emigrants, and his nights in meditation. The Quranic revelations kept pace, but many were more specific than before. They had to be. The cohesiveness and spirit of the community of believers attracted an increasing number of helpers, who would soon outnumber the emigrants. Their requests for guidance rose commensurately, and the revelations began to direct Muhammad on everything from times of prayer to tithing to resolution of marital disputes. As former New York governor Mario Cuomo once put it: "You campaign in poetry, and govern in prose."

Instead of simply receiving the Quranic voice, Muhammad learned to work with it, meditating on an issue or a dilemma and waiting for the voice to guide him. Most trenchantly, the revelations now addressed the relationships between believers and others, and many of their principles would be included in what was to be essentially Muhammad's first major piece of legislation. The clan leaders had invited him to Medina to make peace between them, and the document he drew up within a year of his arrival would do exactly that. But instead of simply resolving their disputes, he aimed higher. In his hands, monotheism would become the means of conflict resolution.

The term "monotheism" to describe the belief in one god didn't exist until the seventeenth century, when it was coined by the English philosopher Henry More, but a far more comprehensive and flexible monotheistic idea had existed for well over two thousand years. As historian James Carroll points out, the Jewish scribes who actually wrote most of the Hebrew bible during the sixth-century BC Babylonian exile conceived of "one god" less as a specific identity than as an affirmation of unity. The personified Yahweh, the territorial god of Israel, gave way to the ineffable Elohim, the universal god—the same god known in Mecca as al-Lah.

In this older and wider concept of monotheism, says Carroll, "the God of this people is the God of all people, associated not with a clan or a tribe or a network of tribes, but with all that exists." God thus becomes "the reconciliation of all oppositions."

Muhammad now translated this concept into political terms. Blending idealism and pragmatism—a master politician's skill if ever there was one—he drew up an arbitration agreement that used the tribal principle to reach beyond tribe. Some historians would rather grandiosely call this agreement "the constitution of Medina," but by whatever name it was still a remarkable document for its time. On the one hand, it resolved the internecine disputes of Medina by taking the form of a mutual defense pact. On the other, it codified a new, inclusive identity as the principle that would bind all the clans and tribes together. The whole of the oasis would be united in the idea that would eventually underlie all of Islam: the *umma*, a term that can be understood as community or people or nation, and would come to mean all these and more.

"This is a document from Muhammad the messenger governing the relations between the believers, both the emigrants and the helpers, and those who are in federation with them," it began. "They are a single community"—*umma*—"distinct from all others."

"Those who are in federation with them" specifically included not only all the clans of the Aws and the Khazraj, whether or not they had formally accepted *islam* at that point, but also the Jewish tribes, named clan by clan. As monotheists, "the Jews are one community with the believers," the document declared, again using the word *umma*. "Each must help the other against anyone who attacks the people of this document. They must seek mutual advice and consultation."

Bloodshed between parties to the arbitration document was henceforth forbidden. "If any dispute or controversy should arise from which disaster is to be feared, it must be referred to God and to Muhammad the messenger of God." This meant that "if the contracting parties are called to make peace and maintain it, they must do so"—called, that is, by Muhammad, who would be the guarantor of the agreement. And in a further clause that was to have far-reaching effects: "The contracting parties are bound to help one another against any attack on Medina." Not that any attack on Medina seemed likely. The danger was not from without, but from Medinan tribes fighting each other, so this clause was understood as a formulaic detail, part of the standard language of inter-tribal alliances.

If some clan leaders had misgivings, they suppressed them for the time being, according equal status to what they saw as the de facto tribe of believers for the sake of the larger goal of establishing peace among all factions in Medina. As they signed on to the concept of the *umma* by fixing their seals to the document, it's unlikely that they realized its potential power to supersede all existing political units. But if they were not aware of it, Muhammad certainly was. In effect, he had persuaded a place in search of an identity to connect with an identity in search of a place.

It's not hard to imagine a collective sigh of relief among the Meccan elite once Muhammad had escaped. Not only had they rid themselves of the threat he posed, but they had done it without any actual bloodshed. If that wasn't quite the way they had planned it, they wasted no time persuading themselves that this was just as good, if not better. They had seen the last of him, they thought, and how perfect that he had fled to a mere date orchard like Medina. He could preach all he liked there and it would make no difference. He had been effectively sidelined. It was, they told themselves, the perfect outcome. Those kinsmen of theirs who had joined him out there in the boondocks would soon come to their senses and return to Mecca. What else were they going to do? Pick dates?

The answer came quickly. The years of harassment and insults, the boycott, the suffering of his followers, that final assassination attempt—all had stretched the limits of non-violence to the breaking point. Muhammad had sought to persuade and even accommodate the Quraysh leadership, but to what now seemed less than no avail. In the insult of exile, turning the other cheek began to seem at best ineffective, at worst self-defeating. So if the Meccan elite anticipated a peaceful life without him, they would not do so for long. Where they had once harassed him, he would now harass them.

The form of harassment he chose was the *razzia*—the raid—which was almost a tradition among Beduin herdsmen, especially during drought years when their flocks were decimated by lack of grazing. Small raiding parties would swoop down on horseback or on fast riding camels to attack trade caravans, often in narrow defiles where the rear of the caravan was especially vulnerable. It was part of the Beduin way of life: you lived off what the desert offered, and when it did not offer grazing, it still offered the tempting targets of those heavily loaded pack camels. For the most part, the mere threat of raiding was enough. Negotiated payments to Beduin chieftains generally assured protection as the camel train passed through their traditional territory, but when territory was disputed or when rogue bands formed to become the highwaymen of the time, the caravans became targets none-theless. Even then, however, a kind of unofficial Geneva Convention held sway. Goods and livestock were fair game, as it were, but human life was not. Kill someone in a raid and the law of blood vengeance swung into action, acting as such an effective deterrent that a *razzia* rarely resulted in loss of life.

There was no reason for the helpers and other Medinans to take part in these early raids ordered by Muhammad, but the emigrants had every reason. Since all the good arable land in Medina was already taken, they could work only as hired hands, if at all. They had relied so far on the kindness of the helpers, but they needed to prove themselves, especially in a culture so strongly based on the idea of virility and honor. Eager to transform the stigma of exile into a banner of proud defiance, they saw raiding as a way to get back at the Meccans where it would hurt them most: in their traders' pockets. Instead of being acted upon, the exiles would be the ones to act.

The early Islamic histories would call these raids military expeditions, but all through the year 623 they were hardly on that level. In fact they were strikingly unsuccessful. In March, for instance, seven months after the *hijra*, thirty emigrants under the command of Muhammad's uncle Hamza tried to intercept a Meccan caravan led by abu-Jahl but "separated without a battle" after the local Beduin chieftain intervened. A month later, the emigrants tried again with double the force, this time attacking a caravan led by abu-Sufyan, but there was "no hand-to-hand fighting" and again the would-be raiders returned with nothing. Several further expeditions "in search of Quraysh" were headed by Muhammad himself, but all with the same non-result. The emigrants seemed to be so ineffective a fighting force that even when

Beduin raided their milk camels just outside Medina and they set off in pursuit, they lost track of them.

But Muhammad can't have expected success in terms of goods and booty. His years of experience on the trade caravans meant that he knew better than most about the arrangements made for protection, and he certainly never expected local Beduin chieftains to give his raiders free rein. He was not aiming for material success so much as to disrupt the smooth working of the caravans. He was making a point, establishing his presence beyond Medina as a force to be reckoned with, and doing so at very little cost. Until, almost by mistake, someone was killed.

It happened in January 624. Muhammad had sent a band of eight emigrants two hundred miles south, deep inside Meccan territory. It's unclear what he intended. His orders were to scout, not to attack, so he may have been aiming for information on the upcoming spring caravan to Damascus. But whatever their mission was, the men he sent had been miserably unsuccessful. Two had carelessly forgotten to hobble their riding camels one night, so had been forced to stay behind and search for them after they'd wandered off into the desert. The remaining six got as far as Nakhla, between Mecca and Taif, where they came across four Meccans traveling with a few camels loaded with raisins and leather. After weeks of frustration and mistakes, the six emigrants couldn't resist such an easy target, however insignificant. No matter that it was the final day of the last of Mecca's three holy months, when fighting was forbidden: they attacked. One of the Meccans escaped, a second was killed, and the remaining two were taken captive.

Expecting a hero's welcome, the emigrants returned to Medina triumphant, captives and laden camels in tow. But any celebration was quickly scotched by Muhammad himself. Mecca was the main market for Medinan produce, and the last thing most Medinans wanted was to disrupt their livelihoods by so openly antagonizing their prime customers. They had doubted the wisdom of even attempting to raid Meccan caravans, and now they feared that what had happened at Nakhla would only invite retaliation. How could it not? It had taken place on the doorstep of Mecca, as it were, which meant that the Meccans had suffered severe loss of face. To kill a Meccan for the sake of a few loads of leather and raisins? This was pure provocation. Had they really invited Muhammad to Medina to make peace between them, only to have him then declare war on someone else?

The whole arbitration agreement he had worked so hard to achieve was suddenly in jeopardy. The mutual self-defense clause was exactly that: for defense, not offense. Yet the fatal Nakhla raid had been undeniably offensive, and doubly so for having taken place during a sacred month. "Fight in the way of God those who fight you, but do not begin hostilities, for God does not like the aggressor," the Quran would say—the crux, of course, being to define the aggressor. The Medinans had agreed on self-defense, but if that was necessary because of prior aggression, they were not agreed at all. In the seventh century as today, there was the ineluctable problem of the difference between self-defense and offense. And then as now, that difference was generally defined by who was doing the defining.

The only way Muhammad could deflect the growing criticism inside Medina was to take the initiative by calling on a recognized higher authority. Revelation was needed, and it came.

"They question you with regard to warfare in the sacred month," the Quranic voice told him. "Say: 'Fighting in that month is a great offense, but still greater offenses in God's eyes are to bar others from God's path, to disbelieve in him, to prevent access to the Kaaba, and to expel its people. Persecution is worse than killing.'"

And to clarify things further: "Permission is granted to those who fight because they have been wronged . . . those who have been driven out of their houses without right only because they said our god is God." In other words, offense was now sanctioned in the name of ex post facto defense. What the Nakhla raiders had done may not have been desirable but it was justified, since as exiles they had been the prior victims here. For the believers, at least, the issue was settled. For everyone else, it had only just begun.

The word used in this initial Quranic sanction of fighting was *qital*, which unequivocally means "physical combat." But then the following verse of the Quran as it was eventually written down and arranged, which was not definitively done until two decades after Muhammad's death, seems to expand on the idea: "Those who have believed, migrated, and striven in the way of God can look forward to God's mercy."

Proximity promotes an association of ideas in which "striving in the way of God" is another way of saying "fighting." But there is no way of knowing whether this sequence of verses reflects the original order or timing of revelation, let alone what exactly is meant by "striving in the way of God." The word usually translated as "striving" is not *qital* but *jihad*, which would only later gain the additional meaning of "holy war."

To some degree, this is a problem of translation. Or rather, of interpretation. With a text as allusive and often mysterious as the Quran, a direct one-to-one correspondence between Arabic and English does not necessarily exist. Like all Semitic languages, Arabic plays on words, taking a three-consonant root and building on it to create what sometimes seems an infinite number of meanings. Even the exact same word can have different connotations depending on the context. And the Quran, God-like, provides no context. It assumes that those who hear it share its frame of reference. But what could be assumed in the seventh century cannot be assumed in the twenty-first; both the language and the frame of reference have changed. Nobody today speaks the seventh-century Hijaz dialect in which the Quran is written, so that Islamic scholars still engage in lifelong arguments about the meaning of specific words, let alone verses.

While the Quran consistently uses terms such as *qital* for combat, its use of *jihad*—struggling or striving—is far less specific. In time, the word would achieve a double meaning: both the inner striving to live a moral life and attain a higher level of spiritual consciousness, and the external armed struggle against those seen as the enemies of Islam. This dual meaning would be enshrined in a famed hadith—literally a report, as in a news report, one of the vast body of such reports compiled after Muhammad's death from claimed memories of what he had said or done—in which he distinguished between the lesser jihad and the greater jihad. The lesser one, he said, was taking up arms in defense of Islam; the greater one was the striving within oneself to come closer to God. The terms themselves indicated which was superior.

For now, it was clear that if Muhammad had once hoped to achieve his mission without violence, this was no longer possible.

The central question, and one to which the Quranic voice would return several times over the next few years, was no longer whether to fight, but under what conditions. And how Muhammad dealt with this question is still the subject of heated debate. The use of violence was destined to become the "hot button" of Islam as the politics of seventh-century Arabia were used, interpreted, and distorted through the centuries by both militant "Islamists" and equally militant anti-Islamists, very few of whom would even be aware of the raid at Nakhla that had begun the debate.

Nakhla forced a turning point. However defense and offense were defined, one thing was clear. Up to now, the revelations had insisted that Muhammad ignore his enemies. He was to turn aside from them and forgive them their ignorance, and the man who patiently put up with years of harassment and concerted opposition in Mecca achieves great moral stature because of this principled refusal to return violence with violence. But that Gandhi-like stand had cost him his home, and almost his life. Now that he was in a position of leadership, the politics of power would dictate a major change.

The term "power politics" might well be considered a tautology, since politics is essentially about power, or as the dictionary would have it, "the science and art of government." Nonetheless, the term now carries a strong negative connotation, one that was challenged by political philosopher Isaiah Berlin in his appreciation of the man practically identified with the idea: Niccolò Machiavelli. Berlin saw him not as the ruthless stereotype imagined by those who have never read his classic *The Prince*, but as the skilled political pragmatist he was. "If you object to the political methods recommended because they seem to you morally detestable, if you refuse to embark on them because they are too frightening," Berlin wrote, "then Machiavelli's answer is that you are perfectly entitled to lead a morally good life, be a private citizen (or a monk), seek some corner of your own. But in that event, you must not make yourself responsible for the lives of others or expect good fortune; in a material sense you must expect to be ignored or destroyed." Or as Machiavelli himself famously put it: "All armed prophets have conquered, and unarmed prophets have come to grief."

Muhammad had been ignored in the past, and almost been destroyed. He had no intention of being either ever again. Where the Quranic voice had formerly been insistent on eschewing violence, it now at least conditionally endorsed it. A new chapter had begun, and just two months later it would erupt into open warfare.

Fourteen

The Battle of Badr was fought on March 17, 624, and if it was not quite what Muhammad had sought, it would turn out to be exactly what he needed. It would be recorded in the early Islamic histories as the first great victory of Islam: a decisive armed encounter that would redound to the honor and reputation of Medina, especially among the surrounding Beduin tribes, who would begin to support Muhammad once he had shown that he could challenge the Meccan monopoly on power and wealth. Yet it appears that it happened as much by miscalculation as by intent.

Badr, between Medina and the Red Sea, was where a large wadi opened out into the coastal flatland. Several wells had been dug into its sides, and cisterns had been hollowed out to hold the residue of winter flash floods. The place was thus a major watering spot, and never more so than when Mecca's big spring caravan stopped there on its way back from Damascus.

To even conceive of a raid on this caravan was a daring proposition. Until now, Muhammad had sent out raiding parties of no more than twenty or thirty men, and the only successful one, at Nakhla, had been highly controversial. Most Medinans, particularly those with family and business ties to the merchant city to the south, had no desire to aggravate the situation further. Nakhla had been bad enough. To follow that up with a challenge of this magnitude risked provoking Mecca into open war. Yet this was a risk Muhammad seemed willing and even eager to take. Minor raids like that at Nakhla had made him merely a thorn in Mecca's side; a major one at Badr would establish him not as a disgruntled exile but as an enemy to be reckoned with. Plus it would bolster his support inside Medina itself, since while their elders advocated caution, younger Medinans were energized by the prospect of challenging the big city, especially when the potential gains were so large.

This would not be a matter of a few loads of leather and raisins. Under the command of the head of Mecca's Umayyad clan, abu-Sufyan, there would be more than two thousand camels returning from Damascus, loaded with luxury goods. And they'd be an easy target: Muhammad's scouts had reported the presence of only seventy armed guards.

Given the size and value of the caravan, seventy guards was a surprisingly low number. The Quraysh leadership seemed to have either failed to register Muhammad's new determination, or were still misled by their disdain for "the provinces." The Nakhla raid had been small fry, after all; an attack on the big annual caravan would be something else altogether, and from their position of power and entitlement, it must have seemed inconceivable. How would anyone dare? But if they underestimated Muhammad, he also seems to have underestimated them.

By the time he led his followers out of Medina for the two-day ride to Badr, they were no longer a mere raiding party but a solid force of over three hundred men. No bloodshed was anticipated, since the caravan's guards would surely act rationally in the face of such numbers and flee. This was intended as a demonstration of presence, not as an armed showdown, much less a battle. On that premise, native Medinans rode out along with emigrants for the first time, and in a sign of Muhammad's growing authority, the helpers outnumbered the emigrants. Expectations ran high, as did talk about them.

Inevitably, with this many people involved, the desert grapevine hummed with information. Word of the impending raid reached the caravan well in advance, and abu-Sufyan sent a fast rider ahead to Mecca with directions for a defensive force to be dispatched immediately. "Come protect your merchandise" was the message.

The Meccans were incensed, all the more since every clan of the Quraysh had shares in the caravan. "Do Muhammad and his companions imagine that it will be like the raid at Nakhla?" roared his old nemesis abu-Jahl. "No, by God, they will find otherwise this time!" Muhammad had three hundred men? They would show him what real numbers were. Overnight, they raised an army nearly one thousand strong and made a forced march north to Badr under abu-Jahl's command, secure in the assumption that Muhammad would never dream of fighting against such overwhelming odds. They'd quash this bumptious crew of outcasts simply by showing up.

Meanwhile, unsure if the army would make it in time, abu-Sufyan decided to bypass Badr by doubling back and leading the caravan safely to the west along the Red Sea. That left two armed forces, one coming north from Mecca, the other west from Medina, converging on a caravan that was no longer there. It was

THE FIRST MUSLIM · 205

a clear recipe for trouble, and abu-Sufyan tried to forestall it by sending a rider to intercept abu-Jahl and his men. "You came out to protect your caravan and your property, oh Quraysh," his message said. "God has kept them safe, so turn back."

But asking abu-Jahl to turn back from a confrontation with Muhammad was like asking a dust storm to stop in its tracks. At the very least, he was spoiling for a fight, even though by doing so he'd be raising Muhammad's profile. As Machiavelli would put it, "There is no doubt that a ruler's greatness depends on his triumphing over difficulties and opposition. So fortune finds enemies for him and encourages them to take the field against him, so that he may have cause to triumph over them and ascend higher on the ladder his foes have provided." In this, the Quraysh, led by abu-Jahl, were now spectacularly cooperative.

In fact for all his aggressive rhetoric, abu-Jahl may have calculated what was at stake more accurately than the calmer abu-Sufyan. This was a matter of Meccan prestige. To have even allowed Muhammad to divert the caravan had been to concede him a kind of semi-victory. Word would spread. The desert grapevine allowed few secrets, especially at a place like Badr where everyone stopped for water, making it a mother lode of gossip and news. For abu-Jahl to turn back now would be a further concession, and he was damned if he'd be the one to make it. Not only would his forces advance on to Badr, he declared, but "we will spend three days there, slaughter camels, and give food to eat and wine to drink to all, so that the Beduin may hear of what we have done and continue to hold us in awe."

Not everyone in the Meccan army agreed. What if it turned out to be more than a show of force, and they actually had to fight? "There is no need to take to the battlefield except in defense of property, and the caravan is safe," argued one clan leader, only to provoke an accusation of cowardice from abu-Jahl: "Your lungs are inflated with fear," he sneered.

Another pointed out that Muhammad's men included emigrants who were kinsmen of theirs: "By God, if you defeat Muhammad in battle, you will not be able to look one another in the face without loathing, for you will see someone who has killed your nephew or your kinsman. Let us turn back." But again abu-Jahl responded with scorn: "You say this only because your own son is among Muhammad's followers. Don't try to protect him." And then he trumped the kinship argument by calling on the brother of the man killed in the Nakhla raid to come forward. "You see your revenge before your eyes," he told him. "Rise and remind them of your brother's murder." By the time the bereaved brother had finished, most of the Meccans were thoroughly riled up for blood vengeance. Though some did turn back, over seven hundred rode on.

They might have had their revenge if the argument over whether to advance had not delayed them. The grapevine had worked both ways, so Muhammad had been informed not only that abu-Sufyan had diverted the caravan but also that a strong Meccan force was on the way. At this point, like the Meccans, he faced a choice: he too could simply retreat and go home. But to do so would be to betray weakness on his part, in the eyes of his own men as well as the eyes of others. This was no longer about the caravan. Nor was it simply an abstract matter of honor. This was about Muhammad and the believers establishing their reputation, and the Meccans defending theirs. Both sides needed to dispel any notion of weakness—the one in order to gain power, the other for fear of losing it.

By the time the Meccan army reached Badr, Muhammad and his men were already there, dug in on the higher ground. That night there was a steady rain, a rarity especially in mid-March. The Meccans hunkered down in field shelters, but Muhammad used the rain as cover. He quietly worked his men to block up the wells and cisterns closest to the Meccans, so that at dawn they'd be forced higher up the wadi, where the believers held the high ground. By controlling access to the water, he would control the whole field.

The fighting began under cloudy skies early the next morning. The believers' ranks held steady, but the Meccan ones—with each clan fighting as a separate unit and no unified command—fractured and broke. By noon, they had been routed. Forty-four Meccans lay dead, including "the father of ignorance," abu-Jahl himself. The kill was claimed by a young emigrant, a former herdsman whom abu-Jahl had once hit in the face. "I struck him a blow which severed his foot and half his leg," the herdsman would say. "By God, when it flew off it was like the pit of a date flying out of a date-wine crusher." And he had the satisfaction of hearing abu-Jahl say as he died: "You have risen high, little shepherd."

Whether abu-Jahl actually said these words or not, the story perfectly expressed the insult of the defeat for the Meccans. "Here the Quraysh have flung their dearest flesh and blood to you," Muhammad told his men as he surveyed the field afterward, as much in sadness as in pride. The crème de la crème of Mecca had fought what they thought was a ragtag group of outcasts, including freed slaves—their own former slaves!—and lost. What had happened at Badr was simply not possible, not in their scheme of things. The natural order of their world had been upended.

The herdsman's story of abu-Jahl's leg flying off so spectacularly is one of many such details in the accounts of Badr. Both ibn-Ishaq's life of Muhammad and al-Tabari's history of early Islam are Homerically resplendent with battlefield gore. Enemy feet and legs are cut off with one slice of the sword so that "the marrow flowed on out." Intestines spill out of gaping bellies. Wounds are bravely suffered, no deterrent to further bravery, so that when an enemy sword leaves one believer's arm hanging by shreds of skin and tendon, "I put my foot on it and stood on it until I pulled it off, then went on fighting."

Exaggerated combat stories had been part of the foundation legends of every culture from the Sumerians down to the Byzantines. They were to be expected. But even as ibn-Ishaq and al-Tabari helped build a heroic Islamic identity, they remained conscientious chroniclers. Alongside the usual tales of death-defying derring-do, they gave realistic accounts of the panic and confusion of battle. The death of each of the fifteen believers killed at Badr is recorded, for example, no matter how ignominious. One fell off a high rock in his excitement and broke his neck. Another was thrown by his panicked horse and fatally kicked in the head. When a third swung his sword hard at an enemy and missed, the momentum carried the blade deep into his own leg, severing his femoral artery.

Like a split screen, the accounts shift back and forth between the conventionally heroic and the humanly fallible, the brave warrior of legend and the terrified human being desperate to survive.

THE FIRST MUSLIM · 209

In the modern era of remote control, it's easy to forget the sheer messiness of face-to-face combat, which was in fact eye-to-eye combat, one on one. Each fighter could smell the rank breath of the other's fear on his face, feel his grip slipping on his adversary's sweat, hear the grunting effort with each thrust and parry. They used not only swords and daggers but stones, fists, elbows, fingers—anything at all in the frantic effort to be the one to survive—and their panic was sharpened by the fact that many found themselves grappling not with an anonymous enemy but with people they knew. Sometimes intimately. In a battle that was all the more ferocious for being so intensely personal, both emigrants and Meccans fought former neighbors, distant cousins and in-laws, uncles and nephews, and even fathers, brothers, and sons.

That afternoon the victors roamed the field of battle, claiming chainmail, swords, horses, and riding camels as booty. Muhammad himself took only two items: an ornate double-edged sword and the prized stud camel that had belonged to his arch-nemesis, the newly deceased abu-Jahl. But the booty was nothing compared with the ransoms they would negotiate with Mecca for the fifty captives they'd taken. These included not only one of abu-Sufyan's own sons but also close kin of Muhammad's: his uncle Abbas as well as a nephew of Khadija's who was also Muhammad's son-in-law, having married his daughter Zaynab. Determined to show no favor, Muhammad held both men along with the others, but when Zaynab sent jewels from Mecca as ransom payment—a good wife, she had stayed with her husband in Mecca rather than emigrate—she included a necklace that had been Khadija's wedding gift to her. Recognizing it, Muhammad broke down and sent both son-in-law and jewels back to her. This was all very close to home.

. . .

By the time they told their battle stories, the believers saw victory in the face of such odds as a sign of divine favor. God had been on their side at Badr. Some would tell of angels descending in clouds of dust to fight alongside them, while Meccans would later explain their unaccountable defeat by recalling "white-robed men on piebald horses, between heaven and earth, for which we were no match and which nothing could resist." As the Quranic voice would soon tell the believers, "It was not you who killed the enemy, but God."

Then as now, everyone loves a winner, all the more an unexpected one. Badr created a huge upsurge in confidence among the believers. As word spread, the magnitude of the victory increased, along with Muhammad's reputation. He had routed the most powerful tribe in Arabia, and in the most public of places, and this only added to the injury for the Quraysh. Where they thought they'd solved their Muhammad problem with his expulsion, it was now infinitely worse. Word of the battle would spread throughout the Hijaz and beyond, over the mountains to the high desert steppeland of the Najd, all the way down to Yemen in the south and up into Syria to the north. The blow to Meccan prestige was particularly painful since like all successful merchants, the Quraysh traded on their reputation; if they could not defend it, their economy would suffer. They knew that Muhammad and the early Muslims would gain respect in direct proportion to the Quraysh loss of it. The challenge to the established order would create a palpable frisson, an excited rustling through the grapevine as old alliances were reconsidered. In the canny assessment of power politics that determined the allegiance of the many tribes of Arabia, nobody could now afford to discount Muhammad.

There was no question that the Quraysh would seek revenge. Further warfare between Mecca and Medina was inevitable, and their Beduin confederates would be drawn into it. The nomadic tribes' main concern was to ally themselves with the winning side, but where that had seemed obvious before Badr, it no longer was. It made sense, then, to cover their bets. Especially when the stories of divine intervention seemed borne out by Muhammad's victory in the face of overwhelming odds.

Even as the captives from Badr were still being ransomed, Muhammad sent out armed delegations with orders to fight the Beduin only if they refused to ally themselves with Medina. The nomads took the pragmatic option, lining up behind the rising new power rather than the fading old one. Time after time, ibn-Ishaq reports, the delegations "made a treaty of friendship and returned to Medina without a fight," and with each such agreement Muhammad expanded his sphere of influence and decreased that of Mecca.

If few of the tribes officially accepted *islam*, that was not a problem. By pledging mutual self-defense and recognizing Muhammad's authority, they were allying themselves with the new *umma*; in time, belief would follow action. The agreements were sealed in the traditional way with tribute and taxes, so that Muhammad was now bringing serious income into Medina. A community treasury was established for the believers, quickly enriched further by successful caravan raids as their new Beduin allies withdrew the protection they'd previously given the Meccans. Money spoke as loud then as it does now, and Muhammad's support within Medina rose further. In just two years he had gone far beyond his role as an arbiter and established himself as a political force. For the first time, perhaps, he could see himself not only as the leader of the believers but as the leader of all of Medina, blending spiritual and political authority into one.

But power was respected only so long as it continued to be demonstrated. This was the political logic of the time, and Muhammad still had to prove himself within its terms. The Quranic voice had advocated forgiveness and tolerance, but that had been when he had only a small minority behind him. If he was to establish his newly made power position, he would need to meet the expectations of his time. A new ruthlessness was called for, and it would be demonstrated nowhere more than in his relations with the Jewish tribes of Medina.

It may be only human to feel the most bitterness not for declared enemies but for those to whom one once felt closest. Only they have the ability to disappoint deeply. The sense of disloyalty—"How could you?"—cuts deep, not least because it's a defense against realizing how much had been assumed, mistaking friendship for unqualified support. When such expectations fall short, there's a tendency to experience this as the fault of the other, and to see it as personal betrayal.

Muhammad certainly assumed that the Jews of Medina would be the most open to his message. Their prophets were his prophets, divinely inspired men who had warned their people just as he had been trying to warn his own people in Mecca. The Quran would honor the great figures of the Hebrew bible from Adam through Abraham down to Joseph and Moses, Solomon and Elijah. Like all Arabians, the Jews spoke of God as al-Lah, the high one, and often used the honorific that would become familiar in the Quran, *ar-Rahman*, the merciful, just as the newly completed Babylonian Talmud used *Rahmana*. It seemed clear to Muhammad that Jews and Muslims were the common descendants of Abraham, the first *hanif*: two branches of the same monotheistic family. They were cousins, not strangers. And since the Jews were the original upholders of *din Ibrahim*, the tradition of Abraham, he took it for granted that he would have not merely their assent, but their enthusiastic support. The superiority of the new message he brought seemed self-evident. How could anyone who claimed to worship God possibly reject it?

Indeed it seemed at first that Medina's Jews were quite open to him. The clans of the three main Jewish tribes had willingly signed on to the arbitration agreement and were part of the *umma*, though only as secondary members—as confederates, that is, of the dominant Aws and Khazraj tribes. The Quranic voice had appealed directly to the original "People of the Book," instructing Muhammad to say: "We believe in that which has been revealed to us and that which was revealed to you. Our God and your God is one." The believers were not to argue with Jews "except fairly and politely," the Quran instructed. They should say, "People of the Book, let us come to an agreement that we will worship none but God, that we will associate no partners with him, and that none of us shall set up mortals as deities alongside God." And then, since that formulation might be understood to exclude Christians, further verses expanded on it: "Believers, Jews, Christians, Zoroastrians, whoever believes in God and the Day of Judgment and does what is right, all shall be rewarded by God . . . We believe in God and in what was revealed to us, in that which was revealed to Abraham and Ishmael, to Isaac and

Jacob and the tribes, and in that which God gave to Moses and Jesus and the prophets. We discriminate against none of them."

The problem was that Medina's Jews saw no more reason to accept Muhammad as a prophet than they had Jesus. They believed that the days of prophecy had ended twelve centuries before, with the Babylonian exile. There could be no more prophets. So just as the Quraysh had declared that they could not abandon the traditions of their fathers, so the Jews were determined to stand firm in the traditions of theirs. In almost two years, hardly any had accepted *islam*, and this appeared to confound Muhammad.

In Mecca, the Quranic voice had been quite accepting of challenges to its teaching. "We have sent down this scripture to you, messenger, with the truth for the people," it had said. "Whoever follows its guidance does so to his own benefit. Whoever strays away from it does so at his own peril; you are not in charge of them." Yet now Muhammad seemed to feel a special responsibility for the Jews. Their lack of interest seemed impossible, the result surely of sheer stubbornness; but the more he tried to convince them, the more they resisted, and in response the tone of the Quranic voice began to change, reflecting his exasperation.

"People of the Book, why do you deny God's revelations when you know they are true?" it said. "Why do you confound the true with the false, and knowingly conceal the truth?" Soon the Jews were no longer addressed directly but referred to only in the third person: no longer "we" but "they." Some of them were "upright and honorable," the voice conceded, but others had "made of their religion a sport and a pastime," as had the Meccans. Couldn't they see that they were betraying their own faith? That the Quran was not a denial of the Judaic message but a renewal of it?

But the Jewish tribes saw no need for renewal, let alone for an outsider telling them that they weren't good enough Jews. Their rabbis rejected the Quranic appeal, leading ibn-Ishaq to devote several pages to scenes in which they argued vehemently with Muhammad, "stirring up trouble" by insisting that his versions of the biblical tales were wrong. It's unlikely that these arguments ever took place, however. While details of the biblical stories as told in the Quran certainly differ from those now accepted in the West as canonical, they were current throughout the Middle East of the time. In fact radically different versions of many of the biblical tales can still be heard today throughout the region, where what seems "wrong" to Western ears is accepted as part of the lore of the Eastern churches.

The real issue was not religious but political. Medina's three Jewish tribes had already been outnumbered by the arrival of the Aws and Khazraj in the fifth century, and now, with the rapid expansion of Muhammad's influence, they feared being marginalized further. Perhaps if they had presented a united front, they could have been a political force to be reckoned with. But they had taken different sides in the inter-tribal conflict that had brought Muhammad to the city as an arbiter, and were thus often as hostile to each other as to anyone else. As the former majority reduced to a divided minority, they saw Muhammad's increasing power as a threat not so much to their religion as to their future in Medina. And in this he would prove them correct.

If it was clear that Muhammad was deeply disappointed by Jewish resistance to his message, it was equally clear that he needed to establish himself as no longer a man to disappoint. Without antagonizing the majority of Medina, he needed to make an example of those who openly challenged him. The smallest of the three Jewish tribes, the Qaynuqa, would now provide that example.

One story has it that "the affair of the Qaynuqa," as ibn-Ishaq calls it, was sparked by a marketplace incident just a month after the Battle of Badr. A young Qaynuqa man was said to have harassed a Beduin girl, trying to get her to lift her veil as she sat selling her produce. The girl swore at him, and a friend of his decided to retaliate by playing a crude practical joke, quietly tying the hem of her dress to a post so that when she stood up, her skirt was ripped off and she was left exposed. A Muslim believer who was passing by saw what had happened and leaped on the laughing men, killing one of them only to be killed himself by others drawn to the fight.

The story places the blame squarely on the Qaynuqa for having instigated the whole affair, and for having taken matters into their own hands after one of them was killed instead of turning to Muhammad for arbitration. With its vivid image of a victimized half-naked girl, it was perfectly calculated to inflame the imagination. Nobody could honorably stand by and allow that to happen. Yet at least part of the story is clearly apocryphal, since no Medinan women, let alone hard-working Beduin, wore veils at that time. The idea of the veil would be introduced only three years later, and then only for Muhammad's wives. Nevertheless, this purported marketplace brawl would serve as the apparent reason to single out the Qaynuqa.

But there were other, more political reasons. One centered on the possibility of collusion with the enemy. After all, somebody had warned abu-Sufyan of the three hundred men planning to raid his caravan at Badr, and though there was no solid evidence against the Qaynuqa, they were suspect by virtue of their close business ties with Mecca. More likely, however, they were never the primary target, but merely pawns in a larger political game in which the real quarry was their chief ally among the Khazraj: Abdullah ibn-Ubayy.

Ibn-Ubayy was a veteran clan leader who was said to have nursed the ambition of becoming "prince of Medina" until Muhammad's arrival. As one rumor had it, he had been "stringing the beads of his crown." It's unclear how he hoped to achieve this given the ongoing rift between his Khazraj tribe and the Aws; perhaps he saw himself as the peacemaker and had accepted *islam* under the illusion that Muhammad would help him. If so, he was soon disillusioned: the distinction between emigrants and helpers made it clear whose role it was to be helped and whose to do the helping. But ibn-Ubayy was far from alone in feeling that Muhammad's spiritual authority did not translate so well into political authority.

It had escaped none of the helpers' notice that Muhammad's closest advisers—abu-Bakr, Ali, and Omar among them—were all emigrants. Though the helpers had welcomed them, many did not quite fully accept them. The emigrants still had the whiff of outsiders, big-city foreigners who had come from another place and were not just taking over, but endangering the whole of Medina by rashly pursuing a policy of confrontation with the city they'd left behind. Along with those who had not yet accepted *islam*, many of the helpers thus had reservations about Muhammad's increasingly political role, and ibn-Ubayy was the most vocal of them.

His voice counted. As a leading figure in Medinan politics, he was used to being listened to, and had been openly displeased when his criticism of raids against Meccan caravans was ignored. He had refused to join the expedition to Badr, but now the victory there had placed his judgment in question, leaving him politically vulnerable. For Muhammad to directly attack him was out of the question; that would only antagonize the Khazraj. Far wiser, then, to undermine ibn-Ubayy by challenging his ability to protect his allies. Charging his Qaynuqa confederates with breaking Medina's arbitration agreement would be an excellent way to subvert his authority, effectively defanging a respected critic and possible rival for leadership.

The last thing the Qaynuqa wanted was to be caught in the middle of a power struggle like this, but caught they were. It made no difference whether what happened was due to a marketplace scrap turned fatal, or payback for suspected collusion with the enemy, or a ploy to disempower a leading critic. Muhammad charged them with disloyalty, and ordered his followers to surround their village, forcing them to retreat into their stronghold.

This was an over-reaction on his part, but that was precisely the point: it was a demonstration of his power and authority, and of ibn-Ubayy's lack of the same. The Qaynuqa held out under siege for fifteen days until they ran out of water, surrendered, and threw themselves on Muhammad's mercy. Like everyone else, they expected him to make the usual demands in such a situation: that they surrender their arms, that their income for the next several years be garnished, even that their leaders be imprisoned for a term. Instead, Muhammad stunned everyone by ordering them all placed in fetters. The punishment, he declared, would be execution for the men, slavery for the women and children, and confiscation of all their property.

Ibn-Ubayy rushed to intercede. The Qaynuqa had been loyal to him, and now his loyalty to them was on the line—his reputation, that is, as a leader of integrity with the power to protect his allies. But the only weapon he had was outrage. "Treat my confederates well!" he shouted at Muhammad. "Seven hundred men who defended me from all comers, and you would now mow them down in a single morning? By God, I do not feel safe with such a decision. It makes me afraid of what the future may hold in store."

Muhammad's only reply was to turn away, and at that ibn-Ubayy saw red. How dare Muhammad turn his back on him? He grabbed him by the collar, and the two men struggled briefly. "Confound you, let me go!" Muhammad yelled, the veins in his forehead throbbing dark and livid with anger. But ibn-Ubayy hung fast: "I will not let you go until you treat them well."

As his followers closed in to help him, Muhammad tore himself free and held up his hand to hold them off. There was no need to go any further. Ibn-Ubayy had just conceded the principle: judgment was Muhammad's to make, and his alone. Only his word could spare the Qaynuqa, and now that ibn-Ubayy had acknowledged this, it was to Muhammad's advantage to compromise. Drawing out the moment, he hesitated as if in thought, and then concluded: "They are yours. Let them go elsewhere." Anywhere but Medina, that is. All two thousand of the Qaynuqa were to be expelled.

The penalty of banishment was not unheard-of, as the poetic meme of the lone outlaw makes clear, but applying it to a whole tribe was. This was collective punishment, and while obviously less extreme than execution and enslavement, it was still inordinately severe. Yet insist as ibn-Ubayy might on more lenient terms, he got nowhere. He had been outmaneuvered, his influence undermined even as it appeared to be bolstered by Muhammad's change of mind.

Three days later, the sad procession of departing Qaynuqa served as due warning to all that Muhammad was now in charge. They filed out of Medina, the women and children on camels, the men on foot, heading for the Jewish-dominated oasis of Khaybar sixty miles to the north. They were allowed to take only what they could carry. What they left behind—land, palm groves, houses—would be divided among the emigrants, with one fifth kept back for the community treasury. The rest of Medina watched silently. If there was irony in the fact that the exiles had now in turn exiled others, nobody cared to comment on it.

The Qaynuqa were not the only ones to pay in the aftermath of Badr. Being a poet could be equally dangerous. However marginal poets may seem in the twenty-first-century West, they were the rock stars of seventh-century Arabia, and not only because of their famed odes and elegies. The other great form of Arabic poetry was satire: verses laced with vivid and often bawdy puns and double entendres, the more biting the better. But if words could be as sharp-edged as a sword, they could also bring the sharp edge of a sword in return.

The price of satire would now be made abundantly clear. One of the pithiest wordsmiths criticizing Muhammad was Asma, whose lines were all the more insulting for coming from a woman.

The wit of her rhyme is lost in translation, but even a literal version conveys her scorn. "Screwed men of Khazraj," she wrote, "will you be cuckolds / Allowing this stranger to take over your nest? / You put your hopes in him like men greedy for warm barley soup. / Is there no man who will step up and cut off this cuckoo?"

In Mecca, Muhammad had had no choice but to put up with such mockery and taunts. Not any longer. "Will nobody rid me of this woman?" he sighed aloud. His wish was the command of one believer who was a kinsman of Asma's. That same night, he went to her house, found her asleep with her youngest child in her arms, and drove his sword through her breast. "Shall I have to bear any penalty on her account?" he asked Muhammad the next morning. The answer was curt: "Two goats shall not come to blows for her."

Another opposition poet, abu-Afak, was mild by comparison: "Here's a rider who has come among us and divided us, / Saying 'This is forbidden and that is permitted.' / But if you believe in power and might, Medinans, / Why not follow a ruler of your own?" But even this was now beyond the pale. All Muhammad had to say was "Who will avenge me on this scoundrel?" and another volunteer obliged. As with Asma, nobody dared demand vengeance.

A third poet, ibn-Ashraf, made good his escape, if only temporarily. A member of the Jewish Nadir tribe, he had headed for Mecca together with some fifty other young men, calling on the Quraysh to take their revenge for Badr. "For such battles, tears and rain flow in torrents," he wrote. "The flower of the Quraysh perished around the wells of Badr, / Where so many of noble fame were cut down." This prompted a taunting rebuke from Hassan ibn-Thabit, who was to become in effect Muhammad's poet laureate: "Weep on like a pup following a little bitch. / God has given satisfaction to our leader / And shamed and cast down those who fought him." Whether bravely or foolishly, ibn-Ashraf returned to Medina eager to out-insult ibn-Thabit in person, only to be quickly assassinated.

And in case anyone else had missed the message of the expulsion of the Qaynuqa, the Quranic voice now intervened with an order to institute a major change in religious practice. The *qibla*, the direction of prayer, was to be reversed. Where the believers had faced north to Jerusalem, as did the Jews, they were now to face south. "We are turning you in a prayer direction that pleases you," declared the Quran, thus implying that the same direction as the Jews was displeasing. "Turn your face in the direction of the noble sanctuary"—the sanctuary of the Kaaba, in Mecca.

This change in *qibla* carried doubly symbolic weight. On the one hand it was a message directed at Mecca. Coming so soon after Badr, it acted as a kind of exclamation mark on the declaration of war against the Quraysh. Just as the Jews swore with their bodies never to forget Jerusalem—"If I forget thee, oh Jerusalem, let my right hand be cut off"—so now the Muslim believers were to use their bodies as a reminder to never forget Mecca. It was not a place of the past but ever present, the focal point of the new faith. Their praying bodies would proclaim it theirs, and they would reclaim it.

But the new direction of prayer also acted as an expression of what some historians were to call "the break with the Jews," especially since it followed so closely on the expulsion of a Jewish tribe. Despite the previous declarations of kinship, the process of Islamic individuation, of defining identity by difference, had begun. Just as Christianity had differentiated itself from its parent Jewish faith six centuries earlier, so the nascent faith of Islam would now begin to do the same. Islam and Judaism shared the same heritage, but the change in *qibla* seemed to indicate that they would no longer share the same future. Perhaps inevitably, as a family split, it was destined to become far more bitter.

Fifteen

It has often been said that you can judge a man by the quality of his enemies. If this holds true, then the "little shepherd" who killed abu-Jahl at Badr played a far larger historical role than he knew, because with "the father of ignorance" dead, the quality of Muhammad's enemies improved sharply. The leadership of the Meccan council now moved to the man who had acted so adroitly to divert the caravan from Badr: abu-Sufyan, the head of the Umayyad clan.

Like all good military commanders, the astute abu-Sufyan believed in measured response rather than heated antagonism. If he had to risk men's lives, it would be not out of personal animosity but out of necessity and duty. In fact it's likely that if abu-Sufyan had been in control earlier, Muhammad and his followers would never have been forced out of Mecca. Where abu-Jahl's fierce opposition had only strengthened Muhammad instead of weakening him, abu-Sufyan would have aimed for containment rather than repression. He might even have co-opted some of Muhammad's social principles, whether out of political calculation or recognition of their value. Though he was sworn to uphold the traditions of his Quraysh fathers, he could see realistically that some measure of reform was necessary. Even his own daughter Umm Habiba had accepted *islam*; she'd been among those who went to Ethiopia during the boycott, but instead of emigrating to Medina on her return, she'd stayed in Mecca, where she seems to have had some influence on her father's thinking. So while abu-Jahl would certainly have opted for immediate and large-scale escalation of the conflict after Badr, abu-Sufyan took a more considered course.

There was no question that some form of retaliation was required. The prestige of Mecca was at stake, and along with it the city's long-term livelihood. But instead of a headlong rush to reprisal, abu-Sufyan took his time. He negotiated a strong coalition with several Beduin allies, waited out the winter months, and the following spring mustered an army ten thousand strong, including hundreds of horsemen, for the ten-day march north toward Medina.

His plan was not to invade Medina, but to force Muhammad out of it. Instead of charging right into the oasis, he stopped on the outskirts and ordered his army to set up camp in the barley fields beneath the hill of Mount Uhud, some three miles to the north. His intention was clear: he had not come to declare war on the whole of Medina, only to settle the score with Muhammad and his followers. And to put aside any doubt, he sent an aide to ride into the settlement with a message for the leaders of the Aws and the Khazraj: "Leave us to deal with our cousin Muhammad, and we will leave you be. We have no need to fight you." This was a matter of Quraysh versus Quraysh, that is. There was no need for other tribes to get involved.

The approach was perfectly calculated. Abu-Sufyan was well informed of the divisions within Medina, and perfectly aware that Muhammad's political authority was still a matter of dispute.

Whether his message was a sincere plea for restraint or an attempt to divide and conquer, it was a powerful one: the gloved hand extended, with the iron fist visible. If the majority of Medinans wanted to risk all-out war, abu-Sufyan was more than ready, but if they stayed out of it, he was happy to respect that. He was not challenging them, only Muhammad and his followers, whom he shrewdly calculated would come out into the open where his army could deal with them quickly and efficiently.

But some of the believers saw through the strategy, chief among them ibn-Ubayy, the clan leader who had tussled with Muhammad over the fate of the Qaynuqa. Muhammad had decided to hold him close rather than alienate him further, and had kept him on his advisory council despite the objections of others. Now ibn-Ubayy argued cogently that the believers should stay put. "By God, we have never gone out of Medina to meet an enemy but that they have inflicted serious losses on us," he said, "and no enemy has ever entered it but that we have inflicted serious losses on them. Leave them alone. If they remain where they are, they will be in the worst possible place. And if they enter Medina, the men will fight them face to face, the women and boys will hurl stones at them from the rooftops, and they will be forced to withdraw."

Abu-Sufyan's cavalry had already trampled the barley fields, he pointed out, so there was nothing left to be defended there. Let them now enter Medina if they dared; the believers would have the advantage of intimate knowledge of every alley and cul-de-sac, every vantage point and hiding place. Then as now, urban warfare was a military commander's nightmare, and ibn-Ubayy calculated that it was not one abu-Sufyan wanted to risk. If the Meccan leader was depending on Muhammad coming out to fight him, why oblige him? Especially since his army could stay camped by Mount Uhud only as long as they could hold out without access to fresh water. Eventually, they'd be forced to break camp and leave. It was merely a matter of waiting them out.

But if discretion was the better part of valor, Muhammad's younger and more ardent followers wanted none of it. Led by the emigrants, still rankling with the insult of exile, they argued that to ignore abu-Sufyan's challenge was to cede the moral high ground. They hungered for something more glorious than hunkering down. They had defeated the Meccans against overwhelming odds at Badr, and now was their chance to prove themselves again against even greater numbers. "Lead us out to these dogs, oh messenger of God," they shouted.

What does a leader do in such circumstances? He can follow what he suspects to be the wiser course, but then he risks disappointing his base—in Muhammad's case, the emigrants. In time, his authority would be strong enough to outweigh popular demand, but he must have realized that he wasn't there yet. And then there was another factor in play. He had acceded to ibn-Ubayy's intervention on the fate of the Qaynuqa and appeared magnanimous because of it, but to accede to him again would only be to enhance the other's prestige. Either way, whether out of a sense of obligation to the emigrants or wariness of giving ibn-Ubayy a greater say, Muhammad allowed his younger followers to override his better judgment. He dressed ceremoniously for battle, with sword, helmet, and chainmail (a double coat to accommodate the increasing girth that had come with age and a sweet tooth). And when ibn-Ubayy tried to argue once more that going out to meet the Meccan army was only to court defeat, he replied that it was too late. "It is not fitting for a prophet to put on his coat of mail only to take it off without fighting," he said.

There was nothing left for ibn-Ubayy to do but to command the three hundred men of his clan to join Muhammad in a gesture of support. But even with the addition of his men, fewer than one thousand followed Muhammad out of Medina that afternoon. Where the odds at Badr had been two to one, they were now ten to one. And as night fell, they would become worse.

Ibn-Ubayy's gesture of support was precisely that: a gesture, that is, and no more. The moment he and his men had reached the outskirts of Medina, he reined in his horse and declared that he would go no further. To engage the Meccans beyond this point would be to turn from defense to offense, he said, and the agreement in the charter of Medina was strictly for defense. "Muhammad refused to listen to me, and listened instead to striplings and men of no judgment," he told his men bluntly. "I see no reason why we should get ourselves killed in this ill-chosen spot." And with that, he ordered his men to turn back, leaving Muhammad to ride on to what ibn-Ubayy clearly thought was inevitable defeat—and himself to pick up the pieces and finally be acclaimed as the leader of Medina.

Left with only seven hundred men, Muhammad again relied on guile to outwit numbers. That night he moved his men through the *harra*—the jagged ancient lava flows on either side of the barley fields, so sharp and stony that they were impassable for the Meccan cavalry. By dawn his men were positioned with Mount Uhud at their back and *harra* to either side. The only way the Meccan horsemen could attack them now was from the front, so Muhammad posted fifty archers on a rise with strict orders to stay put. "Defend us against the cavalry with your arrows," he said. "Whatever happens, whether you see us prevailing over them or them over us, hold your positions, so that we will not be attacked from the rear." It was an excellent strategy—so long as the archers obeyed their orders.

The Battle of Uhud began at daybreak on Friday, March 25, 625, just over a year after the Battle of Badr, but with a very different outcome. By nightfall, it would be a disaster for Muhammad. He would be wounded, and sixty-five of his followers would lie dead. Yet it didn't have to be that way.

There was nothing glorious about this battle. It took place to the sound track not of stirring martial music but of gasps and grunts, clashing steel, swearing men, horses whinnying and snorting in fear, and above it all, the ululations and chants of the women in the rear of the Meccan camp.

This was the traditional martial role of women. They urged on their men and mocked the virility of their enemies, their shrill cries designed to cut through the funk of battle and strike fear into the hearts of the other side, much like the eerie sound of bagpipes swirling through the mist in another part of the world. Abu-Sufyan had selected fifteen widows and daughters of men killed at Badr to accompany his army, and they were led by his own wife, the aristocratic Hind. "Advance, and we'll embrace you on soft pillows," the women chanted. "Falter, and you'll get no tenderness from us."

But what Hind wanted above all was a very personal vengeance. Both her father and her brother had been killed at Badr by Muhammad's uncle Hamza, and she was determined to see him dead. To that end, she'd publicly offered a deal to an Ethiopian slave named Wahshi: his freedom along with a handsome payment in return for seeking out Hamza on the battlefield and killing him.

Perhaps only a slave with so much to gain would have taken on such a task. Hamza was a fearsome warrior, one of those rare men with an appetite for combat. It was easy enough to find him in battle: look for where the fighting was fiercest and there he would be, distinguishable by the ostrich plume he wore on his helmet. One believer would remember him taunting every enemy fighter he came across that day, and in particular a man whose mother was a female circumciser in Mecca, a practice Hamza clearly saw as belonging to the dark days of *jahiliya*, or pre-Islamic ignorance. When confronting others, he'd whirl his sword over his head and yell, "Come get me, you son of a whore!" but he reserved a worse taunt for this man: "Come get me, you son of a clitoris-cutter!" One massive swipe of that sword, and the clitoris-cutter's son was done for.

That was to be Hamza's last kill. While he could defeat any man armed with a sword or a dagger, he was helpless against the Ethiopian weapon of choice. "I balanced my javelin until I was satisfied with it," the slave Wahshi would report, "and then I hurled it at Hamza. It struck him in the lower belly with such force that it came out between his legs. He staggered toward me, and fell." And then, with chilling sang-froid, "I waited until he was dead, and went and recovered my javelin."

Even with the loss of a major figure like Hamza, however, Muhammad's men were on the verge of victory. Every charge by the Meccan cavalry had been repulsed by that solid phalanx of archers on the rise at the foot of the hill, and arrows had maimed many of their horses. As the believers pressed forward, the Meccans broke ranks and turned to flee. And it was at this point that the archers' discipline gave way.

"I saw the women tucking up their skirts in flight and exposing their anklets," one of them would remember. "A cry went up of 'Plunder! Plunder!' Nobody listened to the captain shouting that the messenger's orders were to hold fast. They left their posts and ran onto the battlefield, eager for booty."

Abu-Sufyan's cavalry commander saw his chance. He rallied his horsemen to wheel around and come at Muhammad's men from their now unprotected rear. The infantry charged in after him, and the battle turned. As one believer after another was cut down, the survivors ran for the slopes of Mount Uhud, their flight turning to full-scale panic when Muhammad was knocked down by a blow to the head.

The cry went up that he had been killed. Whether it came first from the Meccans or from his own men is unclear, though it's understandable why people might have thought it. While his helmet had held fast, the force of the blow had smashed its metal faceguard deep into his cheek. It had split his upper lip, broken his nose, and gashed his forehead—a gash that bled copiously, as head wounds do. But none of that concerned Muhammad as aides helped him up and he saw to his fury that his men were in flight. What did it matter if they thought he was dead? Did they have so little faith in *islam*? Did they really think that this was merely about him? "Muhammad is but a messenger," the Quranic voice would say after the battle, reflecting his anger. "Other messengers have come and gone before him, so how can it be that when he dies or is slain, you turn back on your heels?"

He tried to gather his routed followers to him with the cry "To me, servants of God, to me!" But only thirty or so heard him and rallied to his side, and on this too the Quranic voice would comment bitterly: "With God's permission, you were routing the unbelievers, but once he had brought you within sight of your goal, you faltered, disputed the order, and disobeyed. You fled without looking back while the messenger was calling to you from behind, and God rewarded you with sorrow for sorrow." Defeat, in short, was God's punishment of them for having disobeyed Muhammad.

The Meccans eased up their counter-attack as the rumor spread that Muhammad was dead. Since abu-Sufyan had made it plain that their beef was only with Muhammad, their job was done. But not Hind's. While the other Quraysh women set out into the barley fields in search of plunder, gathering up swords, daggers, chainmail, bridles, saddles—anything of value—abu-Sufyan's wife ignored them all. Instead, she strode from corpse to corpse in search of the one she wanted, and when she found it, she uttered a cry of victory that years later still froze the blood of those who had heard her. She stood astride Hamza, gripped her knife with both hands, and plunged it deep into his body, gouging him open to rip out not his heart but a larger and far more visceral organ: his liver. Ululating in triumph, she held it high above her head and then, in full view of all, crammed it into her mouth and chewed, blood streaming down her chin and over her chest and her arms. Some would say that she swallowed Hamza's liver, others that she spat out the pieces, stomped on them, and ground them into the dirt. Either way, she cut an indelible image of terrifying vengeance.

The sight of this ghastly mutilation merely increased the believers' panic, but it also mesmerized the Meccans and thus gave the small group around Muhammad the chance to retreat farther up the lower slopes of Mount Uhud, stoning the few enemy soldiers who still tried to pursue them. It was close to nightfall when abu-Sufyan himself rode up beneath them and called out loud, "In God's name, is Muhammad really dead?"

"No, by God," came the answer from Omar, "he is listening to what you are saying right now."

"Then hear this," abu-Sufyan shouted back. And instead of threatening to finish the job or gloating in victory as might have been expected, he made it clear that his wife's mutilation of Hamza's corpse had not been at his orders: "Some of your dead have been mutilated. I neither commanded this nor forbade it, and it neither gave me pleasure nor saddened me."

Under the circumstances, it was very close to an apology. He had pledged revenge for Badr and gained it, but so far as he was concerned, the score was settled, at least for now. "Wars go by turns," he now declared. "This has been our day for your day." And having established himself, unlike abu-Jahl, as an enemy to respect, he gave the order for his army to break camp and set off back to Mecca.

Even after his nose and cheek had healed, Muhammad would suffer headaches, sometimes as intense as migraines, for the rest of his life. Many of his followers were not in much better shape, and as they straggled back into Medina, nursing both their pride and their wounds, it seemed that ibn-Ubayy's position in the settlement had been strengthened. It had turned out as he'd predicted. Muhammad had placed them all at risk. It had been foolish to engage the Meccan army on open ground, and they should be thankful that abu-Sufyan had decided not to press his advantage and fight on into the oasis itself. Now they could see that

Muhammad's increasing power in Medina worked only to their disadvantage. While he was undoubtedly the messenger, and thus the spiritual leader, Medina would surely be wiser to place political leadership in the capable, prudent hands of ibn-Ubayy himself.

But in this ibn-Ubayy underestimated one of Muhammad's most striking characteristics: the ability to turn reversal to his favor. Any leader can use a victory to his advantage, but one who can turn defeat to his advantage is much rarer. Muhammad had done it before, after being hounded out of Mecca, and now he would do it again, with ibn-Ubayy unwittingly making his task all the easier.

The following Friday, when the believers had gathered at the mosque, ibn-Ubayy stood up to speak. He began by extolling Muhammad, duly emphasizing his relief and gratitude that the messenger's life had been spared. But then he could not resist touting his own wisdom in having advised against open battle with the Meccan army. "Had our brothers heeded me, they would not have been killed," he declared—a statement not exactly calculated to win the hearts and minds of those who were mourning their casualties and smarting from their wounds. In that moment, the crowd turned against him, and he found himself accused of cowardice and worse. "Enemy of God," people shouted, "you are not worthy to speak here after behaving as you have done," and they forced him to cede the floor.

A new word soon appeared in the Quranic revelations: *munafiqun*. Often translated as "hypocrites," it would become the title of Sura 63 of the Quran, which begins: "When the hypocrites come to you, prophet, they say, 'We bear witness that you are the messenger of God.' God knows that this is so and he bears witness that the hypocrites are liars. They professed faith and then rejected it. They use their oaths as a cover and so bar others from God's way.... When you see them, their outward appearance pleases you. When they speak, you listen to what they say. But they are like propped-up timbers. They think every cry they hear is against them. They are the enemy, so beware of them. How devious they are!"

But was ibn-Ubayy really an enemy? Or even a hypocrite? The line between rhetoric and demagoguery is sometimes a very thin one. To translate *munafiqun* as "hypocrites" is to overload the word, which is better if more clumsily rendered as "those who had reservations or held back." Literally, it means "those who crept into their holes," the way desert voles turn tail in fright and dig deep into the earth. In fact ibn-Ubayy neither lied nor rejected *islam*. Instead he reserved the right to question Muhammad's political decisions. Far from hiding his true opinion as the word "hypocrite" implies, he spoke out openly in favor of what in modern terms would be called separation of church and state.

The new coinage was a challenge to all those who had accepted *islam* but did not necessarily accord every statement of Muhammad's the power of divine authority. They distinguished, that is, between the messenger and the politician, and it was this distinction that the Quranic voice now seemed to blur. The messenger was fast becoming the prophet, no longer simply "one of you," but to be thought of as divinely directed in every aspect of his life.

The charge of hypocrisy stuck. Anyone questioning Muhammad's decisions became ipso facto a false believer, no matter the circumstances. For instance, when the grieving father of one of those killed at Uhud was told, "Rejoice, your son is in the gardens of paradise," his despair would allow no such consolation. "By God it is not a garden of paradise," he retorted, "but a garden of rue. You have deluded my poor son into losing his life, and stricken me with sorrow at his death." He too was now called a hypocrite, henceforth to be shunned and distrusted. Fervent believers in the mosque began to forcibly eject anyone whose faith they considered less absolute than theirs, dusting off their hands afterward like nightclub bouncers and shouting, "Don't come near here again!"

The phenomenon is familiar: the tightening of ranks in defeat, the refusal to acknowledge a mistake, the search for some-one else to blame—for the enemy within. In Islam, it would even-tually lead to accusations of heresy and apostasy as the political majority enforced the line. As Edward Said was to write in *Reflections on Exile*: "It is in the drawing of lines around you and your compatriots that the least attractive aspects of being in exile emerge: an exaggerated sense of group solidarity and a passionate hostility to outsiders, even those who may in fact be in the same predicament as you . . . Everyone not a blood brother or sister is an enemy, every sympathizer is an agent of some unfriendly power, and the slightest deviation from the accepted group line is an act of the rankest treachery and disloyalty."

Branding ibn-Ubayy a hypocrite was a political move more than a religious one, and one Machiavelli might have approved when he advised his patron nine centuries later that "some nobles may deliberately and for reasons of ambition remain independent of you. Against nobles such as these, a ruler must safeguard him-self, fearing them as if they were his declared enemies, because in times of adversity they will always help to ruin him."

The label forced the issue. After the insult of being forcibly silenced in the mosque, ibn-Ubayy kept his distance. Among his kinsmen, however, he gave voice to his resentment of the emigrants. "They've tried to outrank us and outnumber us in our own land," he said. "By God, when they say, 'Fatten your dog and he will devour you,' that fits us and them to a tee." In the event, Muhammad would need only one more step in order to neutralize him completely.

Muhammad now focused on expanding his sphere of influence, vying with Mecca for the support of the Beduin tribes on the arid central Arabian steppeland known as the Najd. The Beduin chiefs negotiated this situation cannily, playing one side off against the other as they held out for the best terms of alliance. But this could be a dangerous game, especially when the Meccan–Medinan rivalry served as an excuse to act out power plays within their own tribes, as happened with the Amir.

Their chief had finally pledged his tribe to Muhammad, who sent forty men to instruct them in the new faith. But the chief's nephew wanted alliance with Mecca, not Medina, and saw the chance to discredit his uncle and take over tribal leadership for himself. Carefully maintaining plausible deniability, he arranged to undermine his uncle by having a neighboring tribe ambush Muhammad's delegation as they camped by a well en route to the Amir. The plan might have worked if one believer had not survived. He'd been grazing the camels, and realized what had happened only when he saw flocks of vultures wheeling in the air above the well. He set off back to Medina with the news, and on the way came across two Amir tribesmen fast asleep. Believing that it was their kinsmen who had massacred his colleagues, he killed them in revenge.

The Amir chieftain now held Muhammad formally liable for this one believer's crime. The believers argued that "a mistake is not a deliberate act," but it made no difference. Even though thirty-nine of his own men had been slaughtered, Muhammad was left no honorable recourse but to agree to pay blood money for the killing of the two Amir. Under the terms of Medina's arbitration agreement, he called on all its signatories to contribute, but since the Nadir tribe had their own separate long-standing alliance with the Amir, he demanded that they provide most of the payment.

The Nadir, one of the two Jewish tribes remaining in Medina after the expulsion of the Qaynuqa, did not quite see things this way. They considered themselves no more responsible than anyone else for one believer's mistake. So ibn-Ishaq reports that while they politely welcomed Muhammad when he went to negotiate the matter with them at their Sabbath council meeting, along with his senior aides abu-Bakr and Omar, the Nadir had something else in mind. As he tells it, they asked the visitors to wait outside while they finished their deliberations, and decided to kill Muhammad instead of paying him.

Even as such stories go, this one is strange. The plan was apparently to drop a large boulder from the top of the wall against which Muhammad was sitting and then call it an accident. It was foiled at the last moment, when Muhammad suddenly left "as though to answer a call of nature" and never came back, explaining later that an angel had quietly warned him of the conspiracy. But angel or no, every detail makes it an unlikely scenario. The

council meeting on the Sabbath; Muhammad's departure without abu-Bakr and Omar, presumably leaving them in danger; the
little logistical matter of exactly how a heavy boulder could be
brought to the top of a wall, let alone dropped from it with fatal
precision—none of these seem likely. That is, they are the hall-
marks of a story fabricated to justify what happened next, in the
awareness that it might otherwise not be considered justifiable.

Within the hour, Muhammad sent the Nadir a message:
"Leave my city and live with me no longer after the treason you
have plotted against me." The language itself was telling: not
Medina, nor even the pre-Islamic name Yathrib, but "my city."
And treason charged not against Medina but "against me." It was
a statement of absolute authority: *L'état c'est moi.*

The ultimatum was delivered by a believer who had been a
confederate of the Nadir. Astonished that any confederate could
relay such a message, the Nadir asked why he had agreed to do so.
The reply was a chilling announcement not only of their isolation
but of a whole new political order: "Hearts have changed, and
islam has wiped out the old alliances."

As the Nadir council debated what they could do to avoid
expulsion, ibn-Ubayy sent a message urging them to resist. "I have
two thousand men from the Beduin and from my own people
united around me," he said. "Stay, and they will enter battle alongside you, as will the Qureyz." In fact the Qureyz, the other remaining Jewish tribe, had made no such commitment, but the Nadir
did not know this. Relying on ibn-Ubayy's word, they retreated
into the stronghold in the center of their village, despite the warning of one of their elders that if resistance failed, they might be risk-
ing far worse than expulsion, namely "the seizure of our wealth, the
enslavement of our children, and the killing of our fighting men."

Muhammad's response startled everyone: he gave the order to cut down the Nadir palm groves. In Arabia, trees of any kind were treasured, but date palms especially so. Each one represented generations of careful tending and work, so that to destroy the palms was to destroy not only property but history. Cutting them down was a calculated statement that the Nadir now had nothing left to stay for, and a warning of what might happen to them if they resisted further. Plus it had the additional advantage of unnerving ibn-Ubayy, whose promised two thousand men never materialized. The ensuing siege was a repeat of that of the Qaynuqa the previous year. After fifteen days, with no water left and no future to look forward to in Medina, the Nadir capitulated. They would leave with little more than their lives, allowed to take only one camel-load of goods for every three people.

But this time there would be no sad procession. Unlike the Qaynuqa, the Nadir left Medina in what seemed more like a triumphal parade. They beat drums and tambourines as they went, dressed in their finest clothes and decked out in all their jewelry. As one witness put it: "They went with a splendor and a glory the like of which had never been seen from any tribe in their time." It was an impressive display of protest, a defiant statement by the Nadir that they were the ones who should be proud, and all the rest of Medina ashamed. As they headed north toward the oasis of Khaybar, and on into Palestine and Syria, the manner of their leaving said as much about their expulsion as the reason given for it.

The Quranic voice quickly came into play to counteract the shocking image of believers destroying date orchards: "Whatever you believers have done to their trees, whether cutting them down or uprooting them, was done by God's leave, so that he might disgrace those who defied him." This was the fault not of the believers but of men like ibn-Ubayy: "Consider the hypocrites who say to their fellows, the faithless among the People of the Book, 'We would never listen to anyone who sought to harm you, and if you are attacked, we shall certainly come to your aid.' God bears witness that they are liars." By expelling the Nadir, Muhammad had not only made it clearer than ever that he would tolerate no challenge to his authority; he had again forced his will on ibn-Ubayy.

For the volatile Omar, however, this was not enough. Always the warrior, he urged Muhammad to have done with ibn-Ubayy and give the order to kill him. Instead, he received a political lesson. "What? And let men say that Muhammad slays his companions?" came the reply. To make a martyr of ibn-Ubayy would only be counter-productive; he was far more useful kept close, as a subordinate. Indeed five years later, his power by then unchallenged, Muhammad would return to the issue. "What do you think now?" he'd ask Omar. "By God, if I had ordered ibn-Ubayy killed when you advised it, the chiefs of Medina would have been shaking with fury. But by now if I commanded them directly to kill him, they would do it."

As for the expulsion of the Nadir, the Quranic voice spoke out in angry defense of the decision. Where it had previously maintained that a small number of Jews were creating opposition to Muhammad's message and thus betraying their own faith, it now asserted that there were only a few "good Jews" among them. Verse after verse would build into a bitter polemic whose style and content reflected Muhammad's personal feeling of betrayal. The expulsion of both the Qaynuqa and the Nadir was now justified by labeling them "evil-doers." "It was God who drove the unbelievers among the People of the Book out of their dwellings . . .

They imagined that their strongholds would protect them, but God's scourge fell upon them . . . If God had not decreed expulsion for them, he would surely have punished them in this world." None of which boded well for Medina's one remaining Jewish tribe.

Sixteen

Scrutiny of those in power was no less intense in the seventh century than it is today. Inevitably, Muhammad's private life was now very public, though it may well be anachronistic to even speak of a private life. The concept of privacy is relatively modern, just like the idea of marriage as a romantic union. Through most of history, marriage was an arrangement between men—between fathers and husbands, that is. It was an accepted means of strengthening the bonds of family, which is why marriage between first cousins was common. But for leaders, it was also a means of forming and consolidating alliances. Marriage brought allies close and former enemies even closer. It was a declaration of political amity written, as it were, in the flesh.

In late middle age, then, the man devotedly married for so long to a single wife was multiply married. Within three years of Khadija's death, Muhammad had three wives, with six more yet to come. The first of his late-life marriages, to a quiet widow named Sawda, had been arranged by his followers, who were concerned about the depth of his grief for Khadija. He had also accepted his close friend and supporter abu-Bakr's offer of his daughter Aisha as a bride, and so as not to be seen to favor abu-Bakr above all others, had then married Omar's daughter Hafsa after she'd been widowed at Badr. Two of his closest advisers had thus become his fathers-in-law, while two others became his sons-in-law, one of them doubly so. Not only had the Umayyad aristocrat Uthman married Muhammad's eldest daughter after her first husband had been forced to divorce her; when she died shortly after the Battle of Uhud, he immediately married her sister Umm Kulthum. And Muhammad had personally arranged the marriage between his youngest daughter, Fatima, and his cousin and all-but-adopted son Ali.

This seeming muddle of marriages was part of the traditional and far-reaching Arabian web of kinship, one that beggars the modern Western idea of the nuclear family. It makes a mockery of something as simplistically linear as a family tree, becoming far more like a dense forest of vines. And a very strong one, since it would reach deep into the future. The two fathers-in-law, abu-Bakr and Omar, were to be the first two leaders of Islam after Muhammad's death, each acclaimed as his successor or *khalifa*—caliph in English—and they would be immediately followed by the two sons-in-law, Uthman and Ali. By both giving and taking in marriage, Muhammad was establishing the leadership matrix of the new Islamic community.

But if this was clear to the men, it was not necessarily so to the women involved, and especially not to the youngest, most outspoken, and most controversial of Muhammad's late-life wives, abu-Bakr's daughter Aisha. Where challenges to Muhammad's leadership had previously come from political opponents, now one of the strongest would come from alarmingly close to home.

Certainly Aisha never saw herself as merely a means of political alliance, let alone as just one wife among many. In fact if there was one thing she would insist on all her life, it was her exceptionality. There was the age at which she had married Muhammad, to start with. She had been a mere child, she'd maintain: six years old when she was betrothed and nine years old when the marriage was celebrated and consummated. Few disputed her claim in her lifetime; indeed, few people cared to dispute with her at all. As one of Islam's most powerful politicians would remember years later, "There was never any subject I wished closed that she would not open, or that I wished open that she would not close."

If Aisha was indeed married so young, however, others would certainly have remarked on it at the time. Instead, more restrained reports have her aged nine when she was betrothed and twelve when she was actually married, which makes sense since custom dictated that girls be married at puberty. But then again, to have been married at the customary age would make Aisha normal, and that was the one thing she was always determined not to be. Tart-tongued and quick-witted, she would, at least by her own account, tease Muhammad and not only get away with it but be loved for it. It was as though he had granted her license for girlish mischief. Much as a fond father might indulge a spoiled daughter, he seemed diverted by her sassiness and charm.

Charming she must have been, and sassy she definitely was. But sometimes the charm wore thin, at least to the modern ear. The stories Aisha would later tell of her marriage were intended to show her influence and spiritedness, but there's often a definite edge to them, a sense of a young woman not to be crossed or denied.

There was the time Muhammad spent too long for her liking with another wife who had made a "honeyed drink" for him—a kind of Arabian syllabub, probably, made with egg whites and goat's milk beaten thick with honey, for which he had a special weakness. Knowing that he was very particular about bad breath,

Aisha turned her face away when he finally came to her room, and asked what he had been eating. When told about the honeyeyed drink, she wrinkled her nose in distaste. "The bees that made that honey must have been eating wormwood," she insisted, and was rewarded when Muhammad refused the drink the next time he was offered it.

Other times she went further, as when Muhammad arranged to seal an alliance with a major Christian tribe in the timehonored manner by marrying its leader's daughter, a girl renowned for her beauty. When the bride-to-be arrived in Medina, Aisha volunteered to help prepare her for the wedding and, under the guise of sisterly advice, told her that Muhammad would think all the more highly of her if she at first resisted him on the wedding night by saying, "I take refuge with God from thee." The new bride had no idea that this was the phrase used to annul a marriage; the moment she said it, Muhammad left, and the next day she was bundled unceremoniously back to her own people.

It may have been inevitable, then, that when scandal hit in the form of a lost necklace, the headstrong Aisha would be at the center of it.

It was not just any necklace, of course, though it would have been easy enough to think so. It was only a string of beads, really. Agates, or maybe coral, or even simple seashells—Aisha never did say, and one can see her waving her hand dismissively as though such detail were irrelevant. Enough to say that it was the kind of necklace a young girl would wear, and treasure more than if it had been made of diamonds, because it had been Muhammad's wedding gift to her.

It was lost on the way back from an expedition to the north to seek the support of a large Beduin tribe, the Mustaliq. When Muhammad led such expeditions himself, as he had this one, he usually took one of his wives with him, and none was more eager to go than Aisha. For a spirited teenage girl, this was pure excitement. From the vantage point of her howdah—the canopied cane platform built out from the camel saddle—she saw the vast herds of the camel and horse breeders in the northern steppes; the date-palm oases of Khaybar and Fadak nestled like elongated emeralds in winding valleys; the Beduin warriors of remote tribes, fiercely romantic to a city girl. And when negotiations failed and fighting broke out, as it did this time, her shrill voice carried over the ranks of struggling men, urging them on.

Muhammad's men had prevailed over the Mustaliq, taking captives to be held for ransom or sold as slaves. It was still dark when they began to break camp on the final leg of the journey home, aiming as usual to use the cool early hours of the day to advantage. Before they left, Aisha made her way beyond the encampment to relieve herself behind a spindly bush of broom. She got back just as the caravan was about to move off, and had already settled into her howdah when she put her fingers to her throat and realized that her necklace was gone. The string must have snagged on a branch without her noticing, scattering the beads, but if she was quick about it, there was still time to retrieve them. Without a word to anyone, she slipped down and retraced her steps.

Even for someone so determined, though, finding the beads took longer than she'd thought. Every broom bush looked the same in the early half-light, and when she finally found the right one, she had to sift through the piles of dead needles beneath it to find each bead. By the time she returned with them tied securely into a knot in the hem of her smock, the camp was no longer there. Assuming that she was still safely in her howdah, the expedition had moved on.

The well-trodden route was clear enough, and heavily laden camels move slowly. It would have been a matter of at most an hour or so for a healthy teenage girl to catch up on foot, especially in the early morning when the chill of the desert night still lingers in the air, crisp and refreshing. But instead, in Aisha's own words, "I wrapped myself in my smock and lay down where I was, knowing that when I was missed they would come back for me."

It was inconceivable that her absence not be noted. Unthinkable that the caravan not halt and a detachment be sent back to find her. If there was a murmur of panic at the back of her mind as the sun rose higher and she took shelter under a scraggly acacia tree, she would never acknowledge it. Of course she would be missed, and of course someone would come for her. The last thing anyone would expect was that she, Muhammad's favorite wife, would run after a pack of camels like some Beduin shepherd girl.

But the expedition sent nobody since they never realized she was missing, not even after they reached Medina. In the hubbub of arrival—the camels being unloaded and stabled, the warriors being greeted by wives and kinsmen, the captives being led away—her absence went unnoticed. Everyone simply assumed she was somewhere else. So it was Aisha's good fortune, or perhaps her misfortune, that a young Medinan warrior had been delayed and was riding alone through the heat of the day when he saw Aisha under that acacia tree. His name was Safwan, and in what Aisha would swear was an act of chivalry as pure as the desert itself, he dismounted, helped her up onto his camel, and then led the animal on foot the whole twenty miles back to Medina. Which is how everyone in the oasis witnessed her arrival that evening, seated on a camel led by a good-looking young warrior.

She must have noticed the way people stared and hung back, with nobody rushing up to say, "Thanks be to God that you're safe." No matter how upright she sat on Safwan's camel, how high she held her head or how disdainful her glare, she must have seen the tongues as they started to wag, spreading the word. And must have known what that word was. Muhammad's youngest wife traveling with a virile young warrior, parading through the series of villages strung along the valley of Medina? The news spread rapidly from tongue to tongue, house to house, village to village. A necklace indeed, people would cluck. Alone the whole day in the desert with a single man? Why had she lain down to wait when she could easily have caught up with the expedition on foot? Had it been a pre-arranged tryst? Had Muhammad been deceived by his spirited favorite?

Whether anyone actually believed such a thing was beside the point. Then as now, scandal was its own reward. But more important, this one fed into the existing political landscape. What Aisha and Safwan may or may not have done was not really the issue. In seventh-century Medina as anywhere in the world today, the mere appearance of sexual impropriety was a tried and trusted way to bring down a politician. Soon the whole oasis was caught up in a fervor of sneering insinuation. At the wells, in the walled vegetable gardens, in the date groves, in the inns and the markets and the stables—even in the mosque itself—people reveled in the delicious details, real or imagined.

Muhammad had no doubt as to Aisha's innocence. In fact he did his best to ignore the whole matter until he realized how insidiously it was undermining his authority. He sent her back to her father's house while he decided what to do, but his young favorite had unwittingly placed him in a double bind. If he divorced her, as Ali now advised, that would imply that he had indeed been deceived. On the other hand, if he took her back, he risked being seen as a doting old man bamboozled by a mere slip of a girl. Either way, it would erode not only his own authority but that of his whole message. Incredible as it seemed, the future of the new faith now hung on the reputation of a teenage girl.

For the first time in her life, nothing Aisha could say—and as ibn-Ishaq notes, "she said plenty"—could make any difference. She tried high indignation, wounded pride, fury against the slander, but none of it seemed to have any effect. Years later, still haunted by the episode, she would even maintain that Safwan was known to be impotent—an unassailable statement since by then he was long dead, killed in battle and thus unable to defend his virility. A teenage girl under a cloud, she finally did what any teenage girl would do: she cried. And if there was a certain hyperbole to her account of those tears, that was understandable under the circumstances. As she put it: "I could not stop crying until I thought the weeping would burst my liver."

Aisha's situation was all the more fraught because despite having been married for four years by then, she still had no children. In fact none of the nine women Muhammad was to marry after Khadija's death would become pregnant by him, and this absence of children, and especially of a male heir, itself led to much talk. The whole purpose of his marrying so many times was to bind together the widening *umma* of believers and allies, but such alliances were sealed by children. Mixed blood was new blood, free of the old divisions. What was the point of marriage without offspring?

Certainly any of his later wives would have given her eye-teeth, if not all her teeth, to have children by him. To be the mother of his children would automatically give her higher status than any of the others, especially if she were to give birth to a son, Muhammad's natural heir. So there is no question that every one of them must have done her utmost to become pregnant by him, and especially Aisha. She could only watch in envy as Muhammad doted on his grandchildren—Khadija's grandchildren—and most of all on Hassan and Hussein, the two young sons of Ali and Fatima. One of the few times he was ever seen to laugh was when he played with them, the image of the adoring grandfather as he dandled them proudly on his lap or got down on all fours to let them ride on his back. Aisha saw to her dismay that they were the real joy of his life, not her.

This late-life childlessness of Muhammad's is in sharp contrast to the four daughters he'd had with Khadija, as well as the son who had died in infancy. Since all the wives except Aisha were widows or divorcées and already had children by other husbands, infertility on their part is unlikely. Perhaps, then, despite the highly sexualized image of him in the West, the multiply married Muhammad was celibate. Or since anyone lucky enough to reach his fifties in the seventh century was physiologically far older than he would be today, age may have worked on him to lessen desire, or maybe simply sperm count. But Islamic theologians in centuries to come would posit another explanation. The absence of children with these later wives, they'd say, was the price of revelation. Since the Quran was the last and final word of God, there could be no more prophets after Muhammad, and thus no sons to inherit the prophetic gene. Essentially, they finessed the issue, as theologians often do, in this case by saying that a man so graced with revelation was beyond the simple everyday grace of offspring.

Whatever the reason for Aisha's childlessness, it rankled her. However much she teased and entertained Muhammad, she could never give him what Khadija had. She might be the favorite among the late-life wives, but no matter how hard she tried, she could never compete with the hallowed memory of the one she'd dared to call "that toothless old woman whom God has replaced with a better." And now, with this accusation of infidelity, she was especially vulnerable. Lacking the respect automatically accorded a mother, she could easily be cast off.

Resolution of what would be known as "the affair of the necklace" could come only by grace of a higher authority, and so it did. Even as Aisha swore her faithfulness to him yet again, Muhammad went into the trance-like state of revelation. "When he recovered, he sat up and drops of water fell from him like rain on a winter day," she would remember. "He began to wipe the sweat from his brow, and said, 'Good news, Aisha! God has sent down word of your innocence.'"

She had been slandered, said the Quranic voice. "The slanderers are a small group among you, and shall be punished. But why, when you heard it, did believing men and women not think the best and say, 'This is a manifest lie'? Why did you think nothing of repeating what others with no knowledge had said, thinking it a light matter when in the eyes of God it was a serious one?

Why did you not say, 'This is a monstrous slander'? God commands the faithful never to do such a thing again."

If the slanderers had been telling the truth, the voice added, they would have produced four witnesses to testify to the transgression; the absence of witnesses was itself evidence of their outrageous lie. Aisha's exoneration was thus all the more powerful in that it demanded not one person but four to gainsay her. For a wronged woman, there could have been no better outcome. Her honor was divinely vindicated, and those who had spread the rumors about her were flogged. But if it had all turned out well for her, it would not turn out well for other women.

In the long term, the verses exonerating Aisha would be interpreted in a very different way by conservative Islamic clerics, and used to do the opposite of what had originally been intended: not to vindicate a woman but to blame her. Conflating adultery with rape, they'd argue that any such charge could be valid only if the woman could do the virtually impossible and produce four witnesses. Unless she could do so, a ghastly catch-22 came into effect: the accused rapist was to be declared blameless and the accuser punished not only for slander but for adultery, since by charging rape she had herself testified to illicit sexual relations. Aisha's exoneration was thus destined to become the basis for the humiliation, silencing, and killing of countless women after her.

Even Aisha would not enjoy her triumph for long. With the exception of Khadija, she had so far managed to keep her jealousy of Muhammad's other wives in check. Omar's daughter Hafsa was known more for her mind than her looks (by some accounts she was to play a considerable role in determining the written form of the Quran), while both Sawda and Umm Salama, the woman who had emigrated to Medina alone with her infant son and who had become Muhammad's fourth wife after being widowed at Uhud, were hefty middle-aged matrons. But now Muhammad took a fifth wife: Juwayriya, one of the captives from the battle with the Mustaliq.

"By God, I had hardly laid eyes on her before I detested her," Aisha swore, testifying to the other's beauty. "I knew Muhammad would see her as I did." But then politics was never Aisha's strongest suit. Muhammad had married Juwayriya not for her beauty but in an overture to her conquered tribe. It was a gesture of alliance, a declaration that enmity between them was a thing of the past, and if it was not the one the Mustaliq might have chosen, it was certainly one they now willingly accepted. Aisha might think in terms of passion, but Muhammad's considerations were far more diplomatic. Until, that is, he married yet again.

This time there seemed no doubt that it was out of desire. It could even be seen as reassuringly human that a man in his midfifties could be so carried away with it. But once more the story is a strange one, as though designed to emphasize Muhammad's sexual virility despite the lack of children. He had apparently gone to visit his adopted son Zayd, but found only Zayd's wife Zaynab at home. Expecting her husband and not Muhammad, she was in "a state of disarray," as ibn-Ishaq tactfully puts it. Flustered by the sight, Muhammad rushed away murmuring, "Praise be to God who affects men's hearts!" When Zayd heard about this, he took it as a sign of Muhammad's desire, and in a fit of filial devotion—or possibly, by some accounts, because it hadn't been the best of marriages in the first place—he divorced Zaynab so that Muhammad could marry her instead.

This might have made sense if marriage between a father and

his son's divorced wife was not considered incestuous and thus taboo, even if, like Zayd, the son was adopted. But whatever the real story, it would not be a repeat of the affair of the necklace. This time, Quranic revelation intervened immediately to nip scandal in the bud. The problem was resolved by reasserting the taboo on a father marrying a son's former wife but with careful new wording: the ban now applied to "the wives of your sons who sprang from your loins"—to birth sons, that is, not adopted ones. And since Muhammad had no surviving sons who had sprung from his loins, the revelation took the opportunity to expand further on his paternal status. "Muhammad is not the father of any of you men," it said. "He is God's messenger and the seal of the prophets."

In the face of divine authority, the tart-tongued Aisha had no choice but to accept the marriage to Zaynab, though she made her feelings known nonetheless. "Truly, God makes haste to do your bidding," she told Muhammad, apparently unaware that in light of her own recent exoneration by Quranic fiat, this might be considered a tad ungracious.

All too aware of the tensions between his wives, Muhammad rotated his nights in strict sequence between them. He had no room of his own, instead moving from one wife's room to the next. In keeping with his insistence on simplicity, these rooms were really no more than palm-roofed lean-tos built in a row against the eastern wall of the mosque compound, each with a curtained doorway opening onto the courtyard, and with little furnishing other than a raised stone bench at the back where bedding was spread out at night and rolled up in the morning. The believers kept close tabs on how much time Muhammad spent with which wife, whose honeyed drink he seemed to like best, what mood he was in after spending the night with whom. There could hardly be a more public private life, one far more conducive to stress than to the licentiousness imagined with such envious censoriousness by many Victorian-era European scholars.

Another Quranic revelation from this time seems to reflect the stress created by these multiple marital arrangements. It began by granting Muhammad special dispensation as the leader of the *umma* to marry as many times as he wished. "This privilege is yours alone," it said, "given to no other believer." In principle, it went on, all other male believers could follow traditional practice and take up to four wives. But only in principle. Far from encouraging polygamy, the revelation went on to openly discourage it. Four wives were permitted only so long as each had equal status. But that, said the Quran, was hardly likely. Muhammad was to instruct his followers that "you will never be able to deal equitably between many wives, no matter how hard you try, so if you fear you cannot treat them equally, then marry only one."

For him, that "only one" would always be Khadija. It had been eight years since her death, but as the demands of leadership increased, he seems to have yearned all the more for the monogamy he'd once had. By now his marital situation was beginning to require as much intricate diplomacy as his political one. Far from being a source of warmth and support, it only added to the increasing stress on him as war with Mecca threatened once again, leading to what was destined to become the most controversial decision of his life.

Seventeen

As any reasonably astute political observer can testify, political leaders under pressure domestically can always bolster their popularity with an aggressive foreign policy. It's a strategy that's been played out throughout history, and Muhammad now made good use of it. Even as he continued to weaken opposition inside Medina, he increased the harassment of the Meccan trade caravans, forcing the Quraysh to abandon their usual north–south route for the long and expensive detour through the barren steppelands of the Najd and up through southern Iraq. Even then they were vulnerable. One raid led by the newly divorced Zayd, Muhammad's adopted son, struck deep into the Najd, capturing a whole caravan as its merchants and guards fled for their lives.

The poet Hassan ibn-Thabit celebrated the event, taunting the Meccans with their loss of trade. "Say farewell to the streams of Damascus," he gloated, "for the road is barred by battle." He was kept far busier than any poet laureate today, not least because he also had to glorify the ongoing assassinations of Muhammad's critics, many of whom were rival poets. This could present something of a challenge. One band of believers infiltrated the northern oasis of Khaybar and managed to kill their victim as he slept, only to create a ruckus when one of the more short-sighted among them missed his footing and fell down a flight of stone steps, thus rousing the whole neighborhood. The attackers were forced to take refuge in a drainage ditch, stinking and shivering for hours until they could make good their escape—not exactly the heroic figures lauded by ibn-Thabit as "traveling by night with nimble swords, bold as lions in a jungle lair, setting at naught every calamity."

Such exploits, especially in their hyped-up versions, may have been good for the depleted morale of the believers after the near rout at Uhud, but they only helped solidify opposition to Muhammad. The Meccan leader abu-Sufyan now formed a coalition army in which his most prominent allies were the Ghatafan Beduin from the Najd and the Jewish tribes of Khaybar, where the expelled Nadir were itching to reclaim the lands and property confiscated after their expulsion from Medina. Early in the year 627, abu-Sufyan gave the order to converge on Medina, and this time he had no intention of stopping on the outskirts. The aim was invasion, and a forced end to Muhammad's rising power.

But with thousands of armed men moving through the desert, the grapevine buzzed, and Muhammad had ample time to prepare. First he ordered the early spring crops in the fields around Medina to be harvested, thus depriving the approaching enemy of fodder for their horses and camels. Then he set about digging in. The rough lava fields to the west, south, and east of the oasis were impassable for horses, but the main approach route from the north was the kind of open ground that all but invited a mass charge by abu-Sufyan's powerful cavalry. To thwart this possibility, everyone in the oasis, women and children as well as men, set to work with shovels, digging a dry moat studded with sharply pointed stakes to impale the horse of any rider attempting the leap across. With ten people assigned to dig every sixty feet, the work took six days. By the time it was done, the moat stretched across the whole of the northern entrance to Medina, and the excavated stones and dirt had been heaped into a high defensive berm behind it.

It was the last thing abu-Sufyan's allied armies had expected. Just the idea of a moat—a ditch, as they sneeringly called it—was "dishonorable" and "un-Arab," a shabby trick borrowed from Persia, where it should have stayed. Taunts flew along with arrows. What kind of timid warriors hid behind mounds of earth erected by women and children? "But for this ditch to which they clung, we would have wiped them out," one Meccan poet wrote. "Being afraid of us, they skulked behind it."

The taunts were intended to tempt Muhammad's men out into the open to prove their courage in face-to-face combat, and many would have obliged if he hadn't insisted they hold their positions behind the berm. He was proven right when a few enemy horsemen did try to leap the moat at its narrowest point, only to be thrown when their horses were impaled. For all the numbers ranged on either side of the moat, the Battle of the Trench, as it would be called, would result in only five casualties on abu-Sufyan's side, and three on Muhammad's.

Abu-Sufyan had no option but to settle in for a siege, though he could hardly have expected a successful outcome. To besiege a compact, walled city was one thing, but Medina was still basically a series of villages, each with its own small fortified stronghold. There was no way to seal it off completely. The besiegers had to make do with blocking the main access route and harassing the defenders with volleys of arrows. Still, that was enough to work on Medinan nerves. From behind the berm, they could see hundreds of campfires burning ominously by night, and by day they faced the constant menace of enemy archers taking potshots like rifle snipers. "Muhammad promised us the world," one clan leader was heard to grumble, "and now not one of us can feel safe going to the privy!"

This kind of disaffection with Muhammad was exactly what abu-Sufyan was aiming for, allowing him to seek out the soft spots in Muhammad's support and try to turn them to his advantage. Behind-the-scenes wheeling and dealing—enticements to switch sides, spies acting as double and even triple agents—was as much part of warfare in the seventh century as it is today. Night after night, emissaries slipped back and forth between the oasis and the besieging camps. In Medina, where the mere appearance of a stranger was remarkable even in peacetime, it was almost impossible to keep such overtures secret, but this itself was part of abu-Sufyan's strategy. With nerves frayed and suspicion heightened, the rumor mill worked overtime.

First it was said that Muhammad had secretly offered the Ghatafan Beduin a third of Medina's huge date harvest if they abandoned the Meccan-led alliance. Whether he did or not is beside the point; the rumor itself was enough to cause dissension. Not all the owners of that date crop were pleased with how freely their property had reportedly been offered for barter. Many felt that Muhammad had brought this siege on them by escalating his vendetta with Mecca, and saw no reason why they should have to pay for it, while the more bellicose believers argued loudly against what they saw as a dishonorable attempt to placate the Ghatafan.

Then word had it that abu-Sufyan was trying to entice both the so-called hypocrites and Medina's one remaining Jewish tribe, the Qureyz, into forming a second front inside Medina, promising his full support if they'd rise up against Muhammad. Someone swore that the leader of the expelled Nadir tribe had been seen entering the Qureyz stronghold, and that he'd been heard trying to "twist the camel's hump" by appealing to the Qureyz as fellow Jews to help right the wrong of expulsion.

Every such rumor reached Muhammad, of course, but he would prove himself as adept as abu-Sufyan at psychological warfare, turning the rumors around to his advantage. To this end he employed the services of Nuaym ibn-Masud, a Ghatafan clan leader who had secretly accepted *islam*. "My own tribesmen do not know of this," he told Muhammad, "so instruct me as you will." It must have seemed a heaven-sent opportunity, since Nuaym was perfectly placed to sow disinformation both among dissenting factions inside Medina and within the besieging armies. "Make sure they abandon each other," Muhammad instructed him, "for war is deception."

This canny piece of military wisdom is justifiably famous, but it is not usually attributed to Muhammad. "War is deception" first appears in the sixth-century BC Chinese classic *The Art of War* by Sun Tzu. And while the idea of Muhammad consciously quoting Sun Tzu is an intriguing one, the words were most probably placed in his mouth by ibn-Ishaq, since although Sun Tzu's work was certainly known in the cosmopolitan milieu of eighth-century Damascus, it's doubtful that it had reached the seventh-century oasis of Medina. Nevertheless, Muhammad clearly had an excellent grasp of the principle involved, as evidenced in the intricate triple cross he now orchestrated.

In a tale of the kind calculated to delight by demonstrating how cleverly an enemy can be outwitted, Nuaym went first to the

Qureyz. Assuring them that he was speaking in strictest confidence as a well-wisher, he warned them that any overtures abu-Sufyan had made were not to be trusted, since the Meccans were interested only in booty. Once they had that, Nuaym said, they'd return home, leaving the Qureyz at risk of Muhammad's revenge if they worked against him. Thus they'd be well advised to demand collateral from abu-Sufyan in the form of hostages, so as to ensure that he kept his word.

With the Qureyz thus well primed for suspicion, Nuaym went for the double cross and gained an audience with abu-Sufyan, informing him that the Qureyz had decided to demand Meccan hostages as collateral for their cooperation, but were in fact loyal to Muhammad. Any hostages abu-Sufyan gave them would only be handed over to the believers for execution, so he'd be wise to refuse the demand. Finally, Nuaym tripled the cross by going back to his own tribe, the Ghatafan, and telling them that the Qureyz would demand not Meccan but Ghatafan hostages, and that their ally abu-Sufyan was in on the deal.

As ibn-Ishaq tells it, everyone reacted exactly as planned. The Qureyz demanded hostages as collateral for their cooperation with abu-Sufyan, who instantly saw this as proof of their allegiance to Muhammad. No second front materialized, and the Qureyz defended Medina along with everyone else. The Ghatafan Beduin, convinced that abu-Sufyan had crossed them, struck camp and returned to their tribal lands in bitter regret at the thought of losing all those dates that may or may not have been offered. Stymied by the moat and with his coalition in disarray, abu-Sufyan was soon ready to take advantage of any excuse to declare the siege a lost cause. At the end of the third week, the late-winter weather obliged.

Night temperatures in the high desert can plummet more than forty degrees Fahrenheit below daytime highs, the cold all the more bitter for being in such contrast to the heat of the day. But the last straw for abu-Sufyan was a biting gale-force wind that came howling down through the hills, overturning tents and kettles. "By God, our horses and camels are dying, no pot of ours stays put, no fire of ours keeps burning, no tent of ours holds together," he declared. "Saddle up, we are leaving."

Muhammad had again held off a huge Meccan army, yet his followers gave him little credit for it. They were left full of an intense frustration created by the enforced powerlessness of having been under siege. However successful the defensive strategy of the dry moat, it ran against the grain psychologically. That enemy accusation of having acted in an "un-Arab" way by avoiding battle rather than rushing into it cut deep into their sense of honor. Even for a poet as inventive as ibn-Thabit, it was hard to create the required heroic narrative out of women and children digging a trench.

No leader can afford to alienate his core following. Muhammad needed to rouse the believers with a definitive call to action, and he lost no time issuing it. At noon prayers that Friday, just five hours after the Meccans and their remaining allies had decamped, he declared a new enemy: Medina's last remaining Jewish tribe. The angel Gabriel had appeared to him, he said, and instructed him to "strike terror into the hearts of the Qureyz" in punishment for having considered collaboration with the Meccans.

Why the Qureyz? They were certainly not the only ones in Medina to have suspected that if not for Muhammad's aggressive policies, they would never have come under siege. But the relatively powerless Jewish tribe made for a better target than the "hypocrites," who had at least nominally accepted *islam* and were spread throughout the powerful Aws and Khazraj tribes. The rumors had done their work, and the Qureyz were vulnerable. They were the perfect target of opportunity, and would now provide an outlet for frustration—both Muhammad's own personal frustration with the Jewish refusal to acknowledge him as a prophet, and that of his followers after three weeks of forced inaction under siege. Where the believers had been the besieged, they would now become the besiegers. That same afternoon they surged out of the mosque, grabbed swords, spears, and bows, and surrounded the Qureyz village.

Inside their stronghold, the Qureyz leader called a council meeting and outlined three possible courses of action. The first was to abandon their Jewish identity, accept *islam*, and swear absolute obedience to Muhammad as the prophet. The second: to carry out a surprise counter-attack on the Sabbath, when Muhammad and his men least expected them to. The third was what might be called the Masada option: the men could kill the women and children to save them from capture and slavery, then either kill themselves or fight to the death. But the council was in denial. Far slower than their leader to realize the depths of their predicament, they argued that things had not come anywhere near such a point. They had long been affiliates of the Aws tribe, who would surely vouch for them. As people under threat tend to do, they clung to the established order of things, refusing to acknowledge that as the Nadir tribe had been told just a year earlier, "*islam* has canceled the old alliances."

They appealed to the Aws, pointing out that they had worked

side by side with everyone else to build the defensive moat. If they hadn't been among the fiercest defenders, that was only because the moat was at the northern entrance to the oasis, and their village was eight miles away, at the southern end. They had not worked against Muhammad, they swore; they had merely done what any independent tribe would do, and kept their options open. But the Aws remained silent, and as Muhammad would now make ruthlessly clear, independence was no longer an option.

The Qureyz held out for two weeks, then gave in to the inevitable and surrendered unconditionally. Yet even as they were led out of their stronghold in fetters, many still clung to hope. The worst most of them expected was what had happened to the two other Jewish tribes before them. Expulsion, after all, was one thing. Massacre, quite another.

The fetters were not a good sign. The Aws leaders knew what they meant, and finally tried to intervene for their former affiliates. At least Muhammad could spare the lives of the Qureyz, they argued, as he had done with the Qaynuqa and the Nadir. But Muhammad wanted more than to repeat the past; this time, it seems, he intended to set an example for the future. Not wanting to antagonize the Aws by seeming to ignore their request, however, he made as though to consult with them. "People of Aws," he countered, "will you be satisfied if one of your own passes judgment on the Qureyz?"

They declared themselves well satisfied, assuming that they had thus secured the lives of the fettered prisoners. But it was to be Muhammad, not they, who chose which of their tribe would decide the fate of the Qureyz, and there can be little doubt that he knew exactly what he was doing when he selected Saad ibn-Muad.

This militant hardliner had argued vehemently against the idea of offering the Ghatafan Beduin a single date to abandon the siege of Medina. "Give them our property?" he'd exclaimed. "No, the sword!" His eagerness for blood had been rewarded in kind. Severely wounded by an arrow while defending the trench, he was now dying, and he knew it. Since he was too weak to walk, he was carried to Muhammad on a leather litter, where he took what he presented as the high road of the mortally wounded: "The time has come for me, in the cause of God, not to care for any man's censure." Precisely because he was dying, that is, his decision was assumed to be without prejudice. But his prejudice had always been for the sword, and it was no different now as he passed judgment on the Qureyz: "The men shall be killed, the property divided, the women and children made captives."

Some scholars suspect that the early Islamic historians created this role for Saad in order to absolve Muhammad from responsibility for the massacre. It establishes plausible deniability, since it could then be argued that this was not Muhammad's decision but Saad's, and that Muhammad had no choice but to honor the word of the dying man. But the argument itself reveals a painful awareness that this was something that needed justifying, and so was implicitly not justifiable. It certainly seems unlikely that Muhammad would leave such a drastic decision to someone else, let alone to a man who was not one of his senior advisers. And even if the decision was not made directly by him, it was clearly made at the very least with his consent. Indeed, far from overruling it, Muhammad personally oversaw the executions. Trenches were dug alongside Medina's main marketplace, and when that was done, all the Qureyz men—"all those on whose chins a razor had passed," as ibn-Ishaq puts it—were led out in small groups, made to kneel by the trenches, and beheaded.

This was not easy work. Beheading someone is far harder than conventional battle tales of the time might lead a reader to think. Whole teams of believers went to work in separate morning and afternoon shifts, resting from their labors in the heat of midday. It took three days until they could declare their job done and the trenches were filled in.

Some eyewitness accounts had it that four hundred bodies were buried in these trenches, others as many as nine hundred. Either way, the numbers alone were shocking. The total casualties at Badr and Uhud had come to no more than a few dozen, and that had been in the heat of battle; here, in the center of Medina, hundreds had been methodically executed. It was a demonstratively brutal act that would send shock waves around Arabia. And it had exactly the intended effect. It was now crystal clear to all that there would be no further tolerance of any form of dissent.

Everything the Qureyz had owned—houses, date orchards, personal property—was divided among the believers, with the usual fifth held back for the communal treasury. Most of the women and children were distributed as slaves, with some taken to the Najd and sold in return for horses and arms. But one woman, Rayhana, received very different treatment. Born into the Nadir tribe, she had married into the Qureyz, and this double affiliation may have been why Muhammad now singled her out, but not for punishment. Instead, he made Rayhana his seventh wife.

Since her husband and all her male relatives had been massacred before her eyes, one hardly imagines this was the most loving of unions, but that was not the point. The marriage made a statement: however ruthless Muhammad had proved himself capable of being with those who refused to acknowledge his authority, he would take pains to create new alliances any way he could. Once ruthlessness had been displayed, it was time to rebuild.

There is sometimes a very fine line, if not an invisible one, between reason and rationalization. Innumerable reasons have been given over the centuries for the massacre of the Qureyz. It has been argued that they collaborated with the Meccans, though there is no convincing evidence that they did. That this was standard operating procedure for the time and place, though it was not. That Muhammad did not order it himself, which is only technically true. That the Qureyz themselves expected nothing less, though most of them clearly did. That Muhammad was left with no choice, which ignores the established alternative of expulsion. That the high number of executions is exaggerated, which while quite possible is also impossible to demonstrate. Even that the massacre was justified by the Quran, despite the fact that the Quran demands an absolute end to hostilities the moment an enemy submits.

In fact some Muslim theologians argue that the massacre simply couldn't have happened the way ibn-Ishaq tells it, since it's inconsistent with Quranic values. A few have even gone so far as to argue that it's a deliberate distortion specifically intended to defame Islam and to make the Qureyz look like martyrs. Indeed some Jewish scholars have likened the Qureyz to the rebels of Masada choosing mass suicide over submission to the Romans, even though they specifically rejected that option. Meanwhile,

well-meaning Christian scholars have explained the fate of the
Qureyz by saying that modern Western standards of warfare
cannot be applied to seventh-century Arabia, thus betraying not
only the enduring power of Orientalist condescension but also a
strangely blind eye to the horrors of both medieval and twentieth-
century European history.

The one thing all such explanations have in common is an
almost desperate attempt to make the unpalatable somehow less
so. That vaunted hard-headed realist Machiavelli would define it
as "the question of cruelty used well or badly." But even the master
of realpolitik found himself dogged by the terms of his own question: "We can say that cruelty is used well, if it is permissible to
talk in this way of what is evil, when it is employed once and for
all, and one's safety depends on it, and then it is not persisted in
but is as far as possible turned to the good of one's subjects." That's
four conditional phrases in one sentence—Machiavelli astutely
hedging his bets. Clearly aware that this resolved nothing, he kept
returning to the question. "A ruler must want to have a reputation
for compassion rather than for cruelty," he wrote, "but he must
nonetheless be careful not to make bad use of compassion." Eventually his own logic led him to earn lasting disrepute by arguing
that cruelty can actually be more compassionate than compassion,
coming up with a line that has served as the rationale of repressive
dictators worldwide: "By making an example or two, the ruler will
prove more compassionate than those who, being too compassionate, allow disorders which lead to murder and rapine."

Seen in the light of today's ongoing Middle East conflict, the
massacre of the Qureyz in the year 627 seems to set a terrible
precedent. Since faith and politics are as inextricably intertwined
in today's Middle East as they were in the seventh century, the

arguments given for the massacre in the early Islamic histories are still invoked, alongside the Quran's evident anger at Medinan Jewish rejection of Muhammad's prophethood, to justify the ugly twin offspring of theopolitical extremism: Muslim anti-Semitism and Jewish Islamophobia. In the light of Muhammad's political situation at the time, however, a less emotional analysis may be more to the point. The massacre of the Qureyz was indeed a demonstration of ruthlessness, but they were, in a sense, collateral damage. The real audience for this demonstration was not them but anyone else in Medina who still harbored reservations about Muhammad's leadership. If there had been any doubt that he was dealing from a position of strength, he had now dispelled it.

The principle is both as familiar and as arguable today as it was in Muhammad's time. Only by demonstrating a hard line, the reasoning goes, can a leader establish the authority to make the concessions necessary for the long term. It's a solipsistic argument at best, since there's no knowing what would have happened if a softer approach had been taken. But for Muhammad, it seems to have worked. Having established his willingness to use extreme force, he had gained the leeway to pursue a more peaceful alternative as he looked to the future, and specifically to Mecca.

Eighteen

Perhaps no return in all of history has been as richly symbolic as Muhammad's to the city of his birth. Every exile dreams of return. Not merely going back, but being welcomed back. Being begged to come back, in fact, in a public righting of a great wrong. The place you return to will be the same—the landscape, the people, everything that constitutes the feeling of home—and yet transformed, and your return will itself be a sign of that transformation, a signal of hope for a new start, a better future. This is the vision that sustains you through the years of exile.

Yet for Muhammad there was no single triumphal moment such as the dream might seem to demand. No banners flying, no cheering throngs, no flowers being thrown at his feet and former enemies embracing him in tears of repentance and joy. Instead, his return was an incremental process, so skillfully managed that by the third and final stage it seemed more a matter of completion than of victory.

It began with an actual dream early in the year 628. In it, Muhammad stood in front of the Kaaba with its key in his right hand. His head was shaved pilgrim-style, and he was in *ihram*, the traditional pilgrim's garb consisting of nothing but two seamless pieces of homespun linen, one tied around his waist, the other draped over his shoulders. The moment he woke, he knew what he had to do. He had proven his strength by matching the Meccans three times in battle; now he would approach them in the vulnerability of near-nakedness. Where force of arms could not win the day, the dream said, disarming would.

There were two forms of pilgrimage, both of which would continue into Islam. The greater one, the *hajj*, took place in the twelfth and final month of the year, Dhu al-Hijja, "that of the pilgrimage." But there was also the lesser pilgrimage, the *umra*, or "homage," which could be made at any time of the year. To the dismay of the Meccans, this was what Muhammad now announced he would make.

The whole of the Hijaz buzzed with admiration for the unexpected daring of such a move. Everyone grasped instantly that with this announcement Muhammad was not only calling the Meccans' bluff, but doing it with an act of absolute sincerity. It seemed inevitable that they would try to stop him entering the city, yet how? As the self-declared guardians of the sanctuary, their whole reputation rested on guaranteeing the right of pilgrimage to all who wished. To turn away pilgrims was unthinkable; it would be a major dereliction of their public responsibility, placing in jeopardy their vaunted right to guardianship. And besides, exactly how could they turn Muhammad away? Any armed attack on half-naked pilgrims would be to shed the blood of those they were sworn to protect, defiling the whole idea of sanctuary. By simply declaring his intention to perform this basic act of piety, Muhammad had placed the Meccans in a double bind of their own making.

Seven hundred men made the ten-day journey with him,

THE FIRST MUSLIM · 273

traveling in conspicuously peaceful array. They carried no battle weapons like bows or swords, just the daggers that were as much part of a traveler's equipment as the ubiquitous goatskins full of water. At the head of the procession were seventy specially fatted camels, each one a perfect specimen adorned for sacrifice with the customary woven garlands and necklaces. The most resplendent of them was also the most recognizable: the magnificent silver-nose-ringed male that had once been the pride and joy of Muhammad's nemesis abu-Jahl, and had been chosen by Muhammad as his share of the booty after the Battle of Badr. The symbolism of his bringing it back to Mecca for sacrifice was unmistakable.

As he must have fully expected, the Meccans sent out a mounted squadron to bar the route into the city. But instead of taking one of the two obvious options—confronting them or turning back—Muhammad diverted. He led his followers overnight on "a rough and rugged path among canyons" where horses couldn't follow, and then down into lower ground at Hudaibiya, a few miles north of Mecca, where a single large acacia tree shaded a winter pool. They reached it before dawn and lit fires, knowing that the smoke would announce where they were. They had nothing to hide, after all. They were pilgrims, come in peace, not in enmity. At daybreak they hobbled their camels, laid aside their daggers, and began to wash and change into *ihram*. By the time the Meccan horsemen caught up with them, they were ready to set out for the city as tradition demanded, on foot.

There was nothing the cavalry squadron could do but block the path forward. Instead of battle cries, they'd been met with the pilgrim chant *Labbayka allah-umma labbayka*, "Here I am, oh God of all people, here I am." Instead of a declaration of war, it was a declaration of faith by a mass of men who were unarmed,

unresisting—and unmoving. They would stay right here, Muhammad declared, for however long they had to until the Meccans
allowed them to proceed into the city. All they wanted was to
complete the pilgrimage in peace. Yet the peacefulness was itself
the challenge.

The squadron commander sent riders back into the city to
ask how he should proceed, and abu-Sufyan called an emergency
meeting of the Meccan council. But they were effectively stymied:
damned if they let Muhammad in and damned if they didn't.
Their dilemma was made all the worse when their own Beduin
allies took Muhammad's side. "Not on these terms did we ally
ourselves with you," one chieftain told them. "That you should
turn away those who have come to do honor to the House of
God? Either leave Muhammad free to do what he came to do, or
we will leave you, taking every last one of our men."

Depending on your point of view, this had developed into the
equivalent of either a sit-in or a lockout. Something had to give,
and by now abu-Sufyan must have known that it would not be
Muhammad. The only way to break this impasse was through
negotiation, so over the next few days high-level envoys rode back
and forth between the city and Hudaibiya, some openly, others
less so as they tried to persuade one faction or another of Muhammad's followers to turn back.

Muhammad countered by calling for a renewed pledge of
allegiance from all those with him. One by one they came up to
him as he sat beneath the acacia tree, grasped his hand and held it
close, forearm against forearm, and solemnly renewed their oaths
of loyalty, swearing to obey Muhammad as the messenger of God.
The ceremony made a deep impression on one of the Meccan

envoys. "By God," he reported back, "if Muhammad coughs up a bit of phlegm and a speck of it falls on one of them, he rubs his face with it. If he gives them an order, they vie to be the first to carry out. If he performs ablutions, they almost fight over the water he used. If they speak in his presence, they lower their voices out of respect for him. What he proposes makes sense, and we should accept it."

So it seemed, but then they would be seen as capitulating to Muhammad, and that was out of the question. Both abu-Sufyan and Muhammad needed to save face, and each recognized the other's need. But while Muhammad certainly knew this all along, he could also see that many of his followers did not. That was why he'd called for the renewed vow of obedience under the acacia tree: he needed to be sure that whatever the outcome, his men would accept it. But even that assurance would now be severely tested.

On the face of it, the agreement he hammered out with the Meccan council seemed to concede the day. Known as the Truce of Hudaibiya, it stipulated that there was to be no armed confrontation between Mecca and Medina for the next ten years, and that all Medinan raids on Meccan caravans were to stop. In the meantime, any tribe wishing to ally themselves with either party was free to do so; if they had been allied with Mecca or with Muhammad before, they were now free to switch sides without penalty. But there was to be no *umra*, not this year. Muhammad and the believers were to turn back, so that nobody could say that he had forced Mecca into compliance. In return, Mecca would allow him to enter the city and make the *umra* in a year's time.

This was not what any of the seven hundred would-be pilgrims

276 · LESLEY HAZLETON

had anticipated, especially the emigrants among them. Where they'd been sure they were on the verge of a long-awaited return, they were now faced with what felt like dishonorable withdrawal. The subtleties of the agreement escaped them, especially the clause that freed the Beduin tribes from their former alliances and allowed them to choose between Mecca and Muhammad, thus recognizing Muhammad's authority as the head of an entity on a par with Mecca. Even his closest advisers were divided. Where abu-Bakr and Ali saw the long-term advantages, the warrior Omar saw only weakness. They had come all this way just to be fobbed off with a promise of "next year"? Was this all you got for giving up the right to wage war? Omar's was the most strenuous voice raised in objection, but far from the only one. As ibn-Ishaq would report, "When they saw what they saw—the truce, the retreat, and the obligations Muhammad had taken on himself— they felt so grieved that they were close to despair."

If Muhammad himself was disappointed, he showed no sign of it. There was no telling if he had accepted the agreement in pilgrim-like modesty and humility, or if he knew he had gotten exactly what he wanted and perhaps even more. For now, he presented it as a test of his followers' faith. "Be patient and control yourselves," he told them, "for God will provide relief. We have given and have been given a promise in the name of God. We cannot deal falsely and go back on our word."

He could see that they needed more, however. They had come so far, in such good faith and with such high expectations; it was asking too much to expect them to simply turn round and go home, trailing seventy sacrificial camels behind them. Instead, they would do what they had come to do. If they couldn't perform the pilgrimage in Mecca itself, they would do so right here at Hudaibiya. He stood and gave the order: "Arise, sacrifice, and shave your heads."

But nobody moved. Surely they'd misheard. How could they perform the rituals anywhere but at the sanctuary of the Kaaba? What kind of makeshift pilgrimage was this? Even when Muhammad gave the order a second time, and then a third, they sat in stunned silence.

If anger flared in him at this flagrant breaking of the vows of obedience they'd so recently made, he didn't let it show. If he gave way for a moment to despair, there was no outward sign of it. Instead, Muhammad held all eyes on him as he picked up a dagger and made for the silver-nose-ringed camel that had once been abu-Jahl's. Everyone stared open-mouthed as he recited out loud the plea to God to accept this sacrifice, then pushed the animal's head back to bare its jugular vein, slashed with the dagger, and cut its throat.

Their paralysis broke as the blood gushed out onto the sand, and cries of praise went up throughout the encampment. Muhammad called for an aide to come cut off his long braids and shave his head in the sign that his pilgrimage had been made, and hundreds of men rushed to emulate him. One of them would later stoutly maintain that once they had all been shaven, the mound of tresses and braids was lifted into the air on a sudden breeze and carried the nine miles to the Kaaba in a sign that their sacrifice had been accepted by God.

In time, the truce of Hudaibiya would come to be seen as a strategic masterstroke on Muhammad's part. Ibn-Ishaq would write that "no victory greater than this one had been won previously in Islam. There had only been fighting before, but when the truce took place and war laid down its burdens and all the people felt safe with each other, they met with each other in conversation and debate, and all who possessed understanding and were told about *islam* accepted it." Both Beduin and Meccans were exquisitely attuned to the shift in the balance of power, and many now openly pledged their support for Muhammad. And in case some of the emigrants who'd followed him to Hudaibiya still doubted his judgment in accepting the truce, a Quranic revelation on the way back to Medina effectively silenced them. "God was well pleased with the faithful when they swore allegiance to you under the tree," the voice told Muhammad. "He knew what was in their hearts, and sent down tranquillity among them . . . He has held back the hands of people hostile to you as a sign to the faithful. There are many more gains to come."

If war was deception, so too, in a way, was peace. By disarming his own men, Muhammad had effectively disarmed the Meccans, forcing them into a classic zero-sum game in which compromise was the only possible solution, even as any compromise was to his advantage. Eleven centuries before Clausewitz's famous dictum that war was the continuation of politics by other means, Muhammad had demonstrated quite the reverse. What war could not achieve, politics would. Unarmed confrontation had not only forced Mecca to accommodate him; it had also served as a very public demonstration to all of Arabia that he and his followers were more loyal to "the traditions of the fathers" than the Meccans themselves.

Neither Gandhi nor Machiavelli could have done better. Muhammad had reversed the terms of engagement, turning apparent weakness into strength. He had proved himself as effective unarmed as armed, and used the language of peace as forcefully as that of war. In fact it was precisely this dual aspect of him that would so confound his critics and his followers alike. Whether in the seventh century or the twenty-first, he would frustrate the simplistic terms of those trying to pigeonhole him as either a "prophet of peace" or a "prophet of war." This was not a matter of either/or. A complex man carving a huge profile in history, his vision went beyond seemingly irreconcilable opposites. He had allowed himself to be turned away from Mecca in the full knowledge that he had in fact completed the first stage of his return.

With the Meccan truce in place, Muhammad set about securing what he now considered his hinterland to the north. Just a month after returning to Medina, he headed an expedition of sixteen hundred men against Khaybar, the richest of the oases of the northern Hijaz. Its vast date-palm plantations were divided among seven Jewish tribes, each one with its own fortified stronghold. When abu-Sufyan had led a massive army against Medina, with its similar system of strongholds, he had laid siege to it and failed. Now Muhammad would give practically a textbook illustration of how it should be done.

First he secured the neutrality of Khaybar's Beduin allies, the Ghatafan: the dates they'd forfeited at the siege of Medina would now be theirs in reward for not intervening. Then, instead of trying to lay siege to the whole of Khaybar, he dealt with the strongholds methodically. Starting with the weakest, he forced their surrender one by one—a process made all the easier by offering terms that were graciously munificent compared with those the

Medinan Jews had received. Having established how severe he could be, he had no need to resort to such drastic measures again. Considering what they might have faced, the Khaybar tribes willingly agreed: they accepted Muhammad's political authority and his protection, pledged their support, and surrendered half their annual income in taxes to Medina. Once again the deal was sealed with marriage. Safiya, a beautiful seventeen-year-old whose father was the leading chief of Khaybar, became not only Muhammad's eighth wife, but his second Jewish one.

With Khaybar secured, he marched on to the smaller Jewish-dominated oasis of Tayma, halfway between Medina and the ancient necropolis city of Petra in what is now southern Jordan. The tribes there offered no resistance, and in return received more generous terms than those granted at Khaybar. With the major settled areas of the northern Hijaz now solidly in line behind him, it was only a matter of time until all the Beduin tribes in the region accepted Muhammad's authority. And, to the south, Mecca. He was ready for the second stage of his return.

In February 629, he set out with two thousand followers on the promised *umra*, which was to go down in the history books as the Lesser Pilgrimage of Fulfillment. He led the way mounted on Qaswa, the slit-eared camel he had ridden into Medina seven years before and given free rein until she knelt at the spot where the mosque would be built. The creature that had carried him into exile would now carry him back to Mecca.

Abu-Sufyan kept the word he had given the previous year. As agreed at Hudaibiya, the Quraysh withdrew from the Kaaba precinct and gave free access to Muhammad and his followers. The dream of return that had haunted him day and night for years had come true, and he set foot on his home soil again.

Yet instead of the fulsome account one might expect, the early Islamic historians would treat the event with extraordinary brevity. The usually loquacious ibn-Ishaq devotes a single page to it where one would have expected at least a dozen. He speeds through the details as Muhammad rides to the Kaaba, touches the Black Stone with his staff, then dismounts to circumambulate the sanctuary before making his sacrifice and having his head shaved. There is a distinct sense of anti-climax. Or rather, preclimax. It's as though this pilgrimage, done only with the grudging acquiescence of the Quraysh, was not quite the real thing. If the Quraysh council kept their word and tolerated Muhammad's entry with tight-lipped resignation, they certainly did not welcome him. The real homecoming was yet to happen.

And Muhammad himself? Did he feel resentful eyes boring into him as he rode through the familiar alleys? Was he aware that many Meccans still wished him nothing but ill even as he performed the hallowed rites of pilgrimage? Or was all this rendered null and void by the sheer elation of once more binding himself to his birthplace with those seven orbits of the Kaaba, by the confirmation on his body of what he had known deep inside all along: that he would return, no matter the odds? All we know for sure is that he stayed the full three days allotted him, and that the evident sincerity of his pilgrimage brought many more Meccans over to his side—if not openly, at least by implication.

Muhammad's uncle Abbas, for instance, a leading Meccan banker who had been careful to keep his distance from his nephew over the past seven years, presided over the marriage of his sister-in-law Maymuna to Muhammad on the third day of the *umra*, thus publicly indicating that even if he had not openly accepted *islam*, he was moving closer to it. He was far from the

282 · LESLEY HAZLETON

only one to sense which way the wind was blowing. Maymuna was the aunt of one of Mecca's top military commanders, Khalid, and when Muhammad and his followers departed at the end of the third day, Khalid and another senior commander, Amr, joined them. Both men were greeted with open arms in Medina, welcomed as prodigal sons despite the fact that Khalid had led the Meccan cavalry against Muhammad at Uhud, and was thus responsible for the deaths of several believers. That was now a thing of the past, Muhammad assured him, telling him that his acceptance of *islam* had "erased all debts." Indeed, Khalid was to become such a renowned Muslim commander that he would earn the sobriquet "the sword of God."

Most important of all, though, was one other very public figure with whom Muhammad spoke in those three days in Mecca. They must have met discreetly, given the atmosphere of tension around Muhammad's presence in the city, but meet they certainly did, because shortly after his return to Medina, Muhammad married his ninth wife, the widowed Umm Habiba, who was the daughter of none other than the leader of the Meccan council, abu-Sufyan. She had defied her father by accepting *islam* early on, but the time for defiance was long past. This was about rapprochement. However quietly given, abu-Sufyan's consent to his daughter's marriage now bound him to Muhammad. Between them, father-in-law and son-in-law were to figure out the terms of the third and final stage of Muhammad's return to Mecca.

Just six months later, the Hudaibiya truce was challenged when a long-running feud between two Beduin tribes broke out in renewed violence, encouraged by hardliners on the Meccan council who were looking for any excuse to break the truce. Since one of the tribes was allied with Mecca and the other with Muhammad, the ultimate responsibility for their actions fell on their protectors, which would place Mecca and Medina at logger-heads again. Sure enough, after killing twenty of their opponents, the fighters allied with Mecca fled into the sanctuary city, demanding protection. In response, Muhammad's allies demanded that he force Mecca to hand over the men it was sheltering.

Muhammad would clearly be in the right if he took up arms in defense of his allies, so this time it was abu-Sufyan who made the ten-day journey between Mecca and Medina. The man who had laid siege to Medina just three years before was now obliged to beg for Muhammad's restraint, appealing to him on the grounds that only with Muhammad's cooperation could he contain the hardliners at home in Mecca.

Ibn-Ishaq and al-Tabari concede nothing about Muhammad's response. In fact they go out of their way to insist that Muhammad refused to answer abu-Sufyan at all. Yet this seems not merely impolitic but highly unlikely. The two former enemies had come to respect each other, not only as in-laws but as men of integrity. Even in war, abu-Sufyan had acted honorably, apologizing for his wife Hind's mutilation of Hamza's body at Uhud. He had witnessed Muhammad's devotion during the *umra* and could see that his deportment was more in tune with the spirit and traditions of the sanctuary city than that of many Meccans. But above all, he was a realist. If some members of his council did not yet recognize that their days in power were numbered, abu-Sufyan certainly did. With commanders like Khalid and Amr now among Muhammad's top advisers, there was no longer any doubt that he could take Mecca by force if he decided to. All the

Meccan hardliners had achieved was to bring the reign of the Quraysh very close to an end.

The only question was when and how that end would come, and that is what abu-Sufyan and Muhammad quietly and secretly negotiated. In fact it is still the way most treaties are negotiated. The public meetings take place only after the basics have been privately agreed on in closed sessions far from prying eyes and gossiping tongues. This is where discretion is tested and trust slowly and painfully established. If you are politically wise, you meet publicly only with the negotiated assurance of a good outcome, and this assurance was what abu-Sufyan and Muhammad now hammered out. Basically, they wrote the script for the surrender of Mecca.

So far as anyone else was concerned, the end came abruptly. The moment abu-Sufyan returned to Mecca, Muhammad began to mobilize. He summoned contingents from all his Beduin allies and on January 1, 630, marched south. By the time his army set up camp one day's ride from Mecca, its numbers had been swelled to ten thousand by those fearful of eventual reprisal or eager to be on the right side of history. Or perhaps both.

What happened next can only have been agreed on beforehand. Abu-Sufyan came out of Mecca and rode into the Medinan encampment on a distinctive white horse that belonged to Muhammad, a sign that he was under Muhammad's protection. Not even the most hot-headed believer would dare touch a hair on the head of anyone riding this animal. This was a pre-arranged rendezvous between Muhammad and abu-Sufyan, designed to be part of the public record. And this time their words were recorded.

The exchange between them, far from being antagonistic, seems more like banter: ruefully good-natured on abu-Sufyan's part and almost teasing on Muhammad's. "Alas, abu-Sufyan," he said, "hasn't the time come for you to know that there is no god but God?"

"May my father and my mother be your ransom," abu-Sufyan replied, "you are both forbearing and generous. If there were another god along with God, I think he would have availed me somewhat before now."

It's not hard to imagine Muhammad smiling at this, at least to himself, before pressing his advantage: "Hasn't the time come for you to know that I am the messenger of God?"

"I have indeed been thinking about that," said abu-Sufyan. And referring to Muhammad in the formal third person, he added: "He who with God overcame me, was he whom I had driven away with all my might." At which Muhammad jabbed him playfully in the chest and said, "Indeed you did!"

Then and there, the leader of Mecca formally accepted *islam* by reciting the *shahada*: "I testify that there is no god but God and Muhammad is his messenger." He placed himself and his city under Muhammad's protection, and the pledge was returned as Muhammad swore to ensure safety of life and property for all who did not resist when he and his forces entered. Mecca had formally surrendered.

Abu-Sufyan was given safe conduct back into the city, where he went straight to the Kaaba precinct to announce the terms of the surrender. "People of Quraysh, Muhammad has come upon you with forces you cannot resist," he proclaimed. "Anyone who enters my house will be safe, as will anyone who enters the Kaaba precinct, and anyone who stays at home and bolts his door and withholds his hand from action against Muhammad."

But not even all those closest to him could accept this, least of all Hind. Living up to her fierce reputation as "the liver-eater" of Uhud, she strode up, grabbed her husband's beard in public humiliation, and accused him of cowardice. "Kill that fat greasy bladder of lard," she screamed at him. "A fine leader he is for this people!" Abu-Sufyan was reduced to fighting her off as he appealed again to all of Mecca: "Woe unto you, Quraysh. Do not let her lead you astray, for you cannot resist what will come."

The majority of Mecca was nothing if not realistic. For the most part, those who didn't actively welcome the surrender to Muhammad at least resigned themselves to the inevitable. But there were still hardliners determined to resist no matter what, and in Muhammad's encampment his followers were well aware of this. They pelted him with questions. What if they entered Mecca only to be attacked despite abu-Sufyan's assurance of surrender? If they were met with violence, what were they to do? Could they respond in kind despite the ban on fighting in the sanctuary precinct? But then what if they actually killed someone on sacred ground? Would they be damned to be "companions of the fire," consigned to hell?

The answer came in a new Quranic revelation. Yes, it said, they were permitted to use violence on sacred ground, but only as a last resort. Only, that is, if enemy fighters tried to stop them from reaching the Kaaba, and only if they were attacked first. They were not to initiate any violence. They were to give the Meccans every opportunity to surrender peacefully, and there was to be absolutely no looting or any other form of damage to property:

no booty, no spoils of war. They were entering a holy city, and they were to behave accordingly.

On the morning of the following day, January 11, 630, Muhammad made Mecca his own. He divided his army into four columns, each one entering the city from a different direction. Only the southern column, headed by Khalid, met with resistance when one of his horsemen was killed; twelve of the attackers were quickly dispatched, and the others fled. The *fatah*—literally the "opening" of Mecca, a word that would only later come to mean conquest or victory—had been achieved.

Muhammad's followers thronged the alleys as he rode on in. They cheered and chanted "Praise be to God" as he entered the Kaaba precinct, and the Meccans who had taken refuge there joined in, though whether out of hope or fear was still unclear. No longer the enemy, or even the barely tolerated visitor, he was now the ruler. The man who had grown up on the margins of Meccan society had become its center, the outsider transformed into the ultimate insider. When he struck the Black Stone set into the corner of the Kaaba and shouted *"Allahu akbar!"*—"God is great!"—the cry was taken up throughout the city. It reverberated through the alleys and echoed off the mountains all around, as though to say that this was not a matter of Muhammad returning to Mecca but of Mecca returning to itself. And indeed this was his message as he mounted the steps leading to the door of the Kaaba and addressed the crowd.

"There is no god but God, he has no partner," he declared. "He has fulfilled his promise and helped his servant. He alone has put to flight those who banded together against his servant." This was to be a new beginning, the dawn of an age of enlightenment:

288 · LESLEY HAZLETON

"People of Quraysh, God has taken from you the haughtiness of *jahiliya*," the era of pre-Islamic ignorance. From this point on, the rule of privilege was over. In *islam*, all would be equal, and Mecca would no longer be the fiefdom of a small ruling elite: "Behold, every alleged claim of hereditary privilege, whether by blood or wealth, is hereby abolished. It is as dust under your feet." And then, looking down at the throng of upturned faces, he asked them directly: "People of Quraysh, what do you think I intend to do with you?"

It was a rhetorical question. He knew what they feared: reprisals, enslavement, confiscation of everything they owned. "Only good," came the answer from the crowd, "for you are a noble brother tribesman and the son of a noble brother tribesman." And if they had thought so little of his nobility before that they had driven him out of the tribe, now they not only welcomed him back into it as "one of us" but clamored to acclaim him both as their leader and as the messenger of God.

Muhammad stepped up to the moment. There would be no more bloodshed between them, he declared: "God made Mecca holy the day he created heaven and earth, and it is the holy of holies until the Day of Judgment. It is not lawful for anyone who submits to God and believes in the Day of Judgment to shed blood here. It was not lawful to anyone before me, and it will not be lawful to anyone after me."

There was to be a general amnesty. "Go," he said, "for you are now those whose bonds have been loosed; you are free." And the word he used, *al-tulaqa*, "the freed ones," was resonant with meaning. They were free not only of physical bonds—the shackles and ropes they could have been tied with—but free too of the bonds of the benighted past. This was not a conquest, he was saying, but a liberation: a revolution peacefully achieved, and peacefully accepted.

And with that, almost two years to the day after he'd first dreamed it, he took the key to the Kaaba in his right hand, turned it in the lock, and entered.

Part Three

LEADER

Nineteen

What does one dream of when the dream has been achieved? For the past eight years, Mecca had been the lodestone of Muhammad's life, the focus of prayer, of battle, of every thought about the future. And now it was his. After so many years of resistance and oppression, the exile's dream had come true: not merely return, but return to huge acclaim. Yet Muhammad reveled neither in his victory nor in the ease of it.

The early historians give no sense of elation or exhilaration. Instead there's a feeling almost of letdown, and one can see why. When a man of sixty suddenly achieves the thing he most hoped for, there is none of the triumphalism one might expect in some-one younger. The enormity of his achievement is shadowed by a certain sadness as he reflects not only on how much had to be gone through in order to arrive at this point, but on how much will still be required in the future. As he entered the Kaaba, Muhammad must have sensed the full weight of revolution achieved, and known that to realize a dream was only to wake up to a more complex reality.

Perhaps the closest we can come to how he felt that day is in the recollections of another man who had succeeded against all odds. In 1989, the playwright and former dissident leader Václav Havel became Czechoslovakia's president after the collapse of the Communist regime, and oversaw the first free elections in decades. "It had been a time of excitement, swift decisions, and countless improvisations," he recalled, "an utterly thrilling, even adventurous time . . . It was, in a way, a fairy tale. There were so many things that could have gone wrong. We were traveling on totally unknown terrain. And none of us had any reason to believe that it wouldn't collapse under our feet. But it didn't. And now the time had come when there was indeed reason to rejoice. The revolution, with all its perils, was behind us, and the prospect of building a democratic state, in peace, lay before us. Could there be a happier moment in the life of a land that had suffered so long under totalitarianism?

"And yet," Havel continued, "precisely as that splendid historical moment dawned, a peculiar thing happened to me . . . I was in some sort of profoundly subdued state. I felt strangely paralyzed, empty inside. The pressure of exhilarating events, which until then had aroused in me a surprising level of energy, abruptly vanished, and I found myself feeling exhausted, almost irrelevant. The poetry was over and the prose was beginning. It was only then that we realized how challenging, and in many ways unrewarding, was the work that lay ahead of us, how heavy a burden we had shouldered. Only now could we appreciate the weight of the destiny we had chosen."

This is what one senses in Muhammad: instead of elation, a sudden aching feeling of exhaustion. He was no longer a rebel, no longer a visionary radical, but a man who had achieved the seemingly impossible in just two decades. Yet how much energy can one man have? The toll of the past twenty years was visible in the deep lines creasing his eyes and cheeks, his forehead furrowed against the headaches that had become more and more intense since his injury at Uhud. Now, as he entered the Kaaba, he had to have known that the demands of running an incipient state would only increase this toll, and sensed that from this moment on, his body would begin to fail him.

At all events, he conducted himself with extraordinary restraint. While the popularly accepted image has him demonstratively smashing the idols said to be inside the Kaaba, there is no historical record of this, not least because the sanctuary was almost certainly empty of all physical representation. Neither ibn-Ishaq nor al-Tabari gives any details of what happened when he turned that key and entered, and perhaps that's as it should be. It was a private moment, unrecorded, so that one can only imagine him closing the door behind him and welcoming the hush as the men's shouts of acclaim and the women's ululations of celebration were muffled by the thick stone walls and he was a man alone once more, whispering into the darkness, offering a quiet prayer of praise and thanksgiving. Though he did not yet know it, it was to be one of the last private moments he would ever be willingly allowed.

He emerged to declare the Kaaba formally rededicated to the one god, then gave the order to smash the totems in the precinct surrounding it, and rode to the nearby mound of Safa. There he sat for three days as the Meccans came out of their houses and lined up to swear allegiance to God and to Muhammad as his messenger. Among them, toward the end of the third day, was one elegantly dressed woman who had pulled her shawl over her face. She spoke only when her turn came to take the pledge, and then it was clear who she was, and why she had hidden her face. It was abu-Sufyan's wife Hind, the woman who had so horribly mutilated Hamza's corpse at Uhud.

A tense hush descended on the gathering as they waited to see how Muhammad would deal with her, and they hung on every word of the charged exchange between the two. "Forgive me for what is past," she begged the man she'd so publicly and recently called a bladder full of lard, "and God will forgive you."

"You shall not invent slanderous tales," Muhammad responded, taking his measure of her. She replied with another plea for forgiveness, or at least for forgetfulness. "By God," she said, "slander is disgraceful, but it is sometimes better to ignore it."

He tested her further: "You shall not disobey me in carrying out orders to do good." And now her answer was impatient if not downright impertinent: "We should not have sat all this time waiting to pledge allegiance if we wanted to disobey you in such things." But perhaps she sensed that whatever she said, short of outright hostility, Muhammad had no intention of exacting revenge on her.

The Quran insisted on forgiveness of former enemies once they pledged allegiance, and if Hind's pledge was clearly less than whole-hearted, he would accept it nonetheless, possibly respecting her forthrightness more than the most abject declaration of obedience. This was the opportunity to heal old wounds, and he knew all too well that healing takes time. The massacre of the Qureyz had already established that he was capable of ruthlessness when he deemed it necessary; he had no need to prove it again. On the contrary, to forgo revenge even when it seemed justified would create a sense of obligation and loyalty far more reliable than anything that could be obtained by force. Gracious-ness would be effective not least for being unexpected.

Moreover, Muhammad's public forgiveness of Hind would bind her husband abu-Sufyan all the more closely to him, and this was essential if his vision of unity was to be fulfilled. He did not see this as a conquest where winner takes all, but rather as a reuniting of what should never have been divided. What he envi-sioned was not the enforced subjection of the conquered but a new coalition of the willing, one in which old enmities were abol-ished and all who wanted were welcomed into the *umma* as equal partners. Accordingly, he overrode objections from Omar and other leading advisers, accepting Hind's plea for forgiveness and then reaching across the aisle, as it were, to appoint leading Mec-cans to senior administrative and military positions. Among those favored was not only abu-Sufyan himself but also, strik-ingly, his son by Hind, Muawiya.

Knowingly or not, Muhammad was again creating the future leadership of Islam. Muawiya would become one of his scribes, and within a few years would rise to the powerful position of gov-ernor of Syria after that huge province fell to Muslim control. But his ascendance would not stop there. Just nineteen years after Muhammad's death, when Ali, by then the fourth caliph, was assassinated, Muawiya would assume control of the whole of the Muslim empire and found the Umayyad dynasty, based in Damascus. His mother would be long dead by then, but ever the aristocrat, Hind would doubtless have thought it fitting that her son and his descendants had assumed the caliphate.

If most other Meccans were not so favored, at least there would be no reprisals against them—or nearly none. The sole exceptions were twelve named individuals, among them four woman poets whose satires had been particularly galling, and one man who could conceivably have nothing but hatred for Muhammad: Ikrima ibn abu-Jahl, the son of his old nemesis "the father of ignorance." Muhammad reportedly ordered that these twelve were to be killed "even if they were to be found under the curtains of the Kaaba itself" unless they begged for forgiveness. Half of them did precisely that and accepted *islam*, none more notably or with more demonstrable effect than Ikrima, since Muhammad then appointed him to a senior administrative position in Mecca, turning the son of bitter enmity into an integral part of the new amity.

It was done, it seemed. The city that had expelled him was now formally his. Everything Mecca had rejected for so long had been accepted, and almost entirely in peace. And yet it wasn't done, of course. It never is. There is never a definite point at which it can be said, "There, finished!" Less than two weeks after he had entered Mecca in victory, Muhammad was forced to fight one more battle. Not against the Quraysh this time, but against their enemies.

To the Hawazin, the large confederation of nomadic tribes allied with the mountain city of Taif sixty miles to the southwest, Mecca's surrender only seemed to make the Quraysh still more powerful than before. Since Muhammad himself was Quraysh, they thought in traditional terms and assumed that he was the newly crowned Quraysh king. Taif was clearly next in line for conquest, and nobody there expected any good from that. Just ten years earlier, after abu-Talib's death, they had refused Muhammad's plea for protection. It seemed inevitable that now he'd want revenge.

Headed by Malik, a charismatic thirty-year-old chieftain, the Hawazin decided to force the issue. In a show of determination and confidence, thousands of warriors set out on the road to Mecca, accompanied by their women and children and even their livestock—by some accounts, forty thousand camels alone. Not all agreed that this was a wise move. One aged warrior, reduced by infirmity to riding in a howdah, objected that it merely placed everyone at risk, but he was quickly snubbed by the overly confident Malik. Within a few days the young chieftain would wish he had listened. He never even made it halfway to Mecca. Muhammad and a joint force of Meccans and Medinans met his army near the spring of Hunayn, and the ensuing battle was a rout. Half the Hawazin men were taken captive along with most of the women, children, and livestock, while Malik and his surviving men were forced to flee for refuge inside the walls of Taif, where they closed the gates and prepared for a siege.

The victory would be bittersweet. Among the prisoners, there was one elderly woman who kept insisting, to the amusement of her captors, that she was a relative of Muhammad's. This mere Beduin woman? It was nothing but a pathetic plea for mercy, they thought. But when she was hauled along with her clan in front of Muhammad, she appealed to him directly. "Oh messenger of God," she said, "I am Shayma, your foster sister, who used to look after you when you were a young child among us."

Could it be? Fifty-five years had passed since he had last laid eyes on her. He remembered now that her clan had been part of the Hawazin confederation, but could this frail, white-haired woman possibly have been that adolescent girl? "And where is the proof of that?" he demanded. For answer, she rolled up her sleeve to show her arm. "The scar I still bear here," she said, "from where you bit me that time when I was carrying you on my hip to join the herders at Wadi Sarar."

It was true. Here was the oldest daughter of his foster mother Halima—the girl in whose arms he'd wriggled and fought when all she was trying to do was keep him safe—reduced all these years later to begging him for mercy. Was this what warfare and victory brought? When would it end? Childhood memories crowded in on the newly acknowledged head of state, reminding him of the extraordinary distance he had traveled. Holding back tears, he stunned everyone by spreading out his cloak and inviting Shayma to come sit on it beside him. She could live with him in affection and honor, he said, or go back to her land with her family, taking her pick of the captured camels as compensation for all that had been lost. Beduin to the core, she opted for the latter.

The other Hawazin captives would have Shayma to thank for their lives and their freedom, though they would forfeit their thousands of camels and other livestock, which Muhammad now parceled out as bonuses. A hundred camels each went to leading Meccans like abu-Sufyan and his son Muawiya, fifty each to the heads of Beduin tribes allied with Mecca, and so on down the line of status for "all those whose hearts were to be won over." If there had been any doubt that allegiance to Muhammad was to the direct advantage of his former opponents, the sheer size and number of these bonuses dispelled it. Where they had expected to be subordinated, they now found themselves unexpectedly advantaged, and accepted Muhammad all the more willingly as a result.

Muhammad marched on to Taif, but quickly concluded that time and political momentum would deal with Malik better than a siege of the well-fortified city. With Mecca's surrender, Taifan

THE FIRST MUSLIM · 301

resistance was no longer a practical option. Sure enough, Malik would acknowledge this ten months later, when Taif formally accepted Muhammad's authority.

Malik had been correct in one thing, however: if Muhammad wanted, he could now have declared himself the king of Mecca—indeed of the whole of the Hijaz region. He had been acclaimed; he had received the pledges of allegiance; he was in a more powerful position than anyone in living memory. Yet having done all this, he did none of the things a conquered people might expect. He did not build a mosque in Mecca right by the Kaaba, nor did he build a palace and set up court. He did not even declare Mecca his new capital. In fact he did not move back there at all. Just two months after those four columns of men had marched with him into the city, most of them marched out again, and followed him the two hundred miles back to Medina.

It seems as though he must have struggled with this decision. If his heart lay with one city, his soul lay with the other, though it would be hard to say which was which. Mecca was the city of the Kaaba sanctuary, but Medina was the city that had given him sanctuary. While Mecca was his birthplace, Medina could be seen as the place of his rebirth. His vision had been born in one, but had come to fruition in the other. Surely there was no way to choose between them.

But Muhammad gave no indication that he was even tempted to stay in Mecca, let alone make it the new center of his administration. He had come home, and yet not home. It was as though now that Mecca was his, he was no longer of Mecca—as though by returning, he had freed himself of the need to return. Mecca would always be the center of pilgrimage, and he underscored this when he came back from Hunayn to make the *umra*, the lesser pilgrimage of homage. But then, having spent a total of just fifteen nights in the city, he left. He was to set foot there only once more.

Some of his Medinan followers had been galled at seeing those huge bonuses handed out to leading Meccans and not to them, but as Muhammad now pointed out, where the Meccans got camels, the Medinans would get him. "I mean to live and die among you," he had sworn to them eight years earlier, and as they prepared for the journey back to Medina, he reaffirmed that oath. "If you are disturbed because of the good things of this life by which I win a people over to *islam*, are you not satisfied that other men should take away flocks and herds while you take back with you the messenger of God?"

Though the Quranic word *fatah* would later come to mean "victory," Muhammad clearly did not consider it so. To him, it truly was the opening of Mecca, and this opening was both literal and figurative. Where closed doors separate people, cutting off those inside from those outside, open ones are an invitation, a means of bringing together inside and outside. By the same token with which Muhammad had closed the door on an old era, he had opened the door to a new one. He had united Mecca and Medina in a way that went far beyond physical location. It was no longer a matter of either/or; he had returned to one home, and would now return to the other.

There's no knowing if he sensed that the door had been opened to something much larger, and that this would be achieved not by him but by those closest to him. But then who

could have foreseen such a thing at the time? After all, Muhammad's was not the only return in that year 630. In fact in the great
scheme of things Middle Eastern at the time, his conquest of
Mecca can have been barely a blip on the proverbial radar.

As he returned to Medina at the end of March, what seemed
a far more significant event had just taken place seven hundred
miles to the north, where the Byzantine emperor Heraclius had
ceremoniously returned the relics of the "True Cross" to Jerusalem. To anyone aware of both events at the time, it would have
been self-evident which was the larger and more significant of the
two. Muhammad's achievements would have seemed merely a
pale reflection of those of Heraclius. Yet history would move with
remarkable speed to reverse that equation, making the Byzantine
emperor play a poor second string to Muhammad.

Their struggles over the past decade had developed with
remarkable synchronicity. In 620, when Muhammad had first
faced the prospect of being forced out of Mecca, Heraclius too
had been on the verge of defeat, with the Persians at the gates of
Constantinople. Jerusalem was already in Persian hands, and
now the Byzantine center of Christendom was under siege, ravaged by famine. Heraclius was forced to sue for peace under the
most humiliating terms, then to leave his own capital city in a
kind of self-imposed exile that would be nearly as long as Muhammad's from Mecca. But like Muhammad, Heraclius found
strength in exile, rebuilding his army to renew his challenge to
the Persians.

Just as Mecca and Medina had battled almost continuously
between 622 and 628, so had Byzantium and Persia. In 627, when
Muhammad held off abu-Sufyan's siege of Medina in the Battle
of the Trench, Heraclius won a surprise victory over the Persians

at Nineveh, in what is now northern Iraq. Three months later his army sacked the palace of Khosroe in the Persian capital of Ctesiphon, close to the future city of Baghdad, thus provoking Khosroe's assassination by his own son. At the same time as Muhammad and abu-Sufyan agreed to the Truce of Hudaibiya, the younger Khosroe sued for peace with Heraclius, but to no avail. The Byzantine emperor pursued his advantage, quickly ousting the Persians from Egypt, Syria, Palestine, and Anatolia, and making a triumphal reentry into Constantinople in August 629. As Muhammad performed the *umra* in Mecca, Heraclius played the pilgrim in Jerusalem, returning the True Cross to its rightful place.

There is no sign in the Byzantine records that Heraclius was even aware of what had happened far to the south in Arabia. But then why would he notice? For as long as anyone could remember, the Arabs had played at best a peripheral role in the big dramas of empire being played out to their north. In Byzantine eyes they were mere provincials, negligible in the great scheme of things. Nobody expected that to change, let alone with such remarkable speed.

But there is no doubt that Muhammad and his advisers were fully aware of what was happening. "The Byzantines have been defeated in a nearby land," one Quranic revelation had commented on the temporary Persian ascendance, "but they will reverse their defeat within a few years. God will give victory to whom he will." The news of Heraclius' entry into Jerusalem was confirmation of this prediction, and just nine years later there would be a new interpretation of "victory to whom he will" when Omar led a united Arab army into Jerusalem in one of the most peaceable conquests in that city's overly contested history, establishing Islam as the new power force in the Middle East.

To devout Muslims, the speed of the Arab conquests in the decade after Muhammad's death seems a manifestation of divine will. Even modern historians appear somewhat at a loss to explain it, falling back on hoary Orientalist theories like "a tribal imperative to conquest." In fact such cultural assumptions are not only questionable but unnecessary. Political analysis explains far more, because although Heraclius had forced the Persian Empire to the verge of collapse, the long military conflict had left his own realm in not much better shape. Despite the show of piety in Jerusalem, Byzantine control of the far-flung Christian empire was more tenuous than ever, riven by fierce factionalism rationalized as theological dispute. The two great empires had essentially fought each other to exhaustion, creating a vast vacuum of power in the Middle East.

Any such power vacuum begs to be filled, and for an Arabia newly united under the banner of Islam, the timing was perfect. If Arabia was all but *terra incognita* to the Byzantines and Persians, the reverse was palpably not so. Even before Muhammad was born, well-connected Meccan merchants had established roots in the lands and cities they traded with. They owned estates in Egypt, mansions in Damascus, farms in Palestine, date orchards in Iraq, and thus had a vested interest in these lands. The collapse of the existing political structure was practically an open invitation for a newly established power to enter and take over.

By the year 634, Arab forces would be at the gates of Damascus. In 636, they would decisively defeat Heraclius at Yarmuk, to the southeast of the Sea of Galilee. In 638, they would deal a similar blow to the Persians at Qadisiya, in southern Iraq. One year later, Omar would lead them into Jerusalem, and by the year 640, they would control both Egypt and Anatolia. Barely a century after Muhammad's death, the Muslim empire was to encompass nearly all of both its Persian and its Byzantine predecessors and far more, stretching from Spain in the west to the borders of India in the east, with its capital in the newly built city of Baghdad.

It may be tempting to imagine that as he stood in the Kaaba that day in January 630, Muhammad knew that this was the beginning of a moment in history just waiting to be seized, and that he foresaw how a previously ignored people would unite in his name and that of God to assert a new identity, sweeping out of the wings to become the lead players on the world stage. But as the Quranic voice had constantly reminded him, he was only human, and as his body reminded him, a tired human at that. If he sensed the magnitude of what he had put into motion, that was a matter of God's will so far as he was concerned, not his own. As he stood alone in the darkness of the sanctuary, the moment itself has to have been more than enough. That, and the hope, perhaps, that now he might find some rest. But there was to be none.

Twenty

E very moment of Muhammad's life would now be freighted
with meaning for those around him. Every gesture would
be closely observed, every word and movement scruti-
nized. Whatever he said or did, or was said to have said or
rumored to have done, had become a matter of intense public
interest. Try as he might to insist on simplicity and a lack of
ostentation, the equivalent of a royal court formed around him.
Scribes and poets celebrated him, economic and political advisers
vied for his ear, gatekeepers asserted control over the flood of
petitioners. Even among his closest confidants, intrigues and
resentments simmered as they jockeyed for access, eager to claim
proximity to the locus of power. And to his increasing dismay,
this was true even among his wives.

Not that he had ever been comfortable with his multiple late-
life marriages and the demands they made on his time. Careful as
he was to rotate his nights with each wife in turn, their small
rooms built in a row against the wall of the mosque compound
allowed next to no privacy. Even before the surrender of Mecca,
petitioners had crowded these rooms, begging one wife or another
to intercede with him, even shoving the wives aside in their eagerness for his attention. The "revelation of the curtain" two years

earlier had not done much to help. "If you are invited into the presence of the messenger," the Quranic voice had instructed, "enter, and when you have eaten, disperse. If you ask his wives for anything, speak to them from behind a curtain. This is more chaste for your hearts and theirs."

The curtain in question was just that: a piece of muslin draped over a section of each room, providing at least a modicum of privacy. It applied only to Muhammad's wives, and there is no historical indication that he ever intended it to be taken as an order for any woman to veil. The Quran would advocate modesty for both sexes, but it never specified veiling, which is in any case a misnomer. What would be called "the veil" was in fact a thin shawl, and when it was first adopted in Islam, decades after Muhammad's death, it was to a large degree a matter of status. Much as aristocratic women in ancient Assyria and Persia had worn it as a mark of distinction, so would the women of a rapidly rising Islamic aristocracy. Like an expensive manicure or a pair of Prada shoes today, it was a public indicator, a sign that these women were above any kind of hard work. They had servants, and so could allow themselves the luxury of flamboyantly impractical dress.

There is, of course, a bitter irony at work here, since the whole system of aristocracy by birth and wealth was exactly what Muhammad had opposed all his life. But the proto-democracy he had envisaged would devolve into a succession of ruling dynasties. Class distinctions grew, and with them—as had happened before in both Judaism and Christianity—a rapidly rising all-male clerical elite. These men became the gatekeepers of faith, elaborating the principles of *islam* into the institution of Islam, often by projecting their own conservatism onto the Quran itself. As they built the vast body of Sharia law, they'd attempt to enforce "the veil" on all women, eventually taking the idea so literally that in its most extreme form, the burqa, it would become more like a shroud. Certainly none of Muhammad's wives had any idea that a mere piece of muslin would develop into such a thing, least of all the outspoken Aisha. She might have accepted the shawl as a mark of distinction, but the veil as an attempt to force her into the background and to silence her? The young woman used to high visibility would never dream of being rendered invisible.

But for now, neither curtains nor shawls, let alone veils, could contain the tension among the wives. Marital time had become such a valuable commodity that it could even be traded, with one wife often agreeing to cede "her night" to another in return for a favor, and intense arguments as to who was the favorite. Within a few months of Muhammad's return from Mecca, dissension had built to such a pitch that he simply couldn't take it any longer. In effect, he declared a strike against his role as a multiple husband, and began sleeping alone in a small storeroom on the roof of the mosque. Word of this spread instantly, and along with it the rumor that he was about to divorce all nine of his wives.

The immediate cause of his exasperation was the wives' resentment of a slave girl called Mariya, said to have been sent as a gift from the Coptic Christian patriarch of Alexandria. Muhammad had taken her as a concubine and installed her in a house on the outskirts of Medina, out of sight of both mosque and wives. He began to spend more and more time there, apparently seeking refuge from the public eye. But no matter how discreet he tried to be, his fondness for Mariya was a matter of intense speculation, all the more so when the wives, in an unusual show of unity, publicly protested the amount of time he was spending with her.

Some accounts have it that Mariya had given birth to a son by Muhammad, who had named him Ibrahim, or Abraham. If this was true, it can only have added to the wives' resentment. The very idea that this slave girl had given him what none of them had done would have been intolerable. A son—a natural heir—was the one thing most painfully missing in Muhammad's life. A son's existence would place the wives' own standing in jeopardy, forcing them to play secondary roles to a mere concubine.

It seems strange, however, that while none of the late-life wives had a child by Muhammad, this girl named after the mother of Jesus reportedly did. The symbolic significance is clear. A son of Mary and Muhammad named after the man the Quran honored as the first *hanif*, the Bible's founding monotheist, would appeal to Christians throughout the Middle East. But in all likelihood this infant was born not in reality but in the fond imagination of a male-centered culture. Though the Quran repeatedly asserted that daughters were as valued as sons, Ibrahim's birth would serve as a kind of reassurance of Muhammad's virility. If so, however, it would be an unwittingly cruel one: like Khadija's one son so many years before, Ibrahim would apparently die in infancy, shortly after the conquest of Mecca.

Whether it was grief for Ibrahim that drove Muhammad to withdraw from his wives, or simply the need to escape the pressure of their insistence that he give up Mariya, his night-time retreat to the roof of the mosque created panic throughout Medina. By so demonstratively turning away from his wives, he risked placing the whole power structure of the new *umma* in jeopardy. Nearly all of his marriages were alliances, either with leading advisers like abu-Bakr and Omar, the fathers of Aisha and Hafsa, or with prominent former enemies like abu-Sufyan, the father of Umm Habiba. These were not men to insult by turning his back on their daughters. Not even the messenger of God could do that with impunity.

Aisha cried once more until she thought her liver would burst. Even the usually stolid Umm Salama was seen quietly weeping. For a soldier like Omar, Hafsa's father, all these tears were the last straw. Brusque as ever, he stormed into his daughter's room. "Has he divorced you?" he demanded.

"I don't know," she replied miserably. "He has shut himself up alone in the upper room."

Omar left her to her weeping and went into the mosque, only to find it full of men crying with equal fervor. More enraged than ever, he rushed up to the roof, where the muezzin Bilal stood guard outside the door to the small storeroom. "Ask permission for me to enter," he commanded, but Bilal came out shaking his head: "I announced you, but he said nothing." Omar paced the courtyard until he could stand it no longer, then went back up the stairs to repeat his request. Again Muhammad ignored it. It took one more try for Bilal to emerge and announce: "The messenger will see you now."

His nerves stretched to breaking point, Omar stooped through the low doorway to find Muhammad lying on his side on a rush mat. There was nothing else in the room besides piles of untanned hides—no carpet, no bedding, no sign of common comfort. It was the last place one would expect to find the head of a burgeoning state. Not that Omar wasted any time expressing surprise, let alone sympathy. Ever the man of action, he came to the point immediately. "You have put away your wives?" he asked.

"No, I have not," came the answer, and the moment he heard it, Omar broke out into a loud and sonorous *Allahu akbar*, "God is great." The men gathered below in the mosque understood what the cry meant, and took it up with relief in the knowledge that the crisis had been averted. "But I shall not go near them for a month," Muhammad added quietly when the hubbub had subsided. And with his usual resolve, he kept his word.

Neither ibn-Ishaq nor al-Tabari offer any cogent explanation of why Muhammad insisted on that month of nights alone, but it was as though by withdrawing from his wives he was also withdrawing from the demands of the new world he had created. That sparse rooftop retreat was the Medinan equivalent of Mecca's Mount Hira: a place of contemplation in which to come to terms not only with what he had achieved but also with what lay ahead. He must have realized that there was no room left in his life for personal attachment, and that his relationship with Mariya would end here. His life was no longer his own to determine, but belonged instead to the *umma*. And he certainly sensed that not much of that life remained to him, because when he emerged at the end of the month, he resolved his marital situation with a new Quranic revelation that anticipated his own death.

It would be known as "the verse of the choice," since it spelled out the options for the wives. "Oh messenger, say to your wives: 'If you desire the life of this world and its adornment, then come, I shall make provision for you and send you forth with honor. But if you desire God and his messenger and the future abode of paradise, then God has prepared for you a mighty reward.'" The wives were free to choose divorce, that is, and Muhammad would make sure they were well provided for, or they could freely accept their public role and everything it entailed. That too was spelled out. "The messenger is closer to the believers than their own selves, and his wives are their mothers," the voice instructed. "It is not for you to marry the messenger's wives after him; truly that is grievous in the sight of God."

If the women chose to stay married to Muhammad, they now had to accept that their role went far beyond that of a normal spouse. They would be bound so tightly into the familial fabric of the new Arabia that they would be not merely his wives but the mothers of all the believers: "the Mothers of the Faithful." Given that none of them had mothered a child by him, this was an extraordinary formulation. It introduced the idea of Muhammad himself as the father of the faithful, positioning him as the founding patriarch of what was to become the world's third great monotheistic faith. If he had fathered no biological sons, he had instead fathered a multitude of spiritual ones. In a sense, all male believers were his sons, and thus forbidden to marry their mothers. The wives were to be not only widows after his death, but widows for as long as they lived.

All nine wives chose to stay. They would become, as it were, the vestal virgins of Islam, honored, respected, and celibate. On the personal level, it sounds a harsh fate to modern ears, especially for Aisha and Hafsa, who were both barely twenty. Perhaps they couldn't conceive of Muhammad dying, or perhaps they sincerely accepted the sacrifice of the personal for the political. But for Aisha in particular it would be an ironic fate, even a cruel one. She would be a lifetime mother to all, even as by the same stroke of revelation she would be denied the chance ever to become pregnant and have a child of her own.

For all the honor accorded them, most of the wives would take little part in the formative events of Islam. But then it could be said that Aisha, with her boldness, would play a large enough role for all nine. Two decades after Muhammad's death, she would mount a red camel to lead an army into battle against his cousin and son-in-law Ali, who had just been acclaimed as the fourth caliph. Hurling blood-curdling war cries from within her armored howdah even as her men were being slaughtered at her feet, she cut an indelible figure, so much so that the encounter— just outside Basra, in southern Iraq—would be dubbed the Battle of the Camel. By the time it was done, her howdah would be studded with so many arrows that it reportedly "bristled like a porcupine." One arrow even penetrated the armor and lodged in her shoulder, but that did nothing to stop her, and nobody realized she'd been wounded until she surrendered. Whatever the wisdom of her political judgment, her courage was undeniable.

She returned to Mecca undaunted by defeat. Emphatically outspoken even as she was sidelined by events after that battle, she established herself as the leading Mother of the Faithful: the sole woman who had been a virgin when Muhammad married her; the only one who had been able to tease him and make him smile; the youngest, the liveliest, and always, she insisted, the favorite. Since she outlived all his other widows, nobody was left to dispute her when she described her life with Muhammad. Essentially she wrote her memoirs in the form of thousands of hadiths, the reports of Muhammad's actions and sayings relied on by the Muslim faithful as guidelines for emulation and contemplation. She'd leaven her accounts with images that still tantalize adolescent imaginations, like that of her dangling her toes over his face to tease him—too tantalizing for later Islamic clerics, who'd whittle down her contributions to the body of hadiths from several thousand to a few hundred. As long as she lived, however, few people dared challenge her. Even in forced retirement, she still commanded respect.

The public demands on Muhammad increased by the day. The once marginal palm-grove oasis of Medina was now the power center for hundreds of miles around, with tentacles extending all the way to Bahrain and Oman on the east coast of Arabia, up to the border of Byzantine territory to the north, and south to most of the Yemen. Representatives of Beduin tribes and independent kingdoms alike began arriving in a constant flood of tribute, eager to pledge allegiance and to negotiate the terms of their alliances. This was "the year of delegations," and each one had to be received and given due honor, demanding Muhammad's personal attention.

Dozens of such delegations arrived, but among the most significant was the one from Najran, halfway between Mecca and the coast of Yemen. At a major caravan crossroads, the city had been the home of Arabia's largest Christian population for well over a century. If Najran were to accept *islam*, that would constitute a crucial political statement, especially with the Byzantine Empire seemingly resurgent to the north. In fact its conversion would set the pattern for the whole of the Christian-dominated Middle East.

The Quranic message spoke powerfully to Arabian Christians. The prophetic role of Jesus was fully acknowledged, and there would be more about Mary in the Quran than there was in the Gospels. Yet Najran was divided. It made political sense for the Najranites to ally themselves with Muhammad, but how was this to be reconciled with theology? Those in favor argued that he was the Paraclete, or Comforter, whose arrival Jesus had foretold in the Gospel of John and who was said to embody the Holy Spirit, even to be "the second Jesus." Those against maintained that the Paraclete was supposed to have sons, and since Muhammad did not, it could not possibly be him. Determined to resolve the dispute by debating the matter with him directly, the Najran delegation arrived in Medina only to find that debate was moot.

Instead of meeting the Najranites surrounded by his now customary bevy of counselors, Muhammad dismissed his aides for the occasion. He received the Christians with only four members of his immediate family in attendance: his daughter Fatima, her husband Ali, and their sons Hassan and Hussein. Without saying a word, he slowly and deliberately took hold of the hem of his cloak and spread it high and wide over the heads of this small family. They were the ones he sheltered beneath his cloak, the gesture said. They were his nearest and dearest, the *ahl al-bayt*, or "people of the house"—the House of Muhammad, his flesh and blood.

Whether calculated or instinctive on Muhammad's part, this was a consummate piece of theatricality, the seventh-century equivalent of the perfect photo op. Arabian Christian tradition had it that Adam had received a vision of a brilliant light surrounded by four other lights, and had been told by God that these were his prophetic descendants. The moment the Najran delegation saw Muhammad spread his cloak over the four members of his immediate family, it seemed that the Adamic vision had been fulfilled. The prophetic message that had begun with Adam and been passed down through Abraham and Moses to be embodied in Jesus had now found its final and completed expression in the man the Quran called "the seal of the prophets." They accepted *islam* on the spot.

Muhammad's dramatic staging of this meeting makes it clear that he was acutely aware of how his every gesture was fraught with meaning. Yet that awareness has to have weighed heavily on him. He had begun his mission in full humility, simply as a messenger. Indeed the Quran argued for humility as the highest virtue, continually warning against pride and arrogance. But now the widespread reverence for him threatened to make humility a thing of the past. No matter how much he tried to delegate authority, his revelations were still the word of God, and for the believers it was a small leap to assuming that everything he said, down to the last exclamation or passing comment, was a reflection of divine will. For all the Quran's insistence that he was just a man, obedience to him was sworn in the same breath as obedience to God.

His public role had expanded to consume every moment of his waking life, and now that waking life consumed most of the night as well as the day. The weariness told in his reddened eyes and in the deepening creases of his forehead. As though the headaches of government weren't enough, the physical headaches he had suffered since being wounded at the Battle of Uhud had begun to come with migraine-like intensity, sapping both mind and body. While everyone had expected him to travel to Mecca for the pilgrimage month of Dhu al-Hijja that year, he did not, sending abu-Bakr instead to lead the Medinan pilgrims.

Ibn-Ishaq explains this absence by arguing that Muhammad had declared that this would be the last year anyone who had not accepted *islam* would be allowed to participate in the *hajj*, and thus would not make his own pilgrimage until Mecca was free of all paganism for the duration. But the argument begs the question. Pagans or no, Muhammad had made the lesser *umra* pilgrimage the year before, and the year before that too. A pagan-free Mecca was not the real issue here. Instead, the exhaustion of revolution achieved seemed to be taking its toll. Or was it something more than exhaustion?

Throughout this year, Aisha would recall Muhammad spending nights on end in the graveyard of Medina, standing vigil for the dead. There were so many of them by now. Among the simple stone markers, each one barely higher than a child's knee, were those of two of his four daughters, as well as that of his adopted son Zayd. For a father to outlive his children was not uncommon in those days, but it was no less painful than it is now, fraught with the sense that the rightful order of life and death has been reversed.

Many of his early supporters were here too, some dead of wounds on the battlefield, some of sickness, some—a very few—simply of old age. "Peace be upon you, oh people of the graves," Aisha heard him saying. "Happy are you, so much better off than men here." It was as though he was longing to join them, to escape the demands on him and find rest.

He stood watch equally over the graves of former adversaries like ibn-Ubayy, the leader of the "hypocrites," who had died just a few months earlier. Omar would remember being shocked to see Muhammad at the burial: "I confronted him and said, 'Are you going to pray over God's enemy?' But he smiled and said, 'Leave me be, Omar. I have been given the choice and I have chosen.' Then he prayed and walked with ibn-Ubayy's body until it was lowered into the grave." It was Muhammad's acknowledgment not only of ibn-Ubayy's sincerity, but perhaps also of the value of someone unafraid to challenge his decisions. Now there was nobody left to do so.

The more he was surrounded by people, the more Muhammad seemed aware of his isolation. "God made him love solitude," Aisha would say, trying to explain why he preferred the company of the dead to that of his wives. But even in the dead of night, real solitude was the one thing that was impossible. Though he begged people not to follow him to the graveyard, they did, and even though they kept their distance, he was aware of them hidden in the darkness, standing vigil over him as he stood vigil over others. They did it doubtless out of care and love, but the burden of so much concern for his welfare merely added to the toll on him. They depended on him, he may have feared, for more than he had left to give. Yet however great his weariness, there was one more thing he knew he had still to do: one final return to Mecca, for the *hajj*.

Twenty-one

L ike anyone of sixty-three, an age the body makes known in ways a younger person never imagines, Muhammad certainly knew he would not live forever. When he set out on what his followers called the Pilgrimage of Fulfillment, he seemed to sense that in short order, it would be known as the Final Pilgrimage. "I do not know whether I shall ever meet you again in this place after this year," he would tell the crowd that thronged the Kaaba precinct that March of 632.

The two-week journey from Medina had been an arduous trek, and the five days of the *hajj* itself would be still more tiring, especially with all eyes on him. But that was precisely why he knew he had to complete it, despite the physical toll. This was the only full *hajj* he would ever make as the first Muslim, and as such it would establish the Islamic rites of pilgrimage. Every word, every pause, every gesture, would be etched definitively into the collective memory, and the ancient tradition of the *hajj* renewed. Instead of rejecting the pre-Islamic rituals, Muhammad now officially incorporated them. The sites of prayer, the circling of the Kaaba, the sacrifices, the head-shaving—all these and more were purified and rededicated to God by his example, in the final demonstration of his vision of unity. By absorbing the old into the new, the "traditions of the fathers" into the nascent religious tradition of Islam, he was uniting past and present, and thus establishing the pattern for the future.

He addressed the assembled pilgrims several times over these five days, and on many points the collective memory of his words would be in agreement. There was to be no revenge for any bloodshed in the pre-Islamic days of *jahiliya*. In this new era, "know that every believer is a believer's brother, and all believers are brethren." Nobody was to be forced to convert, and Christians and Jews especially were to be respected: "If they embrace *islam* of their own accord, they are among the faithful with the same privileges and obligations, but if they hold fast to their tradition, they are not to be seduced from it." And perhaps most cogently, in the one sentence most often quoted from these days, Muhammad talked about himself in the past tense: "I have left you one thing with which, if you hold fast to it, you will never go astray: the Quran, the book of God."

To many devout Muslims, this sentence says all that needs to be said. But there are other versions of it, and here is where the collective memory divides. According to these versions, Muhammad said, "I have left you two things," not one. The first of these was still the Quran, but the second would remain in dispute. Either he said "the Quran and the example of his prophet"—the *sunna*, literally the "custom" of the prophet. Or he said "the Quran and the people of the prophet's house"—the *ahl al-bayt*, his blood descendants through his son-in-law Ali and his grandsons Hassan and Hussein.

Both ibn-Ishaq and al-Tabari quote people who were there and who swear they heard one version or the other with their own ears. But as with first-hand testimony today, what they heard may have reflected what they were prepared to hear as much as what was actually said. It would soon be argued that the alternate versions of this one sentence came to essentially the same thing, since the *ahl al-bayt* personified the *sunna* just as Muhammad himself had done. But it would also be argued that since he had been "the seal of the prophets"—that is, the last and final one— his example was unique for all time. It was an argument that would develop into two closely related but very different guidelines for the future structure of Islam, and it would only be deepened by divergent interpretations of another statement Muhammad made just a week later.

The *hajj* completed, the pilgrims returning to Medina had stopped for the night at the spring-fed watering hole known as Ghadir Khumm, the Pool of Khumm. There they were met by Ali, newly returned from a mission to Yemen, where he had quelled the last remaining resistance to Muhammad. Taxes and tribute had been paid and celebration was in the air, so Muhammad ordered a makeshift desert pulpit made out of camel saddles placed on top of stacked palm branches and, after evening prayers, called on Ali to come up and stand alongside him. Raising his son-in-law's hand high in his own, he honored him with a special benediction. "He of whom I am the master, of him Ali is also the master," he declared. "God be the friend of he who is his friend, and the enemy of he who is his enemy."

To the *shiat Ali*, the "followers of Ali" who would soon shorten their name simply to Shia, what this meant was clear: Muhammad had designated his closest kinsman to be his *khalifa*, his caliph or successor. Ali's bloodline would thus be the line of succession, through his sons Hassan and Hussein. But to those who would eventually call themselves Sunni, naming themselves for the *sunna* or practice of Muhammad, this was far from clear. If such was the prophet's intention, why had he not simply said so? The benediction at Ghadir Khumm was certainly a spontaneous demonstration of affection for Ali, and nobody doubted either his closeness to Muhammad or his worthiness. But the idea of a bloodline succession, they'd argue, went against the principles of Islam, by which all were equal before God.

Besides, they'd say, the word translated as "master," *mawla*, like so many words in seventh-century Arabic, had a wide range of related meanings. It could mean leader, or patron, or friend, or confidant, but which one depends on context, and context is infinitely debatable. Moreover, the second part of Muhammad's declaration was no more specific. "God be the friend of he who is his friend, the enemy of he who is his enemy" (a formula much degraded in later political parlance into the misguidedly simplistic "the enemy of my enemy is my friend") was the standard phrasing of the time for alliance or friendship. Under the circumstances, it clearly singled Ali out for honor, but whether it designated him Muhammad's successor was to remain, like so much else, a matter of belief rather than definitive record. None of which, perhaps, would have mattered so intensely if Muhammad had not had only two months left to live.

The illness began just a few weeks after his return to Medina. At first it seemed to be another of those migraine-like attacks, and everyone expected it to pass after a day or two, maybe three at the most. Except it didn't. It came and went, but each time it returned, it seemed worse. And then a fever developed, and with it the headaches intensified, stabbing down the back of

Muhammad's neck in paralyzing spasms. At his insistence, his wives took him to Aisha's room, and there he lay on the raised stone sleeping ledge while they took turns nursing him.

It was the end of May, and the heat of the early desert summer made the small room stifling even for someone in full health. But Muhammad's was rapidly deteriorating as a blinding sensitivity to noise and light developed along with the fever and the terrible head pain. The light could be dealt with by hanging a rug over the doorway, but quiet was not to be had. Aisha's room was now a sickroom, and in the Middle East, then as now, a sickroom was a gathering place. Relatives, companions, aides, supporters— all those claiming closeness to the center of power—came in a continual stream, day and night, with concerns, advice, questions. Even sick, Muhammad could not ignore them. Too much depended on him.

The wives wrapped his head in cloths soaked in cold water, hoping to draw out the fever and ease the pain. But if there was any relief, it was only temporary. As his condition worsened, the women must have realized that this was neither a passing fever nor another migraine but a disease that had been known throughout the Middle East since the start of recorded history.

"Headache roams over the desert, billowing like the wind," reads an ancient Sumerian incantation. "Flashing like lightning, it is loosed above and below. / Bright as a heavenly star, it comes like the dew. / It stands hostile against the wayfarer, scorching him like the day. / This man it has struck and feeds on him, / Like a dread windstorm, bound in death." This was no mere headache but a fatal disease, and indeed the symptoms and the duration of Muhammad's final illness—ten days—are classic for bacterial meningitis.

There's no knowing exactly how he contracted it. Some of his followers would suspect it was the result of his night vigils in the graveyard, which he'd resumed on returning from Mecca. They'd remember him talking to the dead, saying, "Peace upon you, oh people of the graves!" and promising to join them: "God has called another of his servants to him, and soon he will obey the call." Certainly his exhaustion, exacerbated by the stress of government, had made him more vulnerable to infection. So perhaps had the head injury he'd suffered at the Battle of Uhud, since bacteria can enter the skull through a hairline fracture, inflaming the protective membranes of the brain and spinal cord known as the meninges. Even today meningitis is often fatal; in the seventh century, long before antibiotics, it was almost universally so.

Yet despite Muhammad's clear indication during the *hajj* that he did not expect to live much longer, despite that night-time promise to join the dead, despite even the clearly worsening symptoms, it would not be until the tenth and final day of his illness that anyone seemed able to openly acknowledge that he was dying.

Outside the sickroom, the courtyard of the mosque was packed. Unwilling to go home even to sleep, people had camped out there, all wanting to be where news of Muhammad's progress would be heard first. It was as though it was inconceivable that he could die. Right now, with nearly all of Arabia united under his leadership? At the dawn of what felt like a new age? How could the prophet of God possibly die just when the future seemed so full of promise?

Of course their presence in the courtyard testified to the fact that on some level, they knew what was happening. Yet even as they knew it, they refused to believe it, as though denial could change reality and Muhammad was not as mortal as they were. So they waited, and the sound of their prayers and concern built to an unrelenting hum of anxiety that permeated the air of Aisha's small room.

As the days passed and Muhammad did not emerge, even that steady murmur of anxiety grew hushed. The whole of Medina was subdued, face to face with the inconceivable. And hovering on everyone's mind but on nobody's lips—unvoiced, because that would be to acknowledge what was happening—was one paramount question: Who would assume the leadership? Ali, the cousin and son-in-law he had honored at Ghadir Khumm? Abu-Bakr, the companion with whom he had fled Mecca and who inspired both affection and respect? The stern warrior Omar, whose voice, honed to terseness on the battlefield, compelled obedience? Who could claim the authority? Or rather, who could exert it? Now of all times it seemed essential that Muhammad make his will known and clearly anoint a successor. Yet he did not.

Why not? And what did he really intend? These are the questions that were to haunt Islam through the centuries. Everyone would claim to know what Muhammad had been thinking, to have insight into how he saw the future of Islam. Yet in the lack of a clear and unequivocal designation of a successor, nobody could prove it beyond any shadow of doubt. Over the course of those ten days of his illness, all of the men who were to be the first five caliphs of Islam would be in and out of his sickroom: two fathers-in-law, abu-Bakr and Omar; two sons-in-law, Ali and Uthman; and a brother-in-law, Muawiya. But how that would happen, and in what order, was to remain the stuff of discord.

Sunni scholars were to argue that Muhammad had such faith

in the good will and integrity of his aides and companions that he could not bear to decide among them, and trusted to God to ensure that they come to the right decision. "My community"—the *umma*—"will never agree in error," they'd say he declared. That seemed a definitive endorsement of consensus, but it was to have the opposite effect. It would be taken to mean that those who disagreed with the majority were "in error," their dissent proof that they were not truly part of the *umma*. Shia scholars, on the other hand, would argue that Muhammad had already made his choice of Ali as his successor, and that he would have done so again as he lay in that small room against the wall of the mosque compound, had his will not been thwarted.

Divisiveness was the one thing Muhammad had most feared, and now it was the one thing he was helpless to prevent as his sickness gave new life to the resentments and jealousies that had accumulated around him. As the fever ate at him, he began to float in and out of sweat-soaked consciousness, aware of the arguments going on but unable to stop them.

Al-Tabari relates a disturbing exchange that took place on the ninth day of Muhammad's illness, when he mustered the strength to call for Ali, who was praying in the mosque. But nobody fetched him. Aisha lobbied instead for her father: "Wouldn't you rather see abu-Bakr?" she insisted. Her co-wife Hafsa countered by suggesting her own father: "Wouldn't you rather see Omar?" Overwhelmed by their persistence, Muhammad waved assent. Both abu-Bakr and Omar were called for, and Ali was not.

Cajoling a sick man into doing what they wanted may seem unbecoming, even heartless, but then who could blame these young women for pushing their own agendas and promoting the interests of their fathers over those of Ali? They faced a daunting future as lifelong widows, and they knew it. Every person in that crowded sickroom was anxious to safeguard the community, yet each wanted also to safeguard his or her own position. As is the way in politics, everyone was convinced that the collective interest and their personal interest were one and the same, and this could be sensed in what al-Tabari calls "the episode of pen and paper."

With abu-Bakr and Omar present, Muhammad appeared to recover somewhat—the kind of illusory improvement that often precedes the end. He seemed quite lucid as he sat up, sipped some water, and made what many believe was a final attempt to make his wishes known. But even this would come laden with ambiguity. "Bring writing materials that I may dictate something for you, after which you will not be led into error," he said.

It seems a simple enough request, and a perfectly reasonable one under the circumstances, but it produced near panic among those in the room. What did Muhammad want written? Would it be general guidelines for how they should proceed? Religious advice for the community he was about to leave behind? Or was it the one possibility that seemed most called for and yet was most feared: a will. Was the dying prophet about to definitively name his successor?

The only way to know was to call for a scribe to be brought in, but that is not what happened. Instead, everyone began to argue about whether to do it. They voiced concern about the strain on Muhammad, insisting that he rest and that the sickroom be kept quiet. And even as they stressed the need for silence, their voices rose.

It is the strangest scene. There was every sign that the man they were all so deeply devoted to was ready to make his dying wishes known, perhaps even to designate his successor once and for all. It was the one thing everyone in the room wanted to know, but at the same time the one thing nobody wanted to know. Yet it is an altogether human scene. Everyone was concerned, everyone trying to protect Muhammad, to stop the importuning of others and to ease his life even as it seeped out of him. They were all doing their best, and doing it heatedly, their voices rising so that every angry note and high-pitched syllable seemed to pierce the sick man's ears until he could take it no more. "Leave me," he said finally. "Let there be no quarreling in my presence."

He was so weak by then that the words came out in practically a whisper. Only Omar managed to hear him, but that was enough. Using his commanding presence to full advantage, he laid down the law. "The messenger of God is overcome by pain," he said. "We have the Quran, the book of God, and that is sufficient for us."

It would not be sufficient, though. It could have been, and perhaps even should have been—Omar's words are still quoted today as the example of perfect faith—but it was not. The Quran would be supplemented by the *sunna*, the practice of Muhammad as established in the vast body of hadiths as related by those who claimed to be closest to him, and by the ongoing accumulation of clerical rulings that would make up Sharia law. For now, however, Omar prevailed. His words had their intended effect, and the sickroom subsided into a somewhat shame-faced silence. If Muhammad had indeed intended to name a successor, he had left it too late. In the grip of fever, blinded by agonizing spasms, he was no longer in any condition to impose his will. The scribe never arrived, and by dawn the next morning Muhammad could barely move.

He acknowledged now that the end was near. He made one last request, and this one was granted: "Pour seven skins of water from seven wells over me so that I may go out to the men and instruct them." And though he did not say it, all the wives were certainly aware that this was part of the ritual for washing a corpse. When it was done, he asked to be taken to morning prayers in the mosque.

It took two men, Ali and his uncle Abbas, to support him. The few yards across the courtyard to the mosque itself must have seemed an infinite distance, and the shade of the mosque an exquisite relief from the blinding glare of the early-morning sun. Muhammad gestured to be seated beside the pulpit, where his old friend abu-Bakr stood to lead the prayers in his place. Those who were there would remember him smiling as he listened. They'd say his face was radiant, though there's no knowing whether it was the radiance of faith or the flush of fever and impending death. They watched as he listened to the chanting of the words he had first heard from the angel Gabriel, and persuaded themselves that it was not the last time they'd see him. He was on the mend, his energy was returning, all would be well. But once the morning prayers were over and Ali and Abbas had carried him back to Aisha's chamber, he had only a few hours left.

Some were more clear-sighted than others. "I swear by God that I saw death in the prophet's face," Abbas told Ali once they had settled Muhammad back on his pallet and left the sickroom. Now was their last chance to have him clarify the matter of succession. "Let us go back and ask him. If authority be with us, we shall know it, and if it be with others, we will ask him to direct them to treat us well."

But Ali could not bear the idea of placing any more pressure on Muhammad. Or perhaps even he was not ready for too much clarity. "By God I will not," he said. "If it is withheld from us, none after him will give it to us."

Not that it would have helped. Even as the two men were talking, Muhammad lapsed into unconsciousness, and this time he would not recover. By noon of that Monday, June 8 in the year 632, he was dead.

He died, Aisha would say, with his head on her breast, or as the original Arabic has it with vivid delicacy, "between my lungs and my lips." She had been holding him, and realizing suddenly how heavy his head had become, had looked down to find the empty glaze of death in his eyes. Her account would become part of Sunni tradition, but it would not go unchallenged: Shia tradition would maintain that as he died, Muhammad's head lay not on Aisha's breast but on Ali's.

Who held the dying prophet would matter. Whose ears heard that final breath, whose skin it touched, whose arms supported him would matter with particular intensity, as though his spirit had somehow leaped from his body at the precise moment of death to enter the soul of the one who held him. Was it Aisha, the daughter of the man who was to become the first caliph, or Ali, the man who many remained convinced should have been the first?

Whichever it was, no words were needed to carry the news. The wailing did that. Every one of the wives broke into a terrible, piercing howl that sounded for all the world like a wounded animal hiding in the bush to die. It spoke of ultimate agony, of pain and sorrow beyond comprehension, and it spread through the oasis at the speed of sound. Men and women, old and young, all took up the wail and surrendered themselves to it.

"We were like sheep on a rainy night, moving this way and that in panic," one of them would recall. Sheep, that is, with neither shepherd nor shelter. Their wailing was not only for the one who had died but for themselves, leaderless without him. How could it be? Hadn't they just seen him in the mosque, his face radiant as they knelt and bowed and chanted the prayer responses? It was too awful a thing to contemplate, too terrible a thing to accept.

Even Omar, that sternest of warriors, could not absorb it. The man who just the day before had asserted that the Quran was all they needed was no more able than the panicked crowd to accept that death had won the day. Before anyone could stop him, he stood up in the forecourt of the mosque and shouted that it was not so. A curse on those who even entertained such an idea. "By God, Muhammad is not dead," he insisted. "He has gone to his lord as Moses went and was hidden from his people for forty days, returning to them after it was said that he had died. By God, the messenger will return as Moses returned, and will cut off the hands and feet of all men who allege that he is dead!"

But if his intention had been to calm the crowd, the sight of a figure as courageous as Omar in hysterical denial only gave rise to greater panic. That was when the small, stooped figure of abu-Bakr appeared beside him. "Gently, Omar, gently," he said, "be quiet," and he took the towering warrior by the arm and slowly led him aside.

All eyes focused on abu-Bakr as he took Omar's place before the terrified throng. His voice was startlingly strong, not at all what one would expect from such a frail body, as he recited the Quranic revelation that had come after the believers had fled the Battle of Uhud thinking that Muhammad had been killed.

"Muhammad is naught but a messenger," abu-Bakr declaimed. "Why, if he should die or be slain, should you turn back on your heels?"

And then he added what they had all been dreading, yet at the same time what was most needed. "For those who worshipped Muhammad," he announced, "Muhammad is dead. For those who worship God, God is alive, immortal."

There was a stunned silence as the words sank in, and then Omar reacted. "By God," he would remember, "when I heard abu-Bakr say those words, I was so dumbfounded that my legs would not bear me and I fell to the ground, knowing that the prophet was dead." The older man's calm realism had subdued the terrifying giant, turning him into a weeping child. And with this confirmation of mortality, the rituals of grief began. Men and women alike slapped their faces repeatedly, rapidly, with both hands; beat their chests with clenched fists so that their bodies echoed like hollow trees; raked their fingernails over their foreheads until blood streaked down over their eyes and their tears turned red. They scooped up handfuls of dust and poured it over their hair, abasing themselves in despair throughout the afternoon, into the evening, and all through the night.

The burial would be strangely clandestine, done in the dead of night with a matter-of-factness that seems almost shocking in the light of the magnificent tomb and sacred precincts to come.

Ali and three of his kinsmen took over Aisha's room and began the work of the closest male relatives. They prepared Muhammad for the grave, washing him and rubbing herbs over him, wrapping him in his shroud, and sitting in prayer with the body. But others were thinking further ahead. With no clear heir apparent, the "lost sheep" were faced with the daunting task of acclaiming one of their own as their new leader. If Ali trusted that it would be him, that trust would now prove misplaced. Even as the mass of believers grieved in the courtyard of the mosque, the clan leaders of Medina gathered with the rest of Muhammad's senior aides in a *shura*, a traditional council of elders, to decide who his successor would be.

The *shura* went on through that Monday night and far into the following day. Each clan and tribal leader, each elder, had to have his say, and at length. Success would depend on consensus, and while that was a high ideal, in practice it meant that the meeting would go on until those opposed to the general feeling had been either persuaded or simply worn down and browbeaten into going along with the majority.

Ali might have seemed the natural candidate by virtue of his closeness to Muhammad, but that closeness was exactly what now worked against him. It was argued that to choose him as Muhammad's nearest kinsman would risk turning the leadership of the *umma* into a form of hereditary monarchy, and that this was the opposite of everything Muhammad stood for. This was why he had never formally declared an heir, they said. He had faith in his people's ability to decide for themselves, in the sanctity of the decision of the whole community, or at least of their representatives.

It was an argument for democracy, in however limited a form. And since history is nothing if not ironic, it was also an argument against exactly what would happen just fifty years into the future, when abu-Sufyan's son Muawiya would establish the first Sunni dynasty in Damascus by handing his throne over to his eldest son. It was in fact an argument against all the dynasties to come over the ensuing centuries, whether caliphates, shahdoms, sultanates, principalities, kingdoms, or presidencies. And while it won the day immediately after Muhammad's death, it would be destined to lie dormant for thirteen centuries thereafter.

Ali's uncle Abbas urged him to abandon his vigil over the body, offering to keep watch in his place while the younger man asserted his claim to leadership at the *shura*. But as he had done when Abbas had urged him to clarify matters in Muhammad's final hours, Ali refused. To leave the man who had been father and mentor to him before consigning him back to the earth from which he had come? He would not. He stayed with Muhammad's body, and as the light faded on Tuesday evening, the news arrived that the *shura* had finally reached consensus. The first caliph would not be Ali, but abu-Bakr.

By now a full day and a half had passed since Muhammad had taken his last breath, and for reasons all too obvious in the intense June heat, the matter of burial was becoming urgent. Custom decreed that a body be buried within twenty-four hours, but with all the tribal and clan leaders at the *shura*, Ali and Abbas had seen no option but to wait. Now that the leadership had gone to abu-Bakr, however, things were very different. Abu-Bakr would surely make Muhammad's funeral a stage for confirmation of his own election as the successor, so Ali would deny him that opportunity.

In the small hours of that Wednesday morning, Aisha was woken by scraping sounds echoing around the courtyard of the mosque. Since Muhammad's body was lying in her room, she had moved in with her co-wife Hafsa, just a few doors down. Sunk deep in grief, she didn't get up to investigate the noise. If she had, she'd have discovered that what had woken her was the sound of steel digging into rocky soil. With pickaxes and shovels, Ali and his kinsmen were digging Muhammad's grave. And they were digging it in Aisha's room.

Muhammad had once said that a prophet should be buried where he had died, they would later explain, and since he had died on the sleeping platform in this small room, this was where he had to be laid to rest. They dug the grave at the foot of the platform, and when it was deep enough, they tipped up the pallet holding the shrouded body, slid it down into the earth so that it faced toward Mecca as though in prayer, then quickly covered it and laid a simple slab of stone on top.

There was no pomp or circumstance, no elaborate ritual or mass procession, no throngs of mourners, no eulogies. Muhammad was buried in the dead of night, as quietly and inconspicuously as he had been born, and one has to think that this is exactly as he would have wished it. As he entered his grave, he was simply a man again, free of the intense public scrutiny that had hemmed him in. The peace and quiet he had sought would finally be his. At last, he would find some rest.

ACKNOWLEDGMENTS

My deepest thanks to all who have listened as I wrestled these past few years with some of the toughest issues in this biography, and especially to the many Muslims open to this very different way of thinking about Muhammad.

Thanks in particular to Sanaa Joy Carey for her bemused tolerance; to Jonathan Raban, who planted the seed for this book; to TED Global Fellow Nassim Assefi, who invited me to talk on the Quran at the 2010 TEDxRainier; to Olivier D'hose, without whose brilliant IT support I'd be lost in the Inter-tubes; to the University of Washington's Suzzallo Library, which allowed me to keep so much of their collection at home that my houseboat rode low in the water under all the weight; and to the online readers of *The Accidental Theologist* for their patience, encouragement, and good wishes during my extended writing hermitry.

At Riverhead Books, it's been both a pleasure and a privilege to work with editorial director Rebecca Saletan, who "got" what I was doing instantly, and with her executive assistant, Elaine Trevorrow, who kept me gently but firmly on track with regard to time. And last but as far as it's possible to get from least, my love and heartfelt thanks to my longtime friend and agent Gloria Loomis of the Watkins/ Loomis Agency, and to her executive assistant, Julia Maznik. No writer could dream of better.

NOTES

Unless otherwise indicated, all direct speech and dialogue in this book are from either ibn-Ishaq's eighth-century biography of Muhammad, *Sirat Rasul Allah*, or al-Tabari's ninth- and tenth-century history of early Islam, *Tarikh al-Rasul wa'al-Muluk* (see Bibliography under "Primary Sources").

Citations of Quranic verses are numbered according to Abdullah Yusuf Ali's translation (again, see Bibliography under "Primary Sources"). It should be noted that since early Quran manuscripts often omitted verse breaks, some translators, like A. J. Arberry, use a slightly different numbering system in the interest of poetic and thematic integrity.

EPIGRAPHS

Page xi **"Muhammad, say":** Quran 6:14, 6:163, 39:12.
Page xi **"The inner meaning of history":** Ibn-Khaldun, *The Muqaddimah*.
Page xi **"I do not accept":** Desai, *Day-to-Day with Gandhi*.

ONE

Page 3 **He was stockily built:** Details of Muhammad's appearance in, e.g., *The History of al-Tabari*, vol. IX, *The Last Years of the Prophet*, under "The Messenger of God's Characteristics."
Page 8 **"the first Muslim":** Quran 6:14, 6:163, 39:12.
Page 8 **"a man of no importance":** Quran 43:31.
Page 10 **the Jesus Seminar:** Shorto, *Gospel Truth*.
Page 11 **disavowal of the miraculous:** E.g., Quran 17:90–97.
Page 11 **"the hero's journey":** Campbell, *The Hero with a Thousand Faces*.
Page 12 *laylat al-qadr:* Quran 97:1–5.

TWO

Page 18 **Eros and Thanatos:** Sigmund Freud, *Beyond the Pleasure Principle*, trans. James Strachey (New York: Liveright, 1961).
Page 20 **female infanticide:** Kosekenniemi, *The Exposure of Infants*; Piers, *Infanticide*; Pinker, *The Better Angels of Our Nature*.
Page 20 **a practice the Quran would condemn:** Quran 6:14, 6:151, 17:31, 60:12, 81:8–9.

Page 21 **wet-nursing:** Palmer, *The Politics of Breastfeeding.*

Page 23 **life spans:** Jackson, *Doctors and Diseases in the Roman Empire;* Preston, "Mortality Trends."

Page 26 **oral culture:** Finnegan, *Oral Poetry:* Lévi-Strauss, *Myth and Meaning;* Niles, *Homo Narrans;* Whallon, *Formula, Character, and Context.*

Page 26 **Hours-long poems:** Arberry, *The Seven Odes;* Hazleton, *Where Mountains Roar;* Stetkevych, *The Mute Immortals Speak;* Zwettler, *The Oral Tradition of Classical Arabic Poetry.*

THREE

Page 32 **"Tonight I take refuge":** Suras 113 and 114 of the Quran follow the structure of this invocation.

Page 38 **"high-achievement" figures:** Eisenstadt et al., *Parental Loss and Achievement;* Scharfstein, *The Philosophers.*

Page 38 **"The question of morality and conscience":** Eisenstadt, "Parental Loss and Genius."

FOUR

Page 41 **"the invention of childhood":** Ariès, *Centuries of Childhood.*

Page 43 *arish:* Rubin, "The Ka'ba"; Hawting, "The Origins of the Islamic Sanctuary at Mecca."

Page 45 **three hundred and sixty of these "idols":** Ibn-al-Kalbi, *Book of Idols.*

Page 46 **twelve stones for the altar:** Exodus 20:25.

Page 48 **"playing the harlot":** Isaiah 57:3; Ezekiel 16:28–29, 23:20; Jeremiah 2:23–24; Hosea 2:2–3, 2:13, 2:16–17.

Page 51 **"decrepit camels":** Levey, *Medieval Arabic Toxicology.*

FIVE

Page 58 **"alone with the livelong night . . . the lamp of the hermit":** Arberry, *The Seven Odes.*

Page 58 **"monasteries flourishing":** Ward, *The Sayings of the Desert Fathers.*

Page 59 **"like the imprint of a cupping glass":** *The History of al-Tabari,* vol. IX, *The Last Years of the Prophet,* under "The Seal of Prophethood Which He Had."

Page 64 **"Let he who is without sin cast the first stone":** John 8:7.

Page 65 **legends like that of the seven sleepers:** Quran 18:22.

SIX

Page 77 **Meccan thinkers known as *hanifs*:** Gibb, "Pre-Islamic Monotheism in Arabia"; Kister, *Society and Religion from Jahiliyya to Islam;* Rubin, "Hanifiyya and Ka'ba."

Page 78 **"the father of all who believe":** Romans 4:11, 4:16.

Page 79 *tahannut:* Kister, "Al-Tahannuth"; Shoham, *Rebellion, Creativity, and Revelation;* Underhill, *Mysticism.*

SEVEN

Page 88 **"Recite in the name of thy Lord":** Quran 96:1.

Page 91 **"medical materialism"**: James, *The Varieties of Religious Experience*.
Page 91 **"the tuft and final applause of science"**: Preface to *Leaves of Grass*, in Walt Whitman, *Complete Poetry and Collected Prose* (New York: Library of America, 1982).
Page 91 **"the willing suspension of disbelief"**: Samuel Taylor Coleridge, *Biographia Literaria* (London: Oxford University Press, 1954).
Page 91 **"the endeavor to express the spirit of the thing"**: Ralph Waldo Emerson, *Poetry and Imagination* (Boston: Osgood, 1876).
Page 92 **"In the Penal Colony"**: Franz Kafka, *Kafka's Selected Stories*, trans. Stanley Corngold (New York: W. W. Norton, 2007).
Page 95 **"just a messenger"**: E.g., Quran 9:128, 41:6.

EIGHT

Page 99 **dark night of the soul**: *The Collected Works of St. John of the Cross*, trans. Kieran Kavanaugh and Otilio Rodriguez (Garden City, NY: Doubleday, 1964).
Page 100 **leap of faith**: Søren Kierkegaard, *The Concept of Anxiety*, ed. and trans. by Reidar Thomte with Albert B. Anderson (Princeton, NJ: Princeton University Press, 1980).
Page 103 **"By the morning light"**: Quran 93:1–8.
Page 104 **"By the sun and its morning brightness"**: Quran 91:1–10.
Page 104 **"Let the once-dead earth"**: Quran 36:33–36.
Page 104 **"God is the light"**: Quran 24:35–36.
Page 105 **"Be not hasty in your recitation"**: Quran 20:114.
Page 105 **"Be patient"**: e.g., Quran 68:48, 73:10.
Page 109 **"neither begotten nor begetter"**: Quran 10:68.
Page 111 **"Oh you shrouded in your robes"**: Quran 74:1.
Page 112 **"those who amass and hoard wealth . . . not avail them when they perish"**: Quran 104:2, 89:20, 100:8, 104:3, 92:11.
Page 112 **"Know that the life of this world"**: Quran 57:20.
Page 112 **"righteous deeds . . . wealth you amass"**: Quran 34:37, 10:58.
Page 112 **"Blessed are the meek"**: Matthew 5:5.
Page 112 **"We desire to show favor"**: Quran 28:05.
Page 113 **"Say: 'We believe in God'"**: Quran 2:136.
Page 113 **"Before this, the book of Moses was revealed"**: Quran 46:12.
Page 114 **"in a clear Arabic tongue"**: E.g., Quran 20:113, 19:97, 26:195, 44:58.
Page 115 **"When the sun shall be darkened"**: Quran 81:1–14.

NINE

Page 117 **"just a messenger"**: E.g., Quran 9:128, 41:6.
Page 118 **"the first Muslim"**: Quran 6:14, 6:163, 39:12.
Page 120 **"Can you give a dry bone flesh again?"**: Quran 56:47.
Page 120 **"I am come to set a man at variance"**: Matthew 10:35.
Page 121 **"if your fathers, your sons"**: Quran 9:24.
Page 123 **"an eye for an eye"**: Exodus 21:23–25; Leviticus 24:17–21.
Page 123 **"whoever forgoes it out of charity"**: Quran 5:45.
Page 124 **"Give me drink! Give me drink!"**: Mustafa, *Religious Trends in Pre-Islamic Poetry*.
Page 129 **"veiling their hearts"**: Quran 17:46, 18:57.

TEN

Page 133 **singled out by name for condemnation:** Quran 111:1–3.

Page 143 **"Many messengers before you were mocked, Muhammad":** E.g., Quran 6:10, 13:32, 15:10, 15:88, 15:94–97, 21:41.

Page 143 **"We are well aware that your heart . . . Do not let them discourage you":** Quran 15:97, 10:65, 11:12, 16:127, 27:70, 36:76.

Page 143 **"You cannot make the dead hear . . . out of their error":** Quran 27:80–81.

Page 143 **"Even if they saw a piece of heaven":** Quran 52:44.

Page 143 **"Will you worry yourself to death . . . a sport and a pastime":** Quran 18:6, 6:110, 6:112, 6:70, 47:36.

Page 144 **"Turn away from them and wait":** Quran 2:109.

Page 144 **"Ignore them":** E.g., Quran 15:94, 51:54, 53:29.

Page 144 **"Endure what they say":** Quran 16:127.

Page 146 **"'Have you thought on Lat and Uzza'":** Quran 53:19–22.

Page 147 **"'But God annuls what Satan does'":** Quran 50:52.

Page 147 **"They are naught but names":** Quran 53:23.

Page 147 **nineteenth-century Orientalist:** William Muir, *The Life of Mahomet and History of Islam* (London: Smith, Elder, 1858).

Page 149 **The "idea of error . . . is our meta-mistake":** Kathryn Schulz, *Being Wrong: Adventures in the Margins of Error* (New York: Ecco, 2010).

ELEVEN

Page 156 **"wandering king":** Arberry, *The Seven Odes*; Stetkevych, *The Mute Immortals Speak.*

Page 161 **dream incubation:** Covitz, *Visions of the Night*; Eliade, *Myths, Dreams, and Mysteries*; Hopkins, *A World Full of Gods.*

Page 161 **"If there be a prophet among you":** Numbers 12:6.

Page 161 **"During sleep the soul departs":** Midrash, Gen. Rabbah 14:9.

Page 162 **"the master of dreams":** Covitz, *Visions of the Night.*

Page 162 **"lift the veil of the senses":** Ibn-Khaldun, *The Muqaddimah.*

Page 163 **Jacob's dream:** Genesis 28:12–14.

TWELVE

Page 167 **It means uprooting yourself:** Luyat and Tolron, *Flight from Certainty*; Said, *Reflections on Exile and Other Essays.*

Page 174 **Jewish tribes in seventh-century Arabia:** Firestone, "Jewish Culture in the Formative Period of Islam"; Gil, "The Origin of the Jews of Yathrib"; Lecker, *Jews and Arabs in Pre- and Early Islamic Arabia*; Lecker, *Muslims, Jews and Pagans.*

Page 175 **dramatic but ill-fated rebellion against Roman rule:** After Bar Kokhba's rebellion was crushed by six Roman legions in the year 136, Jews were banned from Jerusalem.

Page 176 **"in your own tongue . . . in pure Arabic":** E.g., Quran 20:113, 19:97, 26:195, 44:58.

Page 178 **"have driven out the messenger":** E.g., Quran 60:1.

Page 184 **"They two were in the cave":** Quran 9:40.

THIRTEEN

Page 189 "Exile is the unhealable rift": Said, *Reflections on Exile.*

Page 191 The term "monotheism": Henry More, *An Explanation of the Grand Mystery of Godliness* (London: Flesher and Morden, 1660).

Page 192 "the God of this people": Carroll, *Jerusalem, Jerusalem.*

Page 197 "Fight in the way of God": Quran 2:190.

Page 198 "They question you with regard to warfare": Quran 2:217.

Page 198 "Permission is granted": Quran 22:40.

Page 198 "Those who have believed": Quran 2:218.

Page 200 "If you object to political methods": Berlin, *Against the Current.*

Page 201 "All armed prophets have conquered": Machiavelli, *The Prince.*

FOURTEEN

Page 210 "It was not you who killed": Quran 8:17.

Page 213 "We believe in that which has been revealed": Quran 2:136, 3:84.

Page 213 "except fairly and politely": Quran 29:46.

Page 213 "People of the Book, let us come to an agreement": Quran 3:64.

Page 213 "Believers, Jews, Christians, Zoroastrians": Quran 2:62.

Page 214 "We have sent down this scripture": Quran 39:41.

Page 214 "Why do you confound the true with the false": Quran 3:70–71.

Page 214 "made of their religion a sport and a pastime": Quran 7:51.

Page 222 "We are turning you in a prayer direction that pleases you": Quran 2:144.

Page 222 "If I forget thee, oh Jerusalem": Psalms 137:5.

FIFTEEN

Page 231 "Other messengers have come and gone": Quran 3:144.

Page 232 "With God's permission, you were routing": Quran 3:153.

Page 239 the Qureyz: This tribe's name is usually rendered as "Qurayza." The spelling is adapted here in order to avoid confusion with the Qaynuqa, who had already been expelled from Medina, or with the Quraysh, the ruling tribe of Mecca.

Page 240 "Whatever you believers have done": Quran 59:5.

Page 241 "Consider the hypocrites": Quran 59:11.

Page 241 "It was God who drove the unbelievers": Quran 59:2–3.

SIXTEEN

Page 245 "There was never any subject": The fifth caliph Muawiya, quoted in Abbott, *Aishah the Beloved of Muhammad.*

Page 252 "The slanderers are a small group": Quran 24:4–21.

Page 255 "the wives of your sons": Quran 4:23.

Page 255 "Muhammad is not the father": Quran 33:40.

Page 256 "This privilege is yours alone": Quran 33:50.

Page 256 "you will never be able to deal equitably": Quran 4:129.

SEVENTEEN

Page 261 **the Qureyz:** On the spelling of the tribe's name, see the note for page 210.

Page 264 **the Masada option:** In the year 73, a Jewish splinter group known as "the zealots" held out against Roman siege on this fortified hilltop overlooking the Dead Sea. According to the contemporary historian Flavius Josephus in *The Wars of the Jews*, the siege ended when all 960 men, women, and children killed themselves rather than surrender.

Page 268 **the Quran demands an absolute end to hostilities:** E.g., Quran 2:193.

Page 269 **"the question of cruelty used well or badly":** Machiavelli, *The Prince*.

EIGHTEEN

Page 278 **"God was well pleased":** Quran 48:18.

Page 278 **"He has held back the hands":** Quran 48:20.

Page 278 **"continuation of politics by other means":** Carl von Clausewitz, *On War*, trans. Michael Howard and Peter Paret (Princeton, NJ: Princeton University Press, 1976).

Page 286 **permitted to use violence on sacred ground:** Quran, 2:191–192.

NINETEEN

Page 294 **"It had been a time of excitement":** Havel, *The Art of the Impossible*.

Page 304 **"The Byzantines have been defeated":** Quran 30:2.

Page 305 **"a tribal imperative to conquest":** Crone, *Meccan Trade and the Rise of Islam*.

TWENTY

Page 307 **"revelation of the curtain":** Quran 33:53.

Page 310 **the first *hanif*:** e.g., Quran, 3:67, 3:95, 4:125, 16:123.

Page 312 **"The verse of the choice":** Quran 33:28–31.

Page 313 **"The messenger is closer to the believers":** Quran, 33:6, 33:53.

Page 316 **the Paraclete:** John 14:16, 14:26, 15:26, 16:7.

Page 317 **"the seal of the prophets":** Quran 33:40.

TWENTY-ONE

Page 324 **"Headache roams over the desert":** Tunkel, *Bacterial Meningitis*.

Page 324 **bacterial meningitis:** Brinton, *Cerebrospinal Fever*; Clark and Hyslop, "Post-Traumatic Meningitis"; Tunkel, *Bacterial Meningitis*.

Page 333 **"Muhammad is naught but a messenger":** Quran 3:144.

BIBLIOGRAPHY

Muhammad's life is extraordinarily well documented. In fact if anything, it is over-documented. The biographer's challenge is to assess this mass of information, much of which is only newly available in translation, and to differentiate between history—what actually happened—and the volume of reverential legend that has inevitably accrued over the centuries. This book is thus based on the original eighth- and ninth-century histories, detailed here under "Primary Sources," but it also calls on the perspective and context provided by recent academic research in Middle East history and literature, comparative religion, and social studies, listed under "Secondary Sources."

PRIMARY SOURCES

The early Islamic historians ibn-Ishaq and al-Tabari are outstanding for the breadth and depth of their work, which makes extensive use of both oral history and earlier written sources that have since been lost. The result is not at all the dry history one might expect of classical historical texts. Their work often has the vivid immediacy of reporting, alive with the language and feel of the time.

Western readers used to a progressive chronological structure and a firm authorial point of view, however, may be somewhat disconcerted by their method. For example, the same event or conversation is often told from several points of view. The stylistic effect is almost postmodern, with the narrative thread weaving back and forth in time, and each account adding to the ones preceding it, though from a slightly different angle.

Where versions conflict, both historians ostensibly reserve judgment in the interest of inclusiveness, but indicate their point of view by the amount of space they give differing versions, and by the use of sentences such as "As to which of these is correct, only God knows for sure."

As al-Tabari wrote in the introduction to his monumental history: "In everything which I mention herein, I rely only on established [written] reports, which I identify, and on [oral] accounts, which I ascribe by name to their transmitters . . . Knowledge is only obtained by the statements of reporters and transmitters, not by rational deduction or by intuitive inference. If we have mentioned in this book any report about certain men of the past which the reader finds objectionable . . . know that this has not come about on our account, but on account of one of those who has transmitted it to us, and that we have presented it only in the way in which it was presented to us."

Ibn-Ishaq

Muhammad ibn-Ishaq's *Sirat Rasul Allah*, "The Life of the Messenger of God," is the earliest extant biography of Muhammad. Ibn-Ishaq was born in Medina around the year 704 and died in Damascus in 767. His work was expanded and annotated in the ninth century in Egypt by ibn-Hisham, whose annotated version of ibn-Ishaq's original *Sira* is available in an eight-hundred-page English translation by Alfred Guillaume: *The Life of Muhammad: A Translation of Ishaq's Sirat Rasul Allah* (Oxford: Oxford University Press, 1955).

Al-Tabari

Abu-Jafar al-Tabari's *Tarikh al-Rusul wa-al-Muluk*, "History of the Prophets and Kings," covers the rise of Islam and the history of the Islamic world through to the early tenth century in immense and intimate detail. The volumes on Muhammad's life draw heavily on ibn-Ishaq's work but also incorporate the writings of other early historians whose work has not survived. Al-Tabari was born in 838, and died in Baghdad in 923. His *Tarikh* has been translated into English in a magnificent project overseen by general editor Ehsan Yar-Shater and published in thirty-nine annotated volumes as *The History of al-Tabari*. Quotes and dialogue used in this book are from the following volumes:

The History of Al-Tabari, Volume V: *The Sasanids, the Byzantines, the Lakhmids, and Yemen*. Translated by C. E. Bosworth. Albany: State University of New York Press, 1999.
————, Volume VI: *Muhammad at Mecca*. Translated by W. Montgomery Watt and M. V. McDonald. Albany: State University of New York Press, 1988.
————, Volume VII: *The Foundation of the Community*. Translated by W. Montgomery Watt and M. V. McDonald. Albany: State University of New York Press, 1987.
————, Volume VIII: *The Victory of Islam*. Translated by Michael Fishbein. Albany: State University of New York Press, 1997.
————, Volume IX: *The Last Years of the Prophet*. Translated by Ismail K. Poonawala. Albany: State University of New York Press, 1990.
————, Volume X: *The Conquest of Arabia*. Translated by Fred M. Donner. Albany: State University of New York Press, 1992.
————, Volume XV: *The Crisis of the Early Caliphate*. Translated by R. Stephen Humphreys. Albany: State University of New York Press, 1990.
————, Volume XVIII: *Between Civil Wars: The Caliphate of Mu'awiyah*. Translated by Michael C. Morony. Albany: State University of New York Press, 1987.

The Quran

I have used primarily the following five English-language translations, cross-referencing them with the original Arabic:

Abdel Haleem, M. A. S. *The Qur'an: A New Translation*. Oxford: Oxford University Press, 2008.
Ali, Abdullah Yusuf. *The Holy Qur'an*. New Delhi: Kitab Bhavan, 1996.
Arberry, A. J. *The Koran Interpreted*. New York: Macmillan, 1955.

Bakhtiat, Laleh. *The Sublime Quran*. Chicago: Kazi, 2009.
Dawood, N. J. *The Koran*. London: Penguin, 1956.

SECONDARY SOURCES

Abbott, Nabia. *Aishah the Beloved of Muhammad*. Chicago: University of Chicago Press, 1942.
Abdel Haleem, Muhammad. *Understanding the Quran: Themes and Style*. London: Tauris, 1999.
Ahmad, Barakat. *Muhammad and the Jews: A Re-examination*. New Delhi: Vikas, 1979.
Arberry, A. J. *The Seven Odes: The First Chapter in Arabic Literature*. New York: Macmillan, 1957.
Archer, John Clark. *Mystical Elements in Mohammed*. New Haven, CT: Yale University Press, 1924.
Ariès, Philippe. *Centuries of Childhood: A Social History of Family Life*. Trans. Robert Baldick. New York: Alfred A. Knopf, 1962.
Armstrong, Karen. *Muhammad: A Biography of the Prophet*. San Francisco: HarperSanFrancisco, 1992.
Aslan, Reza. *No god but God: The Origins, Evolution, and Future of Islam*. New York: Random House, 2005.
Berkey, Jonathan P. *The Formation of Islam: Religion and Society in the Near East, 600–1800*. New York: Cambridge University Press, 2003.
Berlin, Isaiah. *Against the Current: Essays in the History of Ideas*. New York: Viking, 1980.
Boswell, John. *The Kindness of Strangers: The Abandonment of Children in Western Europe from Late Antiquity to the Renaissance*. New York: Pantheon, 1988.
Bowersock, G. W. *Roman Arabia*. Cambridge, MA: Harvard University Press, 1983.
Brinton, Denis. *Cerebrospinal Fever*. Baltimore: Williams & Wilkins, 1941.
Brown, Jonathan A. C. *Hadith: Muhammad's Legacy in the Medieval and Modern World*. Oxford: Oneworld, 2009.
Bulliet, R.W. *The Camel and the Wheel*. Cambridge, MA: Harvard University Press, 1975.
Campbell, Joseph. *The Hero with a Thousand Faces*. Princeton, NJ: Princeton University Press, 1949.
Carlyle, Thomas. *On Heroes and Hero Worship*. New York: Dutton, 1954.
Carroll, James. *Jerusalem, Jerusalem: How the Ancient City Ignited Our Modern World*. Boston: Houghton Mifflin Harcourt, 2011.
Clark, Rebecca A., and Newton E. Hyslop. "Post-Traumatic Meningitis." In David Schlossberg, ed., *Infections of the Nervous System*. New York: Springer-Verlag, 1990.
Collingwood, R. G. *The Idea of History*. Oxford: Clarendon Press, 1946.
Cook, Michael A. *Muhammad*. New York: Oxford University Press, 1983.
Covitz, Joel. *Visions of the Night: A Study of Jewish Dream Interpretation*. Boston: Shambhala, 1990.
Crone, Patricia. *Meccan Trade and the Rise of Islam*. Princeton, NJ: Princeton University Press, 1987.
———, and Michael Cook. *Hagarism: The Making of the Islamic World*. New York: Cambridge University Press, 1977.
Desai, Mahadev. *Day-to-Day with Gandhi*, vol. 2. Varanasi: Sarva Seva Sangh Prakashan, 1969.

Dixon, Suzanne, ed. *Childhood, Class and Kin in the Roman World*. London: Routledge, 2001.

Donner, Fred M. *Muhammad and the Believers: At the Origins of Islam*. Cambridge, MA: Harvard University Press, 2011.

———. "Muhammad's Political Consolidation in Arabia up to the Conquest of Mecca." *Muslim World* 69 (1979).

———. "The Role of Nomads in the Near East in Late Antiquity." In Peters, ed., *The Arabs and Arabia on the Eve of Islam*.

Eisenstadt, Marvin. "Parental Loss and Genius." In Eisenstadt et al., *Parental Loss and Achievement*.

———, André Haynal, Pierre Rentchnick, and Pierre de Senarclens. *Parental Loss and Achievement*. Madison, CT: International Universities Press, 1989.

Eisenstadt, S. N., ed. *The Origins and Diversity of Axial Age Civilizations*. Albany: State University of New York Press, 1986.

Eliade, Mircea. *Myths, Dreams, and Mysteries: The Encounter Between Contemporary Faiths and Archaic Realities*. Trans. Philip Mairet. New York: Harper & Brothers, 1960.

Esposito, John L. *Islam: The Straight Path*. New York: Oxford University Press, 2005.

Fahd, Toufic. *La Divination Arabe: Études Religieuses, Sociologiques et Folkloriques sur le Milieu Natif de l'Islam*. Paris: Sindbad, 1987.

Finnegan, Ruth H. *Oral Poetry: Its Nature, Significance, and Social Context*. Cambridge, England: Cambridge University Press, 1977.

Firestone, Reuven. "Jewish Culture in the Formative Period of Islam." In David Baile, ed., *Cultures of the Jews: A New History*. New York: Schocken, 2002.

Geertz, Clifford. *Available Light: Anthropological Reflections on Philosophical Topics*. Princeton, NJ: Princeton University Press, 2000.

———. *The Interpretation of Cultures*. New York: Basic Books, 1973.

Gibb, Hamilton A. R. "Pre-Islamic Monotheism in Arabia." In Peters, ed., *The Arabs and Arabia on the Eve of Islam*.

Gil, Moshe. "The Constitution of Medina: A Reconsideration." *Israel Oriental Studies* 4 (1974).

———. "The Medinan Opposition to the Prophet." *Jerusalem Studies in Arabic and Islam* 10 (1987).

———. "The Origin of the Jews of Yathrib." In Peters, ed., *The Arabs and Arabia on the Eve of Islam*.

Glubb, John Bagot. *The Life and Times of Muhammad*. New York: Stein and Day, 1970.

Groom, N. *Frankincense and Myrrh: A Study of the Arabian Incense Trade*. London: Longman, 1981.

Guillaume, Alfred. *Prophecy and Divination Among the Hebrews and Other Semites*. London: Hodder & Stoughton, 1938.

Havel, Václav. *The Art of the Impossible: Politics as Morality in Practice*. New York: Alfred A. Knopf, 1997.

Hawting, G. R. "Al-Hudaybiyya and the Conquest of Mecca: A Reconsideration of the Tradition About the Muslim Takeover of the Sanctuary." *Jerusalem Studies in Arabic and Islam* 8 (1986).

———. "The Origins of the Islamic Sanctuary at Mecca." In Juynboll, ed., *Studies on the First Century of Islam in Society*.

Hazleton, Lesley. *After the Prophet: The Epic Story of the Shia-Sunni Split in Islam*. New York: Doubleday, 2009.

———. *Where Mountains Roar: A Personal Report from the Sinai and Negev Desert.* New York: Holt, Rinehart and Winston, 1980.

Heath, Peter. *The Thirsty Sword: Sirat Antar and the Arabic Popular Epic.* Salt Lake City: University of Utah Press, 1996.

Henniger, Joseph. "Pre-Islamic Beduin Religion." In Peters, ed., *The Arabs and Arabia on the Eve of Islam.*

Hodgson, Marshall G. S. *The Venture of Islam,* vol. 1: *The Classical Age of Islam.* Chicago: University of Chicago Press, 1961.

Hopkins, Keith. *Death and Renewal.* New York: Cambridge University Press, 1983.

———. *A World Full of Gods: The Strange Triumph of Christianity.* New York: Free Press, 2000.

Hoyland, Robert G. *Arabia and the Arabs: From the Bronze Age to the Coming of Islam.* London: Routledge, 2001.

Ibn al-Kalbi. *The Book of Idols: Being a Translation from the Arabic of the Kitab al-Asnam.* Trans. Nabih Amin Faris. Princeton, NJ: Princeton University Press, 1952.

Ibn-Khaldun. *The Muqaddimah: An Introduction to History.* Trans. Franz Rosenthal. Princeton, NJ: Princeton University Press, 1967.

Jackson, Ralph. *Doctors and Diseases in the Roman Empire.* Norman: University of Oklahoma Press, 1988.

James, William. *The Varieties of Religious Experience.* New York: Longmans, Green, 1902.

Juynboll, G. H. A., ed. *Studies on the First Century of Islam in Society.* Carbondale: Southern Illinois University Press, 1982.

Kennedy, Hugh N. *The Prophet and the Age of the Caliphates: The Islamic Near East from the Sixth to the Eleventh Century.* New York: Pearson/Longman, 2004.

Kister, M. J. "Al-Tahhanuth: An Inquiry into the Meaning of the Term." *Bulletin of the School of Oriental and African Studies* 31 (1968).

———. "Labbayka, Allahumma, Labbyaka: On a Monotheistic Aspect of a Jahiliyya Practice." *Jerusalem Studies in Arabic and Islam* 2 (1980).

———. "The Massacre of the Banu Qurayza: A Re-examination of a Tradition." *Jerusalem Studies in Arabic and Islam* 8 (1986).

———. "Mecca and the Tribes of Arabia: Some Notes on Their Relations." In Kister, ed., *Society and Religion.*

———. *Studies in Jahiliyya and Early Islam.* London: Varorium, 1980.

———, ed. *Society and Religion from Jahiliyya to Islam.* Brookfield, VT: Gower, 1990.

Kosekenniemi, Erkki. *The Exposure of Infants Among Jews and Christians in Antiquity.* Sheffield, England: Phoenix Press, 2009.

Lecker, Michael. *Jews and Arabs in Pre- and Early Islamic Arabia.* Brookfield, VT: Ashgate, 1988.

———. *Muslims, Jews and Pagans: Studies on Early Islamic Medina.* New York: E. J. Brill, 1995.

Lelyveld, Joseph. *Great Soul: Mahatma Gandhi and His Struggle with India.* New York: Alfred A. Knopf, 2011.

Levey, Martin. *Medieval Arabic Toxicology: The "Book on Poisons" of Ibn Wahsiya.* Philadelphia: American Philosophical Society, 1966.

Lévi-Strauss, Claude. *Myth and Meaning: Cracking the Code of Culture.* New York: Schocken, 1995.

Lings, Martin. *Muhammad: His Life Based on the Earliest Sources.* London: Allen & Unwin, 1983.

Luyat, Anne, and Francine Tolron. *Flight from Certainty: The Dilemma of Identity and Exile.* New York: Rodopi, 2001.

Machiavelli, Niccolò. *The Prince.* Trans. George Bull. London: Penguin, 1961.

Madelung, Wilferd. *The Succession to Muhammad: A Study of the Early Caliphate.* Cambridge, England: Cambridge University Press, 1977.

Marty, Martin E., and R. Scott Appleby, eds. *Fundamentalisms and Society: Reclaiming the Sciences, the Family, and Education.* Chicago: University of Chicago Press, 1993.

McAuliffe, Jane Dammen, ed. *The Cambridge Companion to the Qur'an.* Cambridge, England: Cambridge University Press, 2006.

McNeill, William H. *Mythistory and Other Essays.* Chicago: University of Chicago Press, 1986.

Musil, Alois. *The Manners and Customs of the Rwala Bedouins.* New York: American Geographical Society, 1928.

Mustafa, Hafiz Ghulam. *Religious Trends in Pre-Islamic Poetry.* Bombay: Asia Publishing House, 1968.

Newby, Gordon Darnell. *A History of the Jews of Arabia: From Ancient Times to Their Eclipse Under Islam.* Columbia: University of South Carolina Press, 1988.

———. *The Making of the Last Prophet: A Reconstruction of the Earliest Biography of Muhammad.* Columbia: University of South Carolina Press, 1989.

Niles, John D. *Homo Narrans: The Poetics and Anthropology of Oral Literature.* Philadelphia: University of Pennsylvania Press, 1999.

Otto, Rudolf. *The Idea of the Holy: An Inquiry into the Non-Rational Factor in the Idea of the Divine and Its Relation to the Rational.* London: Oxford University Press, 1950.

Palmer, Gabrielle. *The Politics of Breastfeeding.* London: Pandora, 1988.

Peters, F. E. *Muhammad and the Origins of Islam.* Albany: State University of New York Press, 1994.

———, ed. *The Arabs and Arabia on the Eve of Islam.* Brookfield, VT: Ashgate, 1999.

Piers, Maria W. *Infanticide.* New York: W. W. Norton, 1978.

Pinker, Steven. *The Better Angels of Our Nature: Why Violence Has Declined.* New York: Viking, 2011.

Preston, Samuel H. "Mortality Trends." *Annual Review of Sociology* 3 (1977).

Ramadan, Tariq. *In the Footsteps of the Prophet: Lessons from the Life of Muhammad.* Oxford: Oxford University Press, 2007.

Rentchnick, Pierre. "Orphans and the Will for Power." In Eisenstadt et al., *Parental Loss and Achievement.*

Retsö, Jan. *The Arabs in Antiquity: Their History from the Assyrians to the Umayyads.* London: Routledge, 2003.

Reynolds, Gabriel Said, ed. *New Perspectives on the Qur'an: The Qur'an in Its Historical Context.* London: Routledge, 2011.

Rodinson, Maxime. *Muhammad.* New York: New Press, 2002.

Rogerson, Barnaby. *The Prophet Muhammad: A Biography.* Mahwah, NJ: Hidden Spring, 2003.

Rubin, Uri. *The Eye of the Beholder: The Life of Muhammad as Viewed by the Early Muslims.* Princeton, NJ: Darwin Press, 1995.

———. "Hanifiyya and Ka'ba: An Inquiry into the Arabian Pre-Islamic Background of the Din Ibrahim." In Peters, ed., *The Arabs and Arabia on the Eve of Islam.*

———. "The Ka'ba: Aspects of Its Ritual Functions and Position in Pre-Islamic and Early Islamic Times." In Peters, ed., *The Arabs and Arabia on the Eve of Islam.*

————, ed. *The Life of Muhammad*. Brookfield, VT: Ashgate, 1998.

Safi, Omid. *Memories of Muhammad: Why the Prophet Matters*. New York: HarperCollins, 2009.

Said, Edward. *Orientalism*. New York: Pantheon, 1978.

————. *Reflections on Exile and Other Essays*. Cambridge, MA: Harvard University Press, 2002.

Sand, Shlomo. *The Invention of the Jewish People*. London: Verso, 2009.

Scharfstein, Ben-Ami. *The Philosophers: Their Lives and the Nature of Their Thought*. New York: Oxford University Press, 1980.

Schimmel, Anne Marie. *And Muhammad Is His Messenger: The Veneration of the Prophet in Islamic Piety*. Chapel Hill: University of North Carolina Press, 1985.

Shaffer, Robert. *Tents and Towers of Arabia*. New York: Dodd Mead, 1952.

Shoham, Giora S. *Rebellion, Creativity, and Revelation*. New Brunswick, NJ: Transaction, 1980.

Shorto, Russell. *Gospel Truth: The New Image of Jesus Emerging from Science and History*. New York: Riverhead, 1997.

Smart, Ninian. *Dimensions of the Sacred: An Anatomy of the World's Beliefs*. Berkeley: University of California Press, 1996.

Smith, Wilfred Cantwell. *Islam in Modern History*. Princeton, NJ: Princeton University Press, 1957.

Stetkevych, Suzanne Pinckney. *The Mute Immortals Speak: Pre-Islamic Poetry and the Poetics of Ritual*. Ithaca, NY: Cornell University Press, 1993.

Stillman, Norman A. *The Jews of Arab Lands: A History and Source Book*. Philadelphia: Jewish Publication Society of America, 1979.

Sun Tzu. *The Art of War*. New York: Delta, 1983.

Tietjens, Eunice. *The Romance of Antar*. New York: Coward-McCann, 1929.

Tunkel, Allan R. *Bacterial Meningitis*. Philadelphia: Lippincott Williams & Wilkins, 2001.

Underhill, Evelyn. *Mysticism: A Study in the Nature and Development of Man's Spiritual Consciousness*. New York: Dutton, 1955.

von Grunebaum, G. E. "The Nature of Arab Unity Before Islam." In Peters, ed., *The Arabs and Arabia on the Eve of Islam*.

Ward, Benedicta, trans. *The Sayings of the Desert Fathers*. London: Mowbray, 1975.

Watt, W. Montgomery. "Belief in a 'High God' in Pre-Islamic Mecca." *Journal of Semitic Studies* 16 (1971).

————. *Muhammad: Prophet and Statesman*. London: Oxford University Press, 1961.

————. *Muhammad at Mecca*. Oxford: Clarendon Press, 1953.

————. *Muhammad at Medina*. Oxford: Clarendon Press, 1956.

————. "Pre-Islamic Arabian Religion in the Qur'an." *Islamic Studies* 15 (1976).

Whallon, William. *Formula, Character, and Context: Studies in Homeric, Old English, and Old Testament Poetry*. Cambridge, MA: Harvard University Press, 1969.

Zakaria, Rafiq. *Muhammad and the Quran*. New Delhi: Penguin, 1991.

Zwettler, Michael. *The Oral Tradition of Classical Arabic Poetry: Its Character and Implications*. Columbus: Ohio State University Press, 1978.

INDEX

Aaron, 159, 161

Abbas (uncle of Muhammad), 209, 281–82, 330, 335

Abd al-Muttalib (grandfather of Muhammad), 39, 43, 106, 107, 155; childhood custody battle over, 168–70; death of, 53; decline of, 30, 40; Muhammad in home of, 40–42; near-sacrifice of son by, 13, 14–18, 42, 169; neglect of Muhammad by, 22–23; rediscovery of Zamzam well by, 13–14; and water monopoly, 14, 50

Abd Shams clan, 127

Abdullah (father of Muhammad): death of, 18–19; marriage of, 18; and Muhammad's miraculous conception, 18, 22, 35; near-sacrifice of, 13, 14–18, 42, 169

Abraham, 13, 14, 40, 47, 78, 83, 113, 119, 121, 212, 213, 316; Muhammad's Night Journey to, 158–65

Abu-Afak, 221

Abu-Bakr (Attiq ibn-Uthman), 140, 153, 180, 217, 238, 239, 276, 317; adherence to Muhammad's message, 122, 133; and death of Muhammad, 332–33; and harassment of believers, 138, 139; as in-law, 243–44, 311; and Muhammad's escape from Mecca, 183, 184; and Muhammad's final illness, 330; as Muhammad's successor, 122, 335; and naming of Muhammad's successor, 326, 327, 328

Abu-Hakam. *See* Abu-Jahl

Abu-Jahl, 153, 195, 225, 233, 273, 277; campaign against Muhammad, 125–26, 127, 128, 131, 132, 135–36, 137–38, 138–39, 140, 145, 156, 158, 182–83, 224; death of, 207, 224; in fighting between Mecca and Medina, 204, 205–8, 209; and Meccan emigrants, 178–79, 180

Abu-Lahab, 106–7, 108, 133, 135, 155, 156, 183

Abu-Sufyan, 297, 300, 304; acceptance of Islam by, 284–85; and campaign against Muhammad in Mecca, 127–28, 132, 135, 145, 153, 154; and caravan raids, 195, 203, 204–5, 206, 216–17; and counterattack against Medinan believers, 224–27, 229, 231, 233; and death of abu-Talib, 153; as in-law, 282, 311; laying siege to Medina, 258–63, 279, 303; in Muhammad's administration, 297; and Muhammad's pilgrimages to Mecca, 274, 280, 283; and surrender of Mecca, 282–86

Abu-Talib (uncle of Muhammad), 54, 76; adherence to religious traditions, 109, 110–11, 121, 126, 154; and Bahira-Muhammad encounter, 59, 60, 68–69; and boycott against Hashims, 132, 133, 134–35; and caravan trade, 66–67, 68, 73–74; daughter's marriage, 69–70, 75; death of, 154, 164,

Gabriel (angel), 330; and Muhammad's
escape from Mecca, 183; and
Muhammad's Night Journey, 158–59;
and Muhammad's revelations, 88, 89,
90–91, 106, 146; and mystical
dreams, 162; political advice to
Muhammad, 263
Gandhi, Mohandas, 143, 200, 278
Ghadir Khumm benediction, 322–23, 326
Ghatafan tribe, 258, 261–62, 266, 279
Gnostics, concept of the divine, 103
God: fear of, 90; multiple gods,
see Polytheism; one, see Monotheism
Greene, Graham, 99–100

Hadiths: Aisha's contributions to, 314; as
Muhammad's legacy, 329; on
purification ritual, 162; on striving, 200
Hafsa (wife of Muhammad), 243, 253, 311,
313, 327, 335
Hagar, 13, 78
Hajj (pilgrimage), 44–45, 49, 51, 129, 171,
173, 177, 272, 317, 319, 320, 322, 325
Hakam (wise man), 124
Halima: fostering of Muhammad by, 20,
21, 22–25, 29–30, 30–32, 300; and
Muhammad's return to Mecca, 33,
35, 36–37
Hamza (uncle of Muhammad), 75, 153,
154; adherence to Muhammad's
message, 139–40, 141; at Battle of
Uhud, 229–30, 232, 233, 283, 296;
and caravan raids, 195
Hanifs (thinkers), 77–79, 95, 110, 120, 140,
159, 213, 310
Harlotry, and paganism, 48, 49
Hashim, 55, 155, 168
Hashim clan, 16, 22, 30, 37, 54, 182, 183;
boycott of, 131, 132–35, 136–37, 141,
151; expulsion of Muhammad from,
155–57; leadership succession in, 155;
pressure to expel Muhammad from,
122, 125–28, 131, 132, 133, 142–43;
reception of Quranic revelations by,
106–9; water monopoly of, 14, 50
Hassan (son of Ali and Fatima), 251, 316,
321, 323
Havel, Václav, 294

Hawazin confederation, 298–301
Heraclius (Byzantine emperor), 100–101,
175, 303–6
Hijaz mountain chain/region, 31, 67,
79–80, 81, 182, 210, 272, 279,
280, 301
Hijra (hegira), 178–80, 186, 195
Hind, 229, 232, 233, 283, 286, 296–97
Hira, Mount, 78, 82, 312; revelation to
Muhammad on, 5–7, 12, 86–96, 101,
152, 163, 174
History: and group identity, 118–19;
versus tradition, 9–10, 10–11
Hubal (sacred stone and oracle), 15–17, 46,
50, 124, 169
Hudaibiya, Medinan pilgrims at, 273–74,
275, 277, 278
Hudaibiya, Truce of. See Truce of
Hudaibiya
Human sacrifice, laws of, 14, 17–18
Hussein (son of Ali and Fatima), 251, 316,
321, 323
Hypocrites *(munafiqun)*, 234–35, 236, 241,
264, 318

Ibn Abu-Jahl, Ikrima, 298
Ibn-Amt, Zayd, 78
Ibn-Arabi, 162
Ibn-Ashraf, 221
Ibn-Ishaq, 110, 122, 283, 295, 312,
321–22; on Abd al-Muttalib's sons,
15; on Bahira-Muhammad encounter,
59; on Battle of Badr, 208; on
campaign against Muhammad, 126,
129–30, 130–31; on Halima, 25; on
hijra, 181; on Jewish-Muslim conflict,
215, 216, 238; on Khadija, 72, 73; on
Mecca-Medina truce, 276, 277–78;
on Meccan siege against Medina,
261, 262; on Medinan deputation
to Muhammad, 171–72; on
Muhammad's angelic visitation, 33;
on Muhammad's arrival in Medina,
185; as Muhammad's biographer,
9; on Muhammad's escape from
Mecca, 184–85; on Muhammad's
marriages, 75, 250; on Muhammad's
pilgrimages to Mecca, 281, 317–18;

Lesley Hazleton reported on the Middle East from Jerusalem for more than a dozen years, and has written for *Time*, the *New York Times*, the *New York Review of Books*, and *Harper's*, among other publications. Her last book, *After the Prophet*, was a finalist for the PEN Center USA Literary Award. Hazleton lives in Seattle.